D0205834

THE SALMON HANDBOOK

By the same Author

TROUT FARMING HANDBOOK

THE
SALMON
HANDBOOK
*The life and cultivation
of fishes of the
salmon family*

Stephen Drummond Sedgwick
Illustrated by Robin Ade

ANDRE DEUTSCH

SH
167
S17
S 43

First published 1982 by André Deutsch Limited
105 Great Russell Street, London WC1

Copyright © 1982 by S. Drummond Sedgwick
Illustrations copyright © 1982 by Robin Ade
All rights reserved

Photoset by Robcroft Ltd, London WC1
Printed in Great Britain by
Robert Hartnoll Ltd. Cornwall

ISBN 0233 97331 1

OLSON LIBRARY
NORTHERN MICHIGAN UNIVERSITY
MARQUETTE, MICHIGAN 49855

Contents

LIST OF LINE DRAWINGS

LIST OF TABLES

PHOTOGRAPHS

Introduction

The members of the salmon family form the most valuable group of the world's fish species. They have been in the forefront of human interest wherever they occur. Isolated communities in the northern hemisphere have taken the greater part of their livelihood from migratory salmon and charr. The west coast Indians in North America depended on runs of fish homing to their local rivers for winter keep. Other tribes on the east coast fished for Atlantic salmon returning to rivers from Labrador to New Hampshire and Eskimaux in the north trapped and speared the big sea-going Arctic charr. Atlantic salmon in Scotland were put under protective legislation in laws given by William the Lion in the twelfth century. All kinds of political skulduggery have been used through the centuries and are still used to obtain fishing rights and commercially exploit wild stocks of both Atlantic and Pacific salmon. The almost mystical esteem given to these fish probably stems from their strange ability to find a way back to breed in their parent river after years of ocean wandering.

The salmonidae are naturally distributed throughout most of the northern hemisphere, from the temperate zone northwards to beyond the Arctic Circle. There are no native salmon or trout in the southern hemisphere but they have been successfully introduced into South America, Southern Africa and Australasia.

Nearly all members of the salmon family can adapt to life in saltwater. Some species must migrate to the sea or die, most of the others have races which deliberately migrate. A few species have not adapted to life in the sea, mainly because they inhabit isolated freshwaters where they have become land-locked and had no access to a saline environment.

The anadromous salmonids are all hatched and grow for a

time in freshwater before they go down to the sea. They remain feeding and growing either in the oceans far from shore or in mainly estuarial and coastal waters, until the onset of sexual maturity and an increasing urge to spawn sends them home to their parent rivers. The ability of salmon to find their way back to the rivers where they were hatched and spent their parr life period is still a source of wonder to naturalists. The regularity with which different migratory members of the salmon family find their way home varies to some extent between species but the majority return to the right river and some will go back to the gravel bed or even ascend the outfall from the troughs in the hatchery where they were hatched.

Marking has been used for a very long time to demonstrate the consistency of homing in the different salmonid species. Izaak Walton in the Fourth Day of *The Compleat Angler* has Piscator tell us of the salmon: 'that his growth is very sudden; it is said, that after he is got into the sea, he becomes from a samlet not so big as a gudgeon, to be a salmon, in as short a time as a gosling becomes a goose. Much of this has been observed by tying a ribbon, or some tape or thread, in the tail of some young salmons, which have been taken in weirs as they swimmed towards the saltwater, and then by taking a part of them again with the known mark at the same place on their return from the sea.'

Salmon, and to a lesser extent trout and charr, must have developed a sense by which to navigate the seas back to coastal waters. The long-distance migrants return directly and speedily to a short length of coastline near their home rivers, from feeding grounds which may be thousands of miles away across the open seas. It is difficult to believe that they can do this by following only temperature gradients or oceanic currents. It seems posssible that they use the sun, moon and stars like some migratory birds or have a means of sensing variations in the earth's magnetic field. The means by which returning migrants identify the home river or stream is now better understood. The young of anadromous salmonids become imprinted with the chemical characteristics of their freshwater home. The adult fish, once close enough to recognize those characteristics, enter the river and smell their way upstream to waters near their original hatching and rearing ground.

The degree to which the larger members of the salmon family are wholly or partly adapted to migrate to and from the sea varies from some Pacific salmons which are obliged to go to saltwater, to the huchen (*Hucho hucho*) or Danube salmon in Europe and the North American lake trout or charr (*Salvelinus namaycush*) which spend their lives entirely in freshwater. There are other minor sub-species of salmonids mainly in Central Asia and in western North America which do not migrate to the sea. Some of these are close relations of the rainbow trout but chromosome differences indicate true genus differentiation. One of the most attractive is the golden trout (*S. aureolus* or *aquabonita*) found in Mexico. Others with exciting names such as the gila trout (*S. gilae*) and the apache trout (*S. apache*) are found in a few streams in Arizona and New Mexico. Interesting examples in Europe include the marbled trout (*S. trutta marmoratus*) which occurs in streams running into the Soca river basin in Slovenija. These fish might be of interest to fish farmers as they are pisciverous and grow to a weight of up to 10 kg.

A characteristic common to the large quick-growing salmonids in Europe and Asia which do go to sea is that they have a life cycle in freshwater which is analogous to the anadromous species. The adult fish leave the waters of great rivers such as the Danube or Yangste Kiang and migrate into small streams to spawn. The young fish then spend a parr life period in the streams, feeding first on zooplankton and then on insects and other small organisms, until they reach a size at which they migrate downstream to the main river, where they feed mainly on other fish and rapidly increase in size. The lake trout or charr in North America and the lake trout of the great lakes of Norway and Sweden behave in a similar manner.

Wild salmon and trout have been caught and stripped of their eggs, and the eggs artificially fertilized and incubated in hatcheries since the middle of the nineteenth century. But it was not until the early years of the twentieth century that serious thought was given to the commercial possibilities of not only breeding but of on-growing fish of these species as human food. In fact, to domesticate the fish and retain them in captivity throughout their life cycle. Farming rainbow trout in freshwater for the table market got under way in Denmark before the First World War.

The Norwegians found their freshwaters were too cold in winter and the growth season for the fish was too short. The sea temperatures along the north and west coast of Norway are on average higher then those in the rivers. The Norwegians knew that the sea-going race of steelhead rainbow trout were naturally adapted to migrate to the sea when they had grown to a certain size in freshwater. In 1912 the Norwegian Storting approved the culture of rainbow trout in the sea but the original attempts at marine farming were a failure because the sea burst open the pens made to enclose the fish. The failure was the subject of some ridicule at the time and an article in a local paper suggested growing oysters which would not be so likely to escape if the barriers were washed away.

No further attempts of any consequence were made to grow rainbow trout in saltwater in Norway until the mid-1950s. Sea farming then gradually increased over the next ten years and production reached about 500 tons in 1965. Methods initially used were generally a repetition of the original idea of enclosing a bay or an arm of a fjord with a fixed fence of netting. Some farmers tried pumping seawater to earth or concrete fishponds on the shore but this proved to be expensive and was less profitable than other methods. Although the low cost of electricity in Norway and the very small tidal differences kept pumping costs well below those in most other European countries, Norwegian sea farmers have subsequently decided to concentrate on low-cost fixed enclosures, where they could find suitable sites, and otherwise to use floating net cages.

On-growing of rainbow trout in saltwater in the British Isles started in 1960 at Loch Sween on the west coast of Scotland. The fish were first kept in net enclosures in brackish water and then transferred to floating cages in the sea loch. The trials were successful but further commercial development did not take place until the mid-1960s when a farm using fixed enclosures was started in a brackish water loch on the Shetland

Islands. The project was later abandoned because of sub-zero temperatures in the surface water at the site. Similar developments have taken place in Japan and in North America. These have been concentrated mainly on culturing fish belonging to the Pacific salmon species.

The domestication of terrestrial animals, birds and mammals, followed by selection and selective breeding of the most successful species, races and types, has been going on throughout human history. Intensive fish farming most closely resembles the modern methods of production developed for broiler chickens, but development from the time the first red jungle fowl was lured out of the trees to the modern broiler bird has taken thousands of years. We are at the very beginning of the domestication of salmon and trout. The reason that rainbow trout were originally selected for table-market fish farming was because they were relatively easy to rear in captivity. They could be fed and kept healthy, and adapted well to intensive culture. They were not afraid of their human masters and soon came to recognize them as their source of food. It is not proving so simple with some other members of the salmon family.

No doubt, in the not too distant future, races or types of particular species of salmon, trout or charr, or hybrids between them, will be developed for the table market. Such fish may have a combination of desirable features that lend themselves to domestication and to intensive culture. Some progress has already been made in this direction. In the meantime it is proving profitable to go ahead using semi-wild fish. This involves looking at all the available species of salmon, trout and charr in a search for useful characteristics that lend themselves to farming in freshwater and in the sea.

The original intention of this handbook was to confine the subject matter to a discussion of farming Atlantic salmon (*Salmo salar*). In the course of the preparation of material it soon became obvious that it would be of more interest and greater practical benefit to look at all the species and races of salmonids. There are essential differences in the behaviour and environmental requirements of the fish which need to be described and explained. Most of these differences stem from

Fig. 1 Identification guide

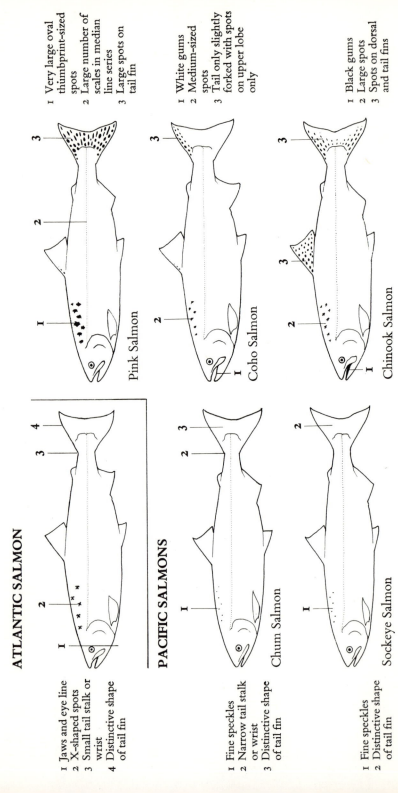

ATLANTIC SALMON

1 Jaws and eye line
2 X-shaped spots
3 Small tail stalk or wrist
4 Distinctive shape of tail fin

PACIFIC SALMONS

Chum Salmon

1 Fine speckles
2 Narrow tail stalk or wrist
3 Distinctive shape of tail fin

Sockeye Salmon

1 Fine speckles
2 Distinctive shape of tail fin

Pink Salmon

1 Very large oval thumbprint-sized spots
2 Large number of scales in median line series
3 Large spots on tail fin

Coho Salmon

1 White gums
2 Medium-sized spots
3 Tail only slightly forked with spots on upper lobe only

Chinook Salmon

1 Black gums
2 Large spots
3 Spots on dorsal and tail fins

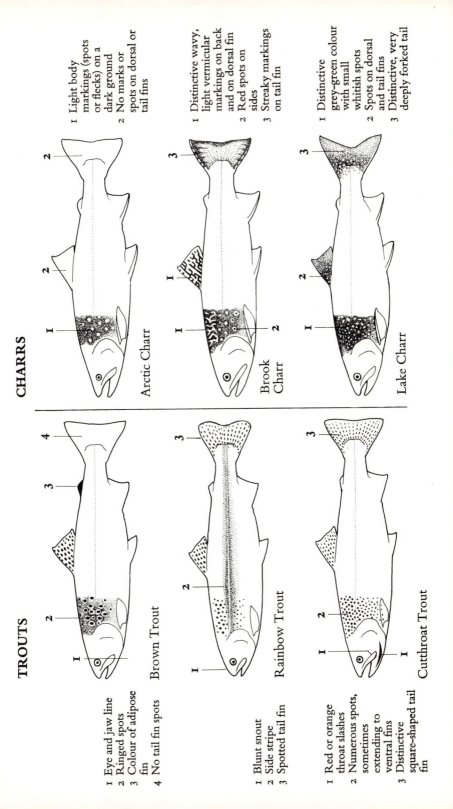

TROUTS

Brown Trout
1 Eye and jaw line
2 Ringed spots
3 Colour of adipose fin
4 No tail fin spots

Rainbow Trout
1 Blunt snout
2 Side stripe
3 Spotted tail fin

Cutthroat Trout
1 Red or orange throat slashes
2 Numerous spots, sometimes extending to ventral fins
3 Distinctive square-shaped tail fin

CHARRS

Arctic Charr
1 Light body markings (spots or flecks) on a dark ground
2 No marks or spots on dorsal or tail fins

Brook Charr
1 Distinctive wavy, light vermicular markings on back and on dorsal fin
2 Red spots on sides
3 Streaky markings on tail fin

Lake Charr
1 Distinctive grey-green colour with small whitish spots
2 Spots on dorsal and tail fins
3 Distinctive, very deeply forked tail

the natural behaviour of the species in the wild and unless they are properly understood can lead to disastrous mistakes when the fish are kept in captivity. A part of this handbook has also been devoted to the relatively new development of ocean ranching which takes advantage of the 'homing' instinct in migratory salmonids that brings them back to the place where they first entered the sea.

Chapter 1

Atlantic Salmon

The marine population of this species is made up of stock from both sides of the North Atlantic. The fish spawn in rivers on the mainland of North America and the larger off-shore islands from the Koksoak river in Ungava Bay to the St Croix which forms the eastern boundary between Canada and the United States. Atlantic salmon have also been re-established in some rivers in the state of Maine. There is a small population in two rivers in S.E. Greenland and salmon enter and spawn in all suitable rivers in Iceland. In the British Isles and on the continent of Europe this species still enters the faster flowing rivers which remain unpolluted and unobstructed from the White Sea to the north coast of Spain, including rivers flowing into the Baltic. Genetic differences between the salmon spawning in rivers in eastern North America and in Britain were demonstrated in the early 1970s. Since that time genetic differences have been shown to exist between races in different rivers in the same country of origin.

Non-migratory populations of *Salmo salar*, which remain throughout their life cycle in freshwater, occur in the USSR, Finland, Sweden and Norway. The Norwegian freshwater race is a dwarf, relict type, but the forms resident in the lakes in south Sweden and in Lake Ladoga in Russia grow at rates comparable to those of marine migrants. Freshwater populations also occur in North America. The form resident mainly in lakes is known as sebago salmon. They grow to a weight of 6-8 kg. Another form occurs in some rivers on the north shore of the St Lawrence and in Northern Quebec Province. These fish are known by the Indian name of *uananiche*. They are a good deal smaller than sebago salmon and do not reach weights of more than 1-2 kg. An interesting fish known as the Adriatic salmon occurs in rivers in Dalmatia.

It has been given the status of a separate species and the name of *Salmothymus obtusirostris* although it is a relict from the last ice age and closely related to both Atlantic salmon and sea trout (*Salmo trutta*).

Differences in the climate and geology affecting rivers throughout the range of Atlantic salmon cause wide differences in growth rates in freshwater and the time of first migration to the sea. Relatively little is known of the marine life of this species but fish from both sides of the ocean meet on their sea feeding grounds. Salmon from the Norwegian rivers are known to feed mainly in the Norwegian and Barents Seas. Stocks from the Swedish, Finnish and Russian rivers draining into the Baltic Sea generally remain entirely within its confines throughout their sea life

The young fish during the period they spend in freshwater are known as parr. The name changes to smolt when they are ready to migrate to the sea. This name derives from the silvery coating which develops on their scales. The fish are seldom seen or captured during the early part of their marine life. At this stage they are known simply as post-smolts. They are silver coloured without visible spots and very slim with a narrow, deeply-forked tail. Although they become deeper and fatter, with some visible black spots on their sides, they retain much of this basic shape for the first or 'grilse' year at sea. The fish which return to their parent rivers as grilse are still recognizable by their streamlined shape and the slim 'wrist' between the body and tail-fin which is appreciably more forked than in older salmon.

The fish of both sexes are bright silver when feeding in the sea and it is sometimes difficult to distinguish males from females. The flesh is red and contains a high proportion of fat. Salmon returning on spawning migration have developing gonads which reduces both the red colour and the fat in their tissues. This change is rather less noticeable in the rivers in the north of Norway which are relatively close to the sea feeding grounds of their native salmon. The flesh of farmed salmon which are fed up to a short time before slaughter on a wet food mixture with added fish oils and sources of carotin has much the same colour and content as that of wild fish caught when feeding hard in the sea, rather than when they are returning to freshwater on spawning migration. The external appearance of the fish, particularly the males, changes radically as the gonads develop. The lower jaw grows to form a hooked 'kype' on the male fish.

The adult fish must spawn in freshwater. At the onset of sexual maturity salmon return to their home rivers and if possible to the area where they hatched and spent their initial freshwater parr life. Atlantic salmon generally spawn in the autumn and winter in the period from October to January, although in some rivers there are stocks which spawn in February and March. Spawning time varies according to geographic distribution. The fish which spawn first inhabit those parts of the range of the species where the rivers freeze over early in the winter. The spawning period goes on longer and starts later at the southern end of the range in Europe where most salmon rivers remain ice-free in winter.

The female fish first selects a site where the gravel is of the right size and of sufficient depth, and where there is an appreciable current of water passing through as well as over the stones in the river bed. She then excavates a hole by turning on her side and flexing her body up and down. In this way she can raise and move quite large stones which weigh comparatively little in the water. Her body does not touch the stones which are lifted through the suction created by her rapid movements. She continues the excavation until, when lying in the trench, it has reached about the same depth as her body. The male fish takes no part in making the nest or redd but often fights with other cock fish on the redds.

When the female fish is ready to spawn, the male moves alongside the female and fertilizes the eggs as they are extruded. Sometimes precocious male parr will slip in and successfully fertilize the eggs ahead of an adult male. The female does not extrude all her eggs at one time. After a resting period she moves a short distance upstream and excavates another trench. The clean gravel from the second trench is washed down and covers the eggs deposited during the first shedding. The process is repeated until the eggs have been extruded. In the final excavation virtually no eggs are left to shed and the gravel serves to fill in the previous trench. A pair of spawning salmon may spend a week or more on the redds, depending on the water temperature. Usually spawning is completed in 2-3 days. Female Atlantic salmon produce between 1200 and 2000 eggs per kg of body weight. Large fish produce more eggs per kg than small fish.

The length of the incubation period for salmon eggs depends on water temperature. When the incubation period has elapsed (approximately 440 day/degrees), the alevins hatch out. Their mouths have not developed and they continue to derive nourishment from the yolk-sacs protruding from the ventral surfaces of their bodies. The yolk-sacs are gradually absorbed over the next three to four weeks, again dependent on water temperature.

The gravel plays a particularly important part in creating the right environment for both incubating eggs and developing alevins. The female fish has deliberately selected a site where there is a current passing through the stones. The chinks between the stones provide individual, quiet resting places for the eggs and subsequently for the alevins. The larval fish do not have to expend any energy in order to maintain their postions which is a vital factor in their survival at a later stage.

The final absorption of the yolk-sac coincides with the development of the mouth, digestive tract and excretory organs and the fry are ready-to-feed. They work their way up through the gravel and take station in a hollow between the stones on the river bed. A dye test will show that there is a vortex in these hollows which prevents the fish from being washed away and allows them to remain in position with the minimum of effort. The fry feed on zooplankton drifted down to them in the current. As they grow bigger they gradually make longer forays after larger food organisms.

Salmon parr spend most of their freshwater life in shallow riffles, where the water is broken and well-oxygenated but the current is not strong. The time taken in freshwater to reach the size of migration to the sea depends on the length of the summer feeding period. At the southern end of their range a fairly high proportion of Atlantic salmon parr reach a length of

12-15 cm, transform into smolt and are ready to migrate to the sea in the spring of the first year after hatching when they are 1+ years old. At the other extreme, in rivers in northern Canada and Arctic Norway, they may take five or six years to reach the smolt stage. The average age at smolting over most of the range of Atlantic salmon is 3+ years. The average in the British Isles is 2+, but most rivers have a proportion of fish which become smolt after 1+ or 3+ years.

No one knows how long Atlantic salmon smolt spend in home coastal waters before putting out to the open sea, and very little is known of the way they take or what directs them to take that way. The salmon, which enter the sea as smolt, feed on a changing diet as they grow in size during their marine life and it is most likely that movements to different areas in the sea depend upon the presence of the right prey.

At each stage of their marine life different races of Atlantic salmon probably go where there is an abundance of the food animals on which they are genetically conditioned to feed. Initially, post-smolt feed on amphipods (small, shrimp-like crustaceans), although very little is known of the feeding habits of the migrants going to the open seas as opposed to the Baltic. Pre-grilse have been caught when feeding on euphausids (krill). At a later stage, salmon certainly become pisciverous and feed mainly on small fish. Favourite food species are capelin (*Mallotus villosus*), sandeels (*Ammodytes spp.*) and members of the herring family, which are all fatty fish forming dense, pelagic shoals. The diet also includes some bigger crustacea such as the Arctic prawn (*Pandalus borealis*). Arctic squid are also taken in some sea areas. One thing is certain, Atlantic salmon feed in northern waters, a fact of the greatest importance to fish farmers.

Sea feeding areas used by Atlantic salmon are known to extend along the edge of the Arctic pack-ice and into the Labrador sea. Salmon from Norwegian rivers feed in the Barents and Norwegian seas between Jan Mayer Island, Svalbard and Novaya Zemlya. The surface waters in these sea areas remain cool in spring and summer, ranging from 2°C to 6°C and not rising above 8°C to 9°C. There is a definite indication that the races of Atlantic salmon feeding in the open

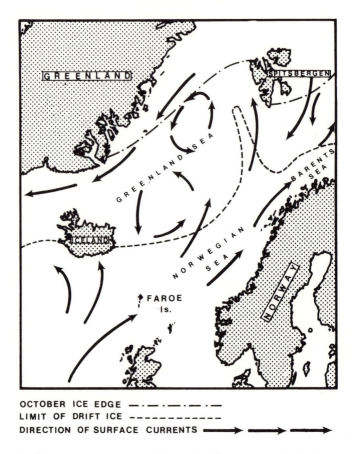

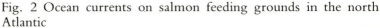

OCTOBER ICE EDGE — · — · — · — · —
LIMIT OF DRIFT ICE – – – – – – – – – – – –
DIRECTION OF SURFACE CURRENTS ➤ ➤ ➤

Fig. 2 Ocean currents on salmon feeding grounds in the north Atlantic

seas prefer colder waters and that their growth rate is slower when the water warms up.

Atlantic salmon stocks in the wild are delicately balanced and are subject to over-fishing, mainly by drift-netting on their marine feeding grounds or at sea while on spawning migration. Survival of the species depends on the preservation of their freshwater environment. Stocks are extremely sensitive to the effects of pollution, obstruction and other man-made changes in the natural regime of their parent rivers.

Wild stocks are generally declining throughout the range of the species, which emphasizes the need to accelerate domestication before it is too late. Serological studies are now providing good reasons for believing that each salmon river may have its own distinct stock of salmon with genetically stable characteristics. This is of great importance to the salmon farming industry because the wild stocks chosen for breeding in captivity can now be selected for attributes which make them most suitable for domestication.

Recognition

There are wide distinctions between the external characteristics of races of Atlantic salmon but the scale arrangement

Fig. 3 Atlantic salmon: adult and grilse in oceanic dress. Insets (clockwise from bottom right): spawning pair; egg, alevin, fry; parr; smolt

and appearance is typical of the species. There are ten to fifteen (usually eleven to thirteen scales) counted in a forward-sloping direction from the adipose fin to the lateral line. The scales are cycloid and show growth rings, the relative position of which can be used to interpret the life history of the fish. They show the length of time it has spent initially in freshwater and the time spent feeding in the sea. Scales also show the occasions when the fish has spawned.

There are ten to twelve rays in the dorsal fin.

The head of the vomer (the bone in the roof of the mouth) has no teeth. The teeth on the shaft of the bone can be shed and replaced.

A recognition feature commonly used, particularly to distinguish salmon parr from small brown or German trout (*Salmo trutta*), is that the posterior end of the maxilla (upper jaw-bone) does not extend back beyond the eye. This can be a useful guide but is also sometimes confusing.

Hybrids can occur in the wild between European sea trout (the sea-going race of *Salmo trutta*) and Atlantic salmon. These fish may have a mixture of the distinguishing features of both species.

Growth, Size and Age at Sexual Maturity

Larval growth in freshwater is slow. The food supply may be limited but the young fish make a better use of the available food animals than other young non-migratory salmonids of the same age sharing the same environment. Larger food animals are taken as the fish descend to brackish estuarial waters and enter the sea, and marine growth becomes progressively more rapid.

A variable proportion become sexually mature and return to freshwater on spawning migration as grilse, after one winter in the sea, when they have reached a length of fifty to sixty-five cm and a weight of 1·5 to 3·5 kg. The fish which remain a second winter in the sea and return to freshwater in the following year when they are approximately two years old are salmon and are normally between 70 cm and 90 cm in length and 4–6 kg in weight. A relatively small proportion of fish (greater from some rivers than from others) remains at sea for three years or longer. These fish become large salmon and after three years sea feeding reach lengths of 90-105 cm and weights of 8-14 kg or more.

The longer Atlantic salmon remain at sea before returning to freshwater on their first spawning migration, the larger they become, but the oldest 'maiden' fish seldom exceeds four

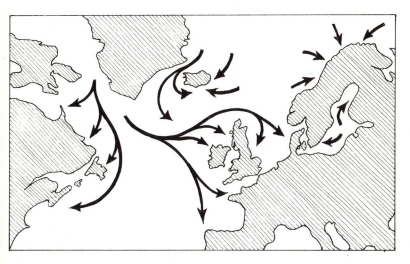

Fig. 4 Return migration routes of Atlantic salmon from major feeding grounds

sea winters in age. The males are generally considerably larger than the females. The biggest Atlantic salmon taken by nets in the Tana River, which is in Finnmark in the far north of Norway and runs into the Barents Sea, exceeded 45 kg (100lb) in weight.

Atlantic salmon appear (from scale reading) to feed continuously throughout their marine life, but more intensively in the spring and summer than during the winter. Indications are that the winter reduction in growth rate is less in the open sea populations than for those in the Baltic, where growth in winter is a good deal slower than during the summer, probably due to surface ice formation and lower water temperatures. On the other hand, growth in summer appears to be proportionately greater in the Baltic salmon. Salmon in water of full oceanic salinity (33 – 34 parts per thousand) appear to continue to feed intensively at lower temperatures than populations in brackish water (and most probably populations in freshwater).

Comparable rates of growth for wild salmon, deduced from scale samples taken from fish caught on their sea feeding grounds in various months of the year, show that the rate of growth of Baltic salmon is generally slightly more rapid than that of salmon in the North-West Atlantic, but neither group grows as quickly as salmon feeding in the seas off the north coast of Norway. These observed patterns of marine growth are probably much more indicative of genetic, racial differences than of the physical characteristics of the marine environment of the fish or the abundance and variety of the species preyed upon as food in the different sea areas.

The growth rates of freshwater races of Atlantic salmon in large lakes in Northern Europe and North America, where shoals of fish species are present, are quite comparable to those attained in the sea. Atlantic salmon held experimentally in freshwater beyond the time of smoltification in Sweden and in Canada grew at a rate equal to fish of same year class in water of full marine salinity. The fact that wild populations of Atlantic salmon can grow as rapidly in a suitable freshwater environment as they can in the sea may have far reaching implications for the future of salmon farming.

Chapter 2

The Pacific Salmons

There are six species of salmon which are native to the rivers flowing into the Pacific and Eastern Arctic Oceans. Five of these species are native to rivers in North America. They also occur naturally in rivers on the Kamchatka peninsula in the USSR which flows into the sea of Okhotsk and in other rivers running out into the Bering Sea and to the far north into the East Siberian and Laptev Seas. The sixth species is a small salmon called masu which runs up the rivers on the islands of Hokkaido in Japan and Sakhalin off the coast of Manchuria. It may also occur in some rivers on the Manchurian mainland.

Two species of Pacific salmon have been successfully introduced into rivers in the southern hemisphere and more recently into rivers in the European Arctic flowing into the White Sea from the Kola Peninsula to the west of Murmansk.

In common with most other members of the salmon family some Pacific species have races which naturally spend their entire life cycle in freshwater and others have been successfully acclimatized to freshwater life, notably in the Great Lakes in Canada. They can grow to full size without going to sea provided there is sufficient food in the freshwater environment. Successful growth on free range in freshwater lakes depends on the presence of a shoaling food fish in sufficiently large numbers, usually belonging to the smelt or herring family. The freshwater populations which have been deliberately introduced have so far had to be supported by hatcheries.

The freshwater introductions in Canada were originally made in order to find a substitute species for the Great Lake trout (*Salvelinus namaycush*) which is in fact a charr. This species, which was of great commercial importance, had been decimated by the colonization of the Great Lakes by the sea lamprey (*Petromyson marinus*) which followed the opening of the St Lawrence seaway. The lampreys spawned in the rivers draining into the lakes. Their progeny no longer needed to migrate to the sea as they could grow to maturity feeding on the larger freshwater fish species. The lampreys were eventually controlled by using a specific poison. The lakes were then stocked with two species of Pacific salmon. These introductions have proved enormously successful, not only in providing the opportunity for a commercial fishery of much greater value than that for the lake trout, but in the contribution the new fishery has made to sporting angling in both Canada and the USA.

The five most important species of Pacific salmon belong to a single, separate genus and they are distinct from Atlantic salmon, the trout and the charrs. The generic name of the Pacific salmon is *Oncorynchus* and this precedes the proper name of each species. The individual species have many different common names. Those used here are generally adopted by the salmon fishing industry in Canada and the USA. They are pink *(gorbuscha),* sockeye *(nerka),* coho or silver *(kisutch),* chum *(keta)* and spring or chinook *(tschawytscha).* The Latin names sound strangely exotic because the species were originally classified by Russian scientists working on rivers on the opposite side of the ocean.

All five species exist in the wild in great abundance. They have been fished for as a staple food by man since pre–historic times. The natives on both sides of the North Pacific originally fished for salmon on their return to spawn in their parent rivers. More recently they have been fished for further and further afield, on their ocean feeding grounds, using sophisticated fishing gear and drift–nets. The inroads made on stocks by increasingly efficient fishing methods have led to the imposition of greater and greater controls, firstly on a national and then on an international basis. Now the catch and spawning escapement in North America is scientifically regulated and a measure of stock management has been achieved.

Recent developments have seen the increasing success of ranching techniques being employed in Japan and in the USA.

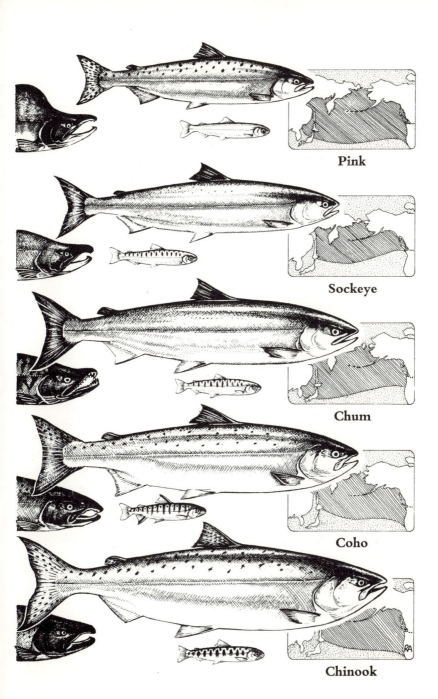

Pink

Sockeye

Chum

Coho

Chinook

Fig. 5 Pacific salmons: showing typical ocean-going adults, fry and heads of spawning males. Maps show sea feeding grounds; stocks from both sides of the Pacific Ocean may meet in the central area

These involve rearing young salmon in an artificial environment, releasing them to feed, free ranging in the sea, and recapturing them commercially on their return to the place where they were released.

All five species must return to freshwater to spawn. The young of two of the five species go down to the sea as fry, either shortly after the yolk-sac has been absorbed or early in the first summer. The other three species have a parr life period of one or two years in freshwater and migrate to the sea as smolt.

The marine diet varies to some extent between the species but consists principally of euphausid shrimps, and the fatty shoal fishes such as pilchards, anchovies, eulachons, smelts and the needlefish *(Cololabis saira)*. The species which migrate as smolt feed initially on a particularly abundant euphausid shrimp (*Thysanoessa spinifera*). This food animal, which is known as the 'red feed' is the main constituent of the diet of sockeye salmon throughout their sea life. This species is less pisciverous than the other four and does not feed, to the same extent, on other fish.

Some species meet on their oceanic feeding grounds and the eastern race of pink salmon from the Kamchatka rivers mingles with the pink salmon from North American rivers feeding in the sea. The marine life before reaching sexual maturity also varies between the species. Pink salmon are the smallest and the youngest at the time of return on spawning migration, having spent one or one and a half years at sea. Sockeye salmon spend two or three years growing to sexual maturity and chum and chinook disappear into the ocean for three or four years. Coho salmon more closely resemble Atlantic salmon and spend one or two years at sea returning to spawn, when they are between three and five years old.

Chum Salmon (*Oncorynchus keta*)

Chum salmon occur in Asia and North America and in Japan. They are most abundant in the Asian rivers. The common names are *keta* in Russian and *sake* in Japanese.

Recognition

The body is elongated and rather compressed looked at from above. The caudal peduncle (junction between body and tail fin) is slender. The head comes to a point at the mouth which has well-developed teeth that turn into fangs when the male fish are in spawning dress. The first gill arch has ten to sixteen rakers and there are 150-160 scales counted along the lateral line. The scales are similar to those of other salmon and show the age of the fish.

The colour in marine feeding dress is metallic blue on the back with a few black flecks. There are no regular black spots. The fins are edged with black particularly in the male fish. The appearance completely changes when the fish shift into spawning dress in freshwater. The males develop distinctive dusky red streaks on their sides which join together below the lateral line and the body colour turns a greenish yellow along the sides of the fish. The heads of the male fish have the elongated and slightly dished appearance typical of the salmon family but the leading end of the lower jaw does not develop the pronounced upward growth or kype typical of Atlantic salmon.

The flesh colour of the fish in marine feeding condition is pale pink and the fat content is 9-11%.

The young fish have green iridescent backs and parr finger-marking on their sides which does not go much below the lateral line.

Spawning

The majority of fish reach their spawning grounds between September and January but in some northern rivers spawning can take place in June or July. The spawning process is similar to that of Atlantic salmon and takes place in fast-flowing, shallow streams with clean gravel beds. The process lasts over three to five days. In very cold regions the female fish appear to select gravel where there are springs in the river bed which maintain a temperature that does not fall below about 4°C.

The number of eggs shed varies between two thousand

and five thousand. The eggs are comparatively large and average about 7 mm in diameter. Both males and females of all the species of Pacific salmon die after spawning.

River Life

Eggs hatch after one hundred to one hundred and twenty days. The alevins average 23 mm in length and this phase lasts thirty to fifty days dependent on water temperature. The larval fish start to feed before the yolk-sac is fully absorbed.

The fry emerge from the gravel some time between March and May depending on the location. They can remain in the river for several months but the majority leave for the sea early in the summer after a few weeks of freshwater life.

Chum salmon fry show an increasing preference for salt-water and become pre-adapted to marine osmoregulation. The fry are very difficult to maintain in freshwater for any period after their normal time of migration.

The average size at migration to the sea is 3·5 cm.

The food in freshwater consists of plankton animals followed by insect larvae.

Marine Feeding and Growth in the Sea

Marine food initially consists of zooplankton followed by copepods, euphausids and other small marine animals including some small fish. The diet contains a high proportion of invertebrates throughout the period of sea feeding.

Most fish reach sexual maturity after three years marine life but some spend only one year in the sea and others as many as six years before returning to their parent rivers on spawning migration.

The average length of the fish when three years old is 50–70 cm and the average weight 2·5 kg. The largest fish, which are six years old, can be up to 6 kg in weight.

Hybrids

Chum salmon have been successfully crossed with pink and

sockeye salmon and the hybrids back-crossed with other hybrids within these species or with the species themselves.

Fish Farming

Chum salmon have not attracted much attention as a species for farming. The reason is most probably that they were not considered a very high-quality fish in North America when compared to the other Pacific species and would cost as much to feed-on to market size in captivity.

The procedures for incubation and hatching are straightforward and chum salmon are now being 'ranched' on a very large scale in Japan. The fry are hatched artificially and released to feed on 'free-range' in the sea. The crop is partly taken by enhanced off-shore marine fishing but the greater proportion of the catch is made by traps as the fish return on spawning migration.

Chum salmon are also ranched in the USSR and have been introduced into the rivers draining into the White Sea. Chum salmon spawned in these rivers have been caught in Norwegian waters.

Sockeye Salmon (*Oncorynchus nerka*)

It can be argued that the differences in the behaviour between the various species of Pacific salmon have developed as a means of avoiding competition and in order to make maximum use of the available freshwater environment for reproduction. Some species have individual races with widely differing patterns of behaviour involving time of return from the sea on spawning migration, habitat during parr life and adaptation to a completely freshwater life.

Sockeye salmon consist of many different races not only present in different rivers but also occurring in different parts of the same river system. The species also has a race completely adapted to spend its entire life cycle in freshwater which occurs in many lakes in British Columbia.

Recognition

The body is less elongated than in chum salmon, which are not unlike sockeye when feeding in the sea, but the species can be easily distinguished from all the other Pacific species by the number of gill rakers (twenty-eight to forty) on the first gill arch.

The fish are bright silver when feeding in the sea and the body and fins are unmarked apart from some fine speckles on the back which is shaded blue-green. In spawning dress the bodies of both males and females turn deep red and the heads become dark greenish grey. The males develop pronounced protrusions on the ends of both the upper and lower jaws.

The flesh during marine feeding is deep red and when canned is regarded as the highest grade.

Sockeye during early life before migrating to the sea have typical parr markings which become obscured during smoltification. Races which remain and grow to sexual maturity in freshwater become silvery but are more spotted than the sea-going form.

Spawning

Sockeye salmon usually spawn in small tributary streams above a lake, often having made a long and arduous journey upstream. Vast numbers, perhaps fifteen million spawning pairs, are concentrated in particular parts of the range of the species, notably the Frazer River in British Columbia and rivers running into Bristol Bay in Alaska. Generally the early returning fish travel furthest upstream. The first runs into the Frazer River start in July and early August and continue into late September and October.

River Life

The young fish hatched in tributary streams drop back to the lakes to feed on zooplankton followed by the typical freshwater diet of young salmonids consisting mainly of insect larvae and small crustaceans. A small proportion of sockeye migrate to sea before they have completed one year of freshwater life but the majority spend one or two years as parr. The proportion of larval fish spending more than two years in freshwater before migrating to the sea increases in the stocks belonging to the Alaskan rivers.

Freshwater Races and Adaptation to Saltwater

The process of smoltification and adaptation to marine life is similar to that of other anadromous salmonids. Races of sockeye can remain throughout their life cycle in their freshwater lake habitat although they are freely able to go to sea. The freshwater races are called kokanees. They feed round the lakes in concentrated shoals and do not grow to a weight of more than about 500–750 gm. Kokanees have not so far been farmed for the table market but they have been extensively stocked as sport fish for angling in many lakes in the Western USA.

Marine Feeding and Growth in the Sea

Sockeye are the least pisciverous of the Pacific salmon and their marine diet consists mainly of small crustacea but includes some small fish.

The fish reach sexual maturity after two or three years feeding in the sea. The age at spawning migration can be a racial characteristic but the typical four-year cycle of Frazer River sockeye, consisting of one year in a freshwater lake, three years in the sea and a return to the parental spawning ground to spawn and die, can vary considerably between fish of the same stock. Some fish may return a year older having spent an extra year in the sea and others a year younger having migrated from freshwater in the first summer of larval life. The proportion of five-year-old and even six- or seven-year-old fish increases in the Alaskan rivers.

The largest fish can grow to a weight of 6–7 kg and a length of 75–80 cm. The average canning weight is generally about 2·25 kg and the fish are generally small in relation to some of the other Pacific salmon.

Fish Farming

Although sockeye salmon eggs can be incubated and hatched without difficulty and there would seem to be no special problems connected with on-growing, they have not so far been of much interest to fish farmers. Their excellent flesh quality and the fact that certain races mature late seem useful attributes and the natural ability to adapt to life in either fresh or salt water also seems an attractive characteristic.

Pink Salmon (*Oncorynchus gorbuscha*)

This species is sometimes called humpbacked salmon because of the ugly cartilaginous 'hump' that forms on the backs of male fish when they are approaching spawning time. It occurs in large rivers in North America and Asia and is the most abundant species in the Alaskan salmon fishery and in the North Pacific. The Russians have introduced pink salmon into rivers running into the White Sea and the species now spawns sporadically in the lower reaches of rivers in north Norway.

Recognition

The first gill arch has twenty-eight rakers. The fish can be distinguished from all the other Pacific salmon species by the large number of small scales. It has 170–240 in the first row above the lateral line.

The overall colour in the sea-life period is silver in both sexes with greenish–blue along the back. The fish are generally distinctively marked with a few large, dark oval marks (about thumb print size) on their backs and on the lobes of the tail. The male fish become brick red in spawning dress as well as developing the characteristic 'hump'.

The flesh is pink, rather than red, which accounts for the common name of the species. They are regarded as being of lesser quality for canning than sockeye salmon.

Spawning

There are many different races of pink salmon with minor differences in behaviour patterns, but in most rivers where the species is native spawning takes place in late summer (August – September) not far above the head of tide. The eggs are shed in nests or redds made by the female fish in fairly shallow, fast-flowing water, typical of the salmon family. The average female fish produces about one thousand five hundred eggs.

River Life

The eggs take approximately 100 – 125 days to hatch and the alevins (newly-hatched young fish) have exceptionally large yolk-sacs. The alevins remain passive in the gravel until the water begins to warm up in the spring which can be as early as March in southern rivers and well into May in northern rivers. The long time which the alevins remain in the gravel makes them vulnerable to suffocation by silting. The fry are silvery when they leave the gravel, without the spots and parr markings of the other salmon fry, and they descend directly to the sea.

Marine Feeding and Growth in the Sea

During the first months of sea life the young fish collect in dense shoals close inshore before moving out to their ocean feeding grounds. The fish feed on crustaceans, squid, sand-eels and other small fish. Marine growth is rapid and pink salmon reach sexual maturity in two years. The short life cycle distinguishes this species from the other Pacific salmon and also from other anadromous salmonids. The weight at maximum sea-growth is 2-3 kg and the length 40-50 cm. A few fish can grow to a weight of 4·5 kg in their short, two-year life span.

There are numerous races of pink salmon and the year classes of different races go through regular cycles of abundance. The fish produced in years of low survival are generally larger than those from the year classes with a high rate of survival to maturity.

Fish Farming

Pink salmon have been reared to maturity in captivity in Europe as well as in North America and Asia. They have proved a useful species to cultivate in sea cages or enclosures.

The prolonged period of alevin development can be shortened if warm water is available but great care must be taken not to over-accelerate the naturally slow absorption of the yolk-sacs. A supply of salt water, preferably of full oceanic salinity is essential, as the fish are too small to be transferred to netting cages, even of the smallest mesh, until they reach a weight of about 200 to the kg.

Pink salmon can be grown to market size in captivity in less time than they take in the wild, using ordinary high-fat salmon diets. The wild races can be farmed successfully, but in the longer term selective breeding or hybridization may lead to the development of a more truly domesticated sub-species.

Coho Salmon (*Oncorynchus kisutch*)

Coho or silver salmon are the Pacific species whose behaviour and life cycle most closely resembles that of Atlantic salmon. They are also a sporting fish for anglers. They are strongly pisciverous and are fished for commercially by trolling with spoons or spinning baits. The species readily adapts to life in freshwater and grows to full-size provided there is an adequate supply of food fish.

Recognition

The internal feature which distinguishes the species from the other Pacific salmons is the low number of pyloric caeca (forty-five to eighty-three). Externally, the tail is less forked than in the other species.

The marine feeding colour is silver with small black spots

on the back and on the lobe of the tail. The gums are noticeably white at the base of the teeth. The male fish become red in spawning dress and develop a kype or hook on the lower jaw.

The flesh is pinkish red in colour, very similar to that of Atlantic salmon. Large quantities of coho eggs are preserved in brine and sold as 'red' or salmon caviar. Unlike the commercial catch of the other Pacific salmon which is generally canned, coho are usually marketed fresh and quick-frozen.

Spawning

Coho are the salmon of the lesser rivers. They make their way into the smaller streams to reach their spawning grounds, which may be close to the head of tide or far up in the head-waters. Spawning behaviour is similar to that of Atlantic salmon.

Female fish can vary considerably in size. The quantity of eggs produced is between 1,500 and 2,000 per kg of body weight. Spawning takes place in the autumn or early winter, earlier in the more northern rivers. Coho do not deteriorate in condition on spawning migration to the same extent as the other Pacific salmon and some spawned-out fish remain alive for several months, although they all die before the spring and there are no survivors.

River Life

The hatching of eggs is controlled by the water temperature and incubation takes approximately four hundred day/degrees. The fry usually emerge from the gravel in late April or May, earlier or later depending on location north or south in the range of the species.

The parr have brown backs and orange fins. Their behaviour, freshwater growth and size at seaward migration resemble more closely Atlantic salmon than the other Pacific species. Coho parr remain in freshwater for one or two years before smolt migration. The average weight at smoltification in one year is about 20 gm.

Marine Feeding and Growth in the Sea

Coho migrate long distances in the sea and their marine feeding behaviour is very similar to that of Atlantic salmon. They spend the first year mainly feeding on crustaceans before becoming almost completely pisciverous. They then feed on high-fat shoal fish such as herrings and needlefish. Growth is very rapid in the second year and the weight increases from 1 to 1·5 kg in March to 5–7 kg in September – October when they start on spawning migration.

The life cycle of most coho consists of one year freshwater parr life followed by two years in the sea. Parr life can extend to two years and adult fish may not return to spawn until they have reached a total age of three to five years.

The average weight of fish at the end of the marine feeding period is normally between 2·5 kg and 6 kg and the length between 60 and 90 cm according to the time spent in the sea.

Fish Farming

Coho is the Pacific salmon species which has attracted most attention from fish farmers in North America and is of increasing interest for sea farming in Europe.

Coho salmon reared in floating net cages in the Puget Sound area of Washington State grew to a weight of 340 gm in six to eight months. A considerable proportion of the coho farmed in the north-west USA are slaughtered and marketed at what is termed 'pan-size' when they have reached a weight of 250-300 gm.

The fish that are grown-on may reach sexual maturity after ten to twelve months in the sea when they weigh between 1 and 2 kg, as opposed to wild fish in the same area which weigh between 2·5 and 5·5 kg when they return on spawning migration. The tendency to mature early may be an additional inducement to slaughter the fish as soon as they reach marketable size.

Initial growth in freshwater can be accelerated if the temperature is raised to between 11°C and 12°C and pre-smolt coho parr can be grown to a weight of 18–20 gm ready for transfer to saltwater in seven to eight months compared to twelve to fourteen months in unheated water. The total growing time taken from fry to slaughter at 'pan-size' can therefore be reduced to about fourteen months, but this is still longer than it takes to grow some other salmonids to a similar size in captivity.

An interesting feature of the natural behaviour of coho is that they can grow to maturity in freshwater without being transferred to the sea. This factor will no doubt play a part in the future development of methods of culturing the species in captivity.

Chinook Salmon (*Oncorynchus tschawytscha*)

The common name of this species is taken from the Chinook Indians, a tribe on the north-west coast of America whose survival was linked to these salmon returning to the Columbia River. Local names include spring and king, and very large fish are called tyee salmon. The natural range in western America extends from California to Alaska. Chinook have also been successfully introduced to rivers in the South Island of New Zealand, where they have formed truly anadromous stocks.

Recognition

They are deep, stoutly made fish with a thick caudal peduncle. Any very large Pacific salmon over 14 kg in weight is almost certainly a chinook and it is only in the middle-size range that they can be confused with coho. They can, however, be easily distinguished internally because they have many more pyloric caeca (140–185).

The backs of the male fish are often very dark and almost black. The sides above the lateral line and the dorsal and caudal fins are heavily marked with fairly large, black spots. The males usually become darker and go reddish round the fins and on the belly while finding the way back from their ocean

OLSON LIBRARY
NORTHERN MICHIGAN UNIVERSITY
MARQUETTE, MICHIGAN 49855

feeding grounds, before they have reached their parent rivers. The male spawning dress is spectacular. The body becomes dark red with a bright red tail fin. A heavy kype develops and the teeth lengthen into fangs. When the fish of both sexes are ripe to spawn, the skin becomes spongy and grows over the scale pockets.

The flesh is pinkish-red but coarser than that of coho. River-caught fish make excellent smokers if they are not too far gone towards spawning.

Spawning

The local name 'spring' salmon originally derived from the early run which enters the Columbia River in April and May. This is followed by other distinct runs, a summer run in June and July and an autumn run in August and September. In some other rivers, the main run of chinook takes place in the spring but some fish continue to enter through the summer and on into the late autumn and winter if the rivers remain ice-free. The early entering fish usually travel furthest upstream to their spawning grounds and the late fish spawn nearer the tideways.

Adult chinook remain in freshwater for some time as they are inhibited from spawning until the water temperature falls below 12°C. Female chinook shed between three thousand and twelve thousand eggs depending on their size and the eggs are 6-7 mm in diameter.

River Life

Chinook can descend to saltwater soon after hatching but a proportion remain in their parent rivers for a parr life of one or two years. They resemble coho and can only be told apart with certainty by the much larger number of pyloric caeca.

Marine Feeding and Growth in the Sea

Chinook are pisciverous from an early age, feeding on herring and other fatty, shoal fish. The majority of young chinook which descend to the sea before they have completed a year of freshwater life return to spawn after three sea winters. In some rivers five and six year olds are common and the very large fish have usually had more than five years of sea feeding. In the most northerly rivers all the young chinook have a parr life of more than one year and most of the female fish returning to spawn are six or seven years old, with the male fish generally a year younger.

Chinook are the largest of the Pacific salmon. The average weight at the end of marine life is about 10 kg, taken throughout the range of the species, but the largest fish can be over 45 kg in weight and more than 150 cm in length.

Fish Farming

Chinook are being farmed commercially in net cages in the sea in western North America but they have not so far been of interest to fish farmers of Europe. The growth rate in wild fish is not as fast as in some other salmonids or other species of Pacific salmon but the fact that some races of chinook appear to mature very late and grow to large size could prove to be an attraction.

Chapter 3

Trouts and Charrs

All species of trout and nearly all the world's charr have races which go down to the sea at some stage in their life history. They are in most cases fully anadromous and undergo physiological changes which enable them to adapt to a saline environment after a genetically prescribed period of early life in freshwater.

The true trouts and charrs are sometimes all deliberately classified together as 'trout'. This may simplify the use of the common names of the different species but it is not correct and only leads to greater confusion.

Most fish have teeth not only on their jawbones but also on other bony structures in their mouths. The basic taxonomic difference between the trouts and the charrs is in the arrangement of the teeth at the anterior end and along the length of the bone from front to rear. The charrs all have the teeth set in a line across the anterior end of the bone and the remainder of the bone is toothless.

The difficulties over common names arose when settlers from Britain first colonized eastern North America. They found Atlantic salmon in many rivers but they also found fish which looked very like the trout they had left behind at home in the West Country of England. They called these fish 'brook trout' to distinguish them from a much bigger obviously troutlike fish in the lakes which they logically called 'lake trout'. Both these species were in fact charrs and have since been classified and given the names of *Salvelinus fontinalis* and *Salvelinus namaycush*.

The proper names of all the true trouts have the prefix *Salmo*. The only trout native to Europe and Asia is *Salmo trutta*. This species is made up of very many different races, some of which have differences sufficient to be classified as sub-

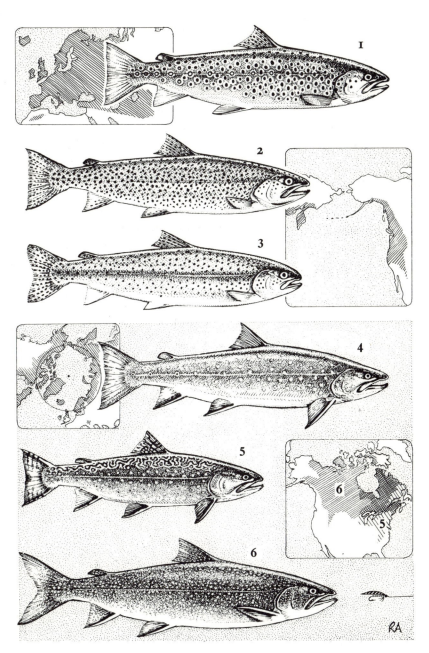

Fig. 6 Trout and charr: **1** Brown trout **2** Cutthroat trout (coastal form) **3** Rainbow trout **4** Arctic charr **5** Brook charr **6** Lake charr

species. There is also more than one sea-going, anadromous race of *Salmo trutta* and a race with a salmon-like life cycle that grows to great size in very large lakes and spawns in their tributary rivers where young fish spend a period as parr before migrating downstream to grow to maturity in the lake.

Two species of trout are native to North America, occurring on the western side of the continent. The common species is the rainbow trout. It has several near relations which are sometimes given status as separate species. These include the golden trout of Mexico, the Californian golden trout, the gila trout and the apache trout.

The cutthroat trout is a genuinely separate species and both rainbow and cutthroat have anadromous races. Sea-going rainbow trout are known as 'steelhead' and they range further in the sea and grow larger than the more coastal-feeding cutthroat.

Native charrs occur in lakes and rivers throughout the northern hemisphere. The most common species is the Arctic charr which is circum-polar in distribution and has non-migratory and sea-going races. Local populations of non-migratory charr inhabiting many European lakes have developed separately since the last Ice Age. In the ten thousand years or so the concentrated gene pools have resulted in the appearance of distinct racial characteristics.

Tate Regan working on the British and Irish charrs in the nineteenth century separated individual populations which he considered to be separate species and classified with different names. This principle was later abandoned and the single species name of *Salvelinus alpinus* was adopted for all the European charr, although there is some justification for the older concept when the very wide range of racial differentiation is taken into consideration.

North America has four distinct species of charr, the Arctic charr, the brook charr or 'trout', the lake charr or 'trout' and the Dolly Varden charr or 'trout'. All these species occur in sea-going form. The Great Lake charr is the only species that does not migrate to sea. A distinctive feature of the charrs as opposed to the trouts, is that most species have races that can spawn in suitable parts of lakes and do not need running water.

Only rainbow trout out of all the species of trout and charr have so far been selected for large-scale commercial farming as a table-market fish, although all the species have been cultured at some time or other for re-stocking rivers and lakes. Several species of charr are now being experimentally grown for the table market.

There are other less well-known but interesting members of the salmon family that might usefully be domesticated and bred in captivity. These include the two related species of freshwater 'salmon' called huchen and taimen that live in very large Eastern European and Asiatic rivers, and the Adriatic salmon trout which is found only in rivers on the Dalmatian Coast of the Mediterranean Sea.

Wild stocks of rainbow trout and of the North American charrs have been established in European waters and under suitable conditions in the southern hemisphere. The common European brown or German trout (*Salmo trutta*) have also been transplanted and acclimatized in North America and in the southern hemisphere. It is therefore quite possible to cultivate these members of the salmon family anywhere in the world if the correct environment can be provided in temperature and water quality.

Brown or German Trout (*Salmo trutta*)

The most widely distributed of the world's trout, this species occurs naturally in many different, racially distinct forms throughout Europe, parts of North Africa and the Middle East and the western side of Asia. The most familiar form is perhaps the typical river trout of Western Europe.

Recognition

The species has ten or less branched rays in the anal fin. There are less than 130 scales along the lateral line and fourteen to nineteen scales counted in a downward, diagonal direction between the adipose fin and the lateral line.

Life History and Behaviour

There are three basic types of *Salmo trutta* which have developed different patterns of behaviour in accordance with their environment.

River Trout

This is the most familiar form and the fish are hatched and live out their life cycle in a river or stream. They can remain dwarfed in size, never reaching a length of more than 20-30 cm and mature early when they are only two or three years old. In rich chalk streams with alkaline water and a plentiful food supply river trout can grow to a weight of 2-5 kg becoming sexually mature after three to four years and surviving for ten to fourteen years.

The external appearance of river trout can vary greatly. The young fish develop typical salmonid parr markings like finger-prints on their sides. These disappear before sexual maturity and the red and brown spots along the sides of the fish become larger and ringed with white. The colour darkens and in rivers where the young fish tend to be silvery this coating is lost and never returns.

The food of river trout consists initially of plankton animals. As the fish grow the diet includes insects, crustacea and small fish. The trout in smaller rivers and streams become territorial from a very early age and take up a station which they continue to occupy until a better place becomes vacant through the disappearance or absence of the previous occupant. The largest and most aggressive fish take over the most favourable positions for the collection of any food brought downstream in the current.

In large rivers some individuals change to pisciverous feeding. Their growth rate then increases rapidly and they soon greatly exceed in size others of the same year class. The trout which start to feed on other fish no longer occupy a territory but hunt their prey over a wide area. There is no apparent explanation for the change to pisciverous feeding which seems to occur at random and to have no clear genetic explanation.

Lake Trout

Salmo trutta inhabiting most lakes have a life history and growth rate not unlike that of river trout. Fish in small lakes will ascend any tributary stream to spawn and the young fish feed and grow to sexual maturity in the lakes. Rich, eutrophic lakes will usually support a population of fast-growing fish. Oligotrophic lakes producing little in the way of food fauna but also having little available spawning ground may still have a small population of fairly large, slow-growing trout. On the other hand, lakes of this type with good spawning ground in tributary streams will have a large population of small fish.

The average growth rate for *Salmo trutta* in lakes is generally similar to that of river trout in water of a comparable chemistry. The fish in larger, richer lakes tend to take longer to reach sexual maturity and during the initial years of lake life are silvery in colour. At this stage they often form small schools which roam as a group in search of food. In most lake systems spawning takes place in tributary rivers but in some lakes, particulary those on high ground, the adult fish may move downstream into the outlet river to spawn.

Salmo trutta in the largest lakes which are virtually inland seas may adopt a completely different behaviour pattern compared to other members of this species. The huge lakes where this racially distinct type of trout is to be found are usually on big rivers. The trout behave very much like Atlantic salmon and eventually grow to comparable size although they take longer to do so and spawn a number of times. The environmental factor which appears to induce this life-style is the presence in the lake of a large population of some food fish, usually a corregonid or whitefish. They are fully migratory and usually spawn in the main river flowing into the lake. Although they may not be ripe to spawn until late September and October, the adult fish may enter the river as early as June or July and run upstream for fifty miles or more before reaching their spawning grounds. The young fish spend one to three years of parr life in the river before migrating downstream to the lake. The growth rate is quite comparable to that of the anadromous race and the fish can reach a weight of more than 15 kg. Very large trout of this variety have been taken from the innsjø in Norway and from lakes in Switzerland, Austria and Germany such as the Chiem See, where a trout over 27 kg was once taken in the commercial nets.

Sea Trout

The anadromous, sea-going form of *Salmo trutta* occurs in European rivers from the White Sea to the north coast of Spain. Related forms migrate to and from the rivers running into the Black and Caspian Seas. The seaward migration of young fish usually takes place in the spring or early summer when they have reached a length of 15–25 cm and an age of one to five years, taking longer to reach migratory size in the more northern rivers. They do not range far to sea usually remaining well inside the continental shelf during their marine life.

Some immature or precocious fish return to freshwater after having spent only a few months at sea. Most fish return after having spent one to three years at sea and having reached a weight of 1–2 kg, but some spend up to five years marine feeding and grow to a weight of 7–8 kg before returning on first spawning migration.

Sea trout can survive to spawn many times in either successive or alternate years, returning to sea to feed in the interim. Spawning takes place in October/November and in northern rivers may take place after Atlantic salmon have finished spawning.

The largest anadromous form of *Salmo trutta* is the Caspian race. Fish of over 45 kg are occasionally taken while on spawning migration into rivers in the USSR and a monster of 50 kg was reported from the Kura River in Azerbaijan.

Spawning

All races of *Salmo trutta* spawn in the typical salmonid fashion, the female fish making a redd or nest in the gravel in which she deposits her eggs. The average number of eggs shed is approximately 1,500 per kg of body weight and more than ten thousand eggs are sometimes produced by large female fish. The eggs can be 3-7 mm in diameter according to the size of the parent.

The eggs of *Salmo trutta* take approximately 410 day/ degrees to incubate. The fry can be distinguished from those of Atlantic salmon because the fingerprint parr markings are less clearly defined. They can also be distinguished from rainbow trout fry because they do not have any spots on their tail fins.

Farming

Salmo trutta have been cultivated in captivity for re-stocking rivers and lakes since the middle years of the nineteenth century. For some reason they have not attracted attention as a fish to be farmed for the table market. It is difficult to understand why this should be so because in many respects certain races of *Salmo trutta* have much to recommend them to fish farmers.

Brown trout are not so easy to domesticate as rainbow trout and do not grow so quickly in their first summer, although they can grow equally well in the second summer. The principal advantage of brown trout over rainbow trout would seem to be that some races grow to comparatively large size before reaching sexual maturity. The most interesting possibility seems to be the culture of the racial type occurring in very large freshwater lakes or inland seas. These fish might be grown-on in cages in freshwater to a size comparable to that achieved by Atlantic salmon. There is also the possibility of using sea trout of the truly anadromous race as an alternative to rainbow trout of the 'steelhead' type to cultivate in cages or enclosures in the sea.

Rainbow Trout (*Salmo gairdneri*)

The home range of this species extends from the Kuskokwim River in Alaska south through British Columbia to Baja in California. It is primarily a native of the coastal rivers of western North America but also occurs on the eastern side of the Great Divide in the headwaters of the Peace River in British Columbia and the Athabasca in Alberta. There is also a native population in the Rio Casa Grandes in the Mexican province of Chihuahua. The migratory race of sea-going steelhead grow more quickly and are generally bigger than the non-migratory race which lives out its life cycle in rivers but the largest rainbow trout are found in freshwater lakes. A near relative is the Far Eastern trout (*Salmo mykiss*) which occurs in the Kamchatka rivers in Asia.

The species is the hardiest of the salmonids and tolerates a wider range of environmental differences. It has been success-fully introduced into many rivers and lakes in the southern hemisphere where it has established self-sustaining, wild populations. Stocking proved particularly successful in the highlands of Peru, notably in Lake Titicaca, where fish of over 15 kg were not uncommon in commercial catches.

Rainbow trout are the fish farmers' fish and have been domesticated and cultured for the table market since the late nineteenth century. They now form the basis of an industry which has developed and continues to grow in importance in practically every country which can provide a suitable fresh or salt water environment in both hemispheres.

Recognition

There are ten or less branched rays in the anal fin. The west coast race in North America has 120 - 140 scales counted along the row immediately above the lateral line. The kamloops and shasta races may have up to 180 scales in the lateral line series.

The back and sides of the body and the fins are densely spotted with black spots. There is a pink band extending from the gill covers along the sides of the fish to the caudal peduncle, above and below the lateral line.

Life History and Behaviour

The life cycle of rainbow trout on their native range in North America resembles that of brown trout in Western Europe. The anadromous, coastal races of both species spend one to five years of parr life in their parent rivers before migrating to sea. In the most northerly rivers, the steelhead trout in northern Alaska and in the North West Territories are replaced by sea-going Arctic charr, as are the sea trout in some rivers in the far north of Norway and in Iceland.

The spawning behaviour of rainbow trout differs from that of brown trout which are autumn spawners. The spawning season of the different native races can be any time from September to April extending through the autumn and winter months to the spring. Rainbow trout transplanted to the southern hemisphere retain the same seasons for spawning but this provides the opportunity for a useful exchange between fish farmers who can obtain eyed eggs in practically any month of the year.

Female rainbow trout shed 1,000 - 1,400 eggs per kg of body weight and the eggs take approximately 400 day/degrees to hatch. The parr retain about twelve clearly defined, dark parr finger-marks on their sides until they reach a length of 15-20 cm.

Growth in rivers with a good food supply is faster than brown trout and the fish can reach a weight of 250 gm in the first summer. The anadromous race can grow to 7-9 kg after three years feeding in the sea.

The largest rainbow trout come from freshwater lakes and the fish of the kamloops race which is native to lakes in inland British Columbia are particularly notable for their great size. The record rainbow trout caught on rod-and-line was taken by an angler trolling a bait on Jewel Lake. It weighed 21·8 kg (48 lb).

Cutthroat Trout (*Salmo clarki*)

The natural distribution of this species corresponds to that for rainbow trout. The coastal race occurs in most rivers and streams from Alaska down to the Eel River in northern California. The inland form occurs in rivers and lakes on both sides of the Great Divide. Native populations in lakes in Nevada and Utah and more particularly in the Yellowstone Lake in Idaho were at one time classified as sub-species under the names of *S.c. henshawi* and *S.c. lewisi*.

The sea-going race is not completely anadromous although most coastal cutthroat migrate to sea some time during their life cycle. They do not range far in the sea and remain mainly in estuarial water. Some young coastal cutthroat like steelhead do not migrate to sea but remain as breeding populations in freshwater, as do populations of both cutthroat and rainbow trout which are resident in rivers above impassable falls. Like rainbow trout, the largest cutthroat trout have been reported from freshwater lakes. The species has not been transplanted to any great extent outside North America, although there are small stocks held in Europe and in other parts of the world. Cutthroat seem to be poor competitors and often fail when introduced into rivers with natural stocks of other salmonids.

Recognition

Cutthroat, particularly the young fish, can be confused with rainbow trout which are fairly close relations. The scale counts in the rows immediately above the lateral line range from 150 - 180 in the inland, non-migratory races and from 122 -188 in the coastal forms. The number of pyloric caeca is variable. There are generally reckoned to be twenty-seven to forty-five for cutthroat compared to thirty-nine to eighty for rainbow trout but as with the scale count there is a considerable overlap between species.

The simple recognition feature is the pair of red grooves on the underside of the jaw which gives the name of cutthroat and the absence of the pink band on the sides. The coastal fish are heavily speckled with black spots, more densely below the lateral line than in rainbow trout, but they often become silvery in saltwater and the red throat marks can disappear. The inland forms have fewer but larger spots and may have a reddish tinge on the sides.

Life History and Behaviour

Cutthroat are early spring spawners and the main spawning

time for the coastal race is January–February compared to March–May for steelhead.

The various inland populations differ considerably in growth rate, age at sexual maturity and the number and size of eggs produced by the female fish. In some rivers, fish of the coastal race make only brief, random excursions into saltwater, usually during the summer, with an average stay of about three months between spawnings. The fish which migrate early in life may spend up to a year in tidal water.

The majority of coastal cutthroat mature in the third year when they have reached 400–500 gm and subsequently grow to a maximum weight of about 4 kg. The lacustrine races grow to the largest size. The record cutthroat was taken from Pyramid Lake in Nevada and weighed 18 kg (41 lb). Cutthroat in this lake were said to have died out in the early 1940s but it was re-stocked and by the late 1950s fish up to 7 kg were reported. Inland cutthroat up to 10 kg also occur in other lakes in Nevada.

Hybridization

Wild cutthroat are known to hybridize with rainbow. The species have frequently been hybridized in hatcheries. The proportion of fertile eggs obtained in the cross is generally as high as for either parent species fertilized separately but fry mortalities are abnormally high in the F 1 generation although the F 2 generation yields rather better results. Some additional hybrid vigour has been noted. The close similarities between the species are almost sufficient for cutthroat to be regarded as a sub-species of rainbow trout. The ease of hybridization and the fact that the hybrids appear to be both vigorous and fertile might be of future interest to fish farmers.

The Arctic Charr (*Salvelinus alpinus*)

This is the most widely distributed species of charr. It is present with racial variations in most of the rivers and lakes in the more northern land areas round the Pole. It is primarily an

Arctic species and the anadromous races occur only in the far north of Europe, Asia and North America, including rivers in Greenland. Fishing for the sea-going races was of basic, economic importance in the lives of the native Eskimaux and Yakut peoples. The completely freshwater form exists mainly at the southerly end of the range of the species and there are numerous racially distinct relict varieties in lakes throughout the sub-Arctic and temperate zones in the northern hemisphere. The individual characteristics of the separate stocks have developed through isolation since the last Ice Age. Both the non-migratory and migratory forms can occur in the northern part of the range of the species.

Recognition

In common with all the charrs, the shaft of the vomer bone is toothless. The scales are small with 190 – 240 in the lateral line series.

The colour is a bluish-black back with lighter sides, overlaid with silver in sea-going dress. The back and sides are fairly uniformly covered with pale spots. Spectacular changes take place at the onset of sexual maturity. The colour of the back deepens, the belly becomes blood-red, deeper in the male fish, and the leading ends of the pectoral, pelvic and anal fins become edged with brilliant white.

Life History and Behaviour

The life cycle of the sea-going race is fairly constant throughout the range of the species. There are two forms, one of which returns to spawn in the shallow waters of lakes while the other type remains in running water and spawns there. The spawning season is September to October. The female fish produces 3,000 – 4,000 eggs per kg of body weight which measure 3-4 mm in diameter. The lake spawning variety does not make a redd or nest but spawns over rough, stony ground where the eggs lie between the stones until they hatch. The kelts or spawned out fish return to sea on the spring floods after the ice melts in late May or June of the following year.

The newly hatched fry measure 15 mm in length and have a large yolk-sac which is absorbed in about thirty days. The young fish migrate to sea after a variable period of parr life, some of which may be spent in brackish water.

The marine food consists mainly of small fish and the growth rate varies considerably between different stocks. The fish may take three to six years to become sexually mature reaching a weight of 1-3 kg.

The static population in lakes belong to one of several different basic types which can be either autumn or spring spawning and vary greatly in growth rate and eventual adult size. More than one of these basic types can exist in the same lake. The commonest type is relatively slow-growing and feeds on invertebrates, either planktonic crustacea, or small bottom fauna in comparatively shallow water. A less common race lives in deep water on a pisciverous diet, growing rapidly to reach a weight of 1-2 kg at sexual maturity and continuing to grow-on so that the largest individuals eventually attain weights of 8-10 kg.

There are also two dwarf races, one of which lives in shallow and the other in deep water. The different groups of non-migratory Arctic charr have developed differences in choice of spawning ground and spawn at different times. It is this distinction which has probably served to prevent cross-breeding and the eventual loss of separate characteristics in behaviour.

The quick-growing, pisciverous, non-migratory race and the sea-going race are of interest to fish farmers. They are hardy, easy to domesticate and grow comparatively quickly in captivity. The pisciverous race has an ability to retain carotin and quickly becomes red-fleshed. The species, either on its own or hybridized with another salmonid, seems to have considerable potential as a farmed fish.

Brook Charr (*Salvelinus fontinalis*)

The Eastern brook trout of North America is in truth a fish of the cold 'fountains'. In hot weather, when the rivers are low and warm, they search out the springs in the bogans or backwaters and collect there and in the deeper, cooler water above the beaver dams. The lacustrine form thrives best in the cold, very clean, well-oxygenated water of lakes deep in the woods where in summertime they share the green shade with moose feeding on the lily roots.

The natural distribution of the species is from the New England states northwards to the rivers running into Ungava Bay. They have been introduced, primarily for angling, to many rivers and lakes throughout North America. They were imported to Europe in the late nineteenth century at the same time as rainbow trout and wild self-sustaining stocks have since become established in most European countries. There was a revival of interest in this species as a possible table-market fish in the 1960s. The anadromous and sedentary races are present in the same river systems.

Recognition

The colour varies from pale olive green to blue-grey or black, with a white belly. The most distinctive feature is the vermiform pattern of light markings on the back. The sides are spotted with small, pale spots above and below the lateral line. Some fish have red spots and these may be surrounded with bluish rings. The dorsal and caudal fins are spotted, and the leading ends of the body fins are edged with black and white stripes. The colour deepens on the approach of sexual maturity and the lower sides below the lateral line become suffused with red. The sea-going race is generally lighter in colour and silvery during the marine feeding period.

Life History and Behaviour

Brook charr are autumn or winter spawners. They mature earlier than trout and some male fish can develop functioning gonads in the first winter. Male fish usually reach sexual maturity when they are two to three years old and the females take a year longer.

The spawning time varies from September in the far

north of the natural range of the species to February in ice-free rivers at the southern end of the range. Spawning takes place in fast-flowing, shallow water over a gravel bed and the female fish excavate a nest or redd in which they bury their eggs.

The freshwater as well as the anadromous races migrate in search of spawning gravel in spring-fed streams, where their eggs will not be frozen in the redds. The female fish of average size produce about 2,000 eggs which are approximately 4 mm in diameter. The eggs do not hatch out until the spring. The fry, in their natural environment where the water is cold, grow to a length of 4-7 cm in the first summer.

Brook trout can tolerate a fairly wide range of water temperatures from near freezing point up to 20°C, but the optimum temperature for food conversion and growth is 12° – 15°C. They are voracious feeders on a mixed diet of aquatic and land insects, crustacea and small fish; availability, as with many salmonids, determines the choice of food species. They grow more slowly than either rainbow or brown trout. Fish of three to five years old may reach a length of 30-40 cm and a weight of 0·5-1 kg. Stunted races are common in oligatrophic lakes.

The original importations of brook charr to Europe were made as potential table-market fish but their culture was soon given up in favour of the quicker-growing rainbow trout. In the mid-1960s, the interest of fish farmers in this species was aroused because when crossed with rainbow trout it produced a sterile hybrid. The brook charr x brown trout is well-known to anglers as tiger trout. Brook charr have also been crossed with other salmonids including other species of charr. The ability of this species to store carotin and develop bright red flesh of excellent quality and flavour may encourage further use of brook charr in fish farming either directly or for use as breeding stock to produce a useful hybrid.

Great Lake Charr (*Salvelinus namaycush*)

This is the largest of the North American charrs. Its natural habitat is in the Great Lakes in central and northern Canada and in the northern part of the USA. It also occurs in some Canadian rivers running north into the James and Ungava Bays. It has been introduced into Europe and there are breeding populations in large lakes in Sweden and Switzerland.

Recognition

The body is greenish-grey covered all over, including head, gill covers and dorsal and tail fins, with pale spots. The tail is very deeply forked.

Life History and Behaviour

This species of charr prefers the coldest lakes. Spawning takes place over a gravel bed from September to November, earliest in the most northern waters. The eggs are small and large female fish shed about 2,000 per kg of body weight.

The lake-hatched fry feed initially on invertebrate, bottom fauna but soon move into deep water and become pisciverous.

The fish reach sexual maturity when five to eight years old and may live for twenty-five years. The species is commercially important and fish of 80-90 cm and 7-8 kg are caught in gill nets. The record fish weighed 46·3 kg (102 lb).

The species has not proved of much interest to fish farmers probably because of its slow growth. It has some interesting characteristics, notably that it is easily hybridized with other charr and is late maturing. It merits more consideration for its potential for domestication.

Dolly Varden Charr (*Salvelinus malma*)

Who was Dolly Varden who gave her name to the common charr of the Pacific north-west? She is not remembered in song like Clementine but perhaps she was a fisherman's daugher. 'Dolly trout' like the other North American charr do well in the coldest lakes and rivers. There are coastal populations which migrate to and from the sea, either before or after reaching sexual maturity.

Recognition

The back and sides are dark green-grey shading to yellowish white below the lateral line. The bodies are spotted with orange and red but unlike the other charrs, Dolly Varden have no spots on their fins.

Life History and Behaviour

Spawning time for both sea-going and non-migratory races is the autumn and winter, earliest in the far north.

The young fish soon turn to pisciverous feeding and are regarded as damaging predators in salmon rivers.

The average weight of Dolly Varden in rivers is 0·5-1 kg but the coastal race grows up to 5 kg. The largest fish are generally those that live in lakes although the record rod-caught Dolly Varden, which weighed 16 kg (35 lb) came from the Duncan River in British Columbia.

Dolly Varden have not been of any interest to fish farmers although they grow relatively quickly compared to some other charr and are very good to eat, often having pink or red flesh.

Huchen and Taimen (*Hucho hucho* and *Hucho taimen*)

The Danube salmon or huchen inhabits the middle and upper reaches of the River Danube and is occasionally found in lakes. It does not migrate to the Black Sea. The taimen lives in the great Siberian rivers and also in large lakes. They are neither salmon, trout or charr but are unique species. They are included here because they are the less well-known members of the salmon family and may at some time in the future be of interest to fish farmers.

Recognition

Huchen and taimen are very similar in appearance. Both are relatively long and round in cross-section, rather than deep. The colour is generally greenish-grey with sometimes a coppery tinge along the sides. The species are distinguished by huchen having sixteen gill rakers on the first gill arch while taimen only have eleven or twelve.

Life History and Behaviour

Both species spawn in the spring from March to May, as soon as the rivers are ice-free. In rivers, spawning takes place over gravel in fast-flowing water, where the females excavate a shallow redd. The lake variety usually spawn over gravel in the mouths of incoming rivers. The female fish produce about 1,000 eggs per kg of body weight. The eggs are 5 mm in diameter and hatch after four to five weeks' incubation at $8° - 10°C$.

The food during the first summer consists mainly of invertebrates but growth is rapid. The young fish usually reach a length of 15 cm in the second spring by which time they have become pisciverous. From then on the diet consists almost entirely of other species of freshwater fish.

Both species normally become sexually mature when they are five years old, having reached a length of about 70 cm and a weight of 2-3 kg. They can live for at least fifteen years reaching great size. The largest fish of this species are known to have been about 150 cm in length and over 50 kg in weight.

Neither huchen or taimen have been of interest to fish farmers, certainly in Western Europe and North America, probably because they are thought to be technically difficult to breed in captivity. They could, however, prove to be a valuable species for cage culture in freshwater.

Chapter 4

Fish in their Environment

The anatomy and physiology of the salmonids and particularly of those which are of most concern to fish farmers are basically similar. The adults of the various species are generally fairly easily recognizable but the very young fish are difficult to distinguish without long practice.

Salmonids have the typical arrangement of fins common to most freshwater fish. The leading pair are the pectoral fins on either side of the lower half of the body. These are followed by a second pair of pelvic fins on the ventral surface or belly of the fish and a single, anal fin immediately behind the anus. There are two fins on the back, the dorsal fin and a degenerated adipose fin. The body ends in a caudal or tail fin. All the fins except the adipose fin are supported by bony rays.

The skin over the whole of the body surface, apart from the head and fins, is protected by overlapping scales and an outer coating of slime. The larval fish when newly hatched

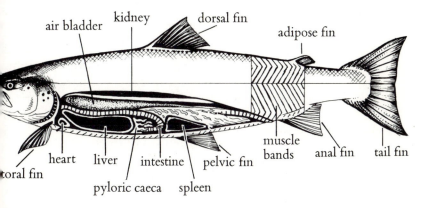

Fig. 7 Main internal and external features of salmonid fish

have no scales and scale growth does not start until the fish reach a length of about 3 cm. Scale growth begins with the laying down of platelets in the region below the adipose fin. The scales lie partly embedded in pockets in the skin and grow with the fish. They are cycloid and the outer, overlapping part is smooth.

Scale growth takes place at the periphery of each scale. Keratinous material is laid down in the form of visible, thickened rings on the embedded portion of the scale. The fish's body and the scales which cover it grow more quickly in summer than in winter. The parts of the scale surface where the growth rings are closer together or wider apart represent periods of winter and summer growth from which it is possible to read the age of wild fish. This is not so easy and is sometimes impossible in farm fish as growth can be more or less continuous and the different growth periods become indistinguishable.

The basic pigmentation of the body surface, green, brown, red or gold, is produced by colour cells or chromatophores in the skin. These cells have the ability of either releasing or withdrawing microscopic colour particles from the cell walls. This accounts for the fish's ability to change colour when against different backgrounds. Most pelagic fish and salmonids in the sea are often partially or wholly silver-coloured along their sides. The highly reflective, silver coating is formed by microscopic, colourless crystals of a metabolic bi-product called guanin, which is laid down on the scale surfaces and in the surrounding chromatophores.

The body is supported by a flexible vertebral column which links together the head, body and tail fin. Propulsive power for swimming is provided by the main blocks of muscles on each side of the back-bone which are supported by bony ribs. The thick, bony structures of the head protect the brain and specialized sense organs. Behind the semi-circular canals, which are organs of balance on each side of the hind-brain or cerebellum, are cavities each containing an otolith. This is a small free-floating portion of hard calcium carbonate. The otoliths rest on hairy cilia lining the cavities and act as balance mechanisms by indicating body aspect to the fish's nervous system. Otoliths grow with the fish and when ground thin and polished show dark and light rings corresponding to winter and summer growth periods.

The heart is at the leading end of the body cavity, behind the head and below the vertebral column. The body cavity extends back to the anal opening which is between the leading ends of the pelvic fins. Food passes through the oesophagus into the stomach to the distensible walls of which are attached a number of blind appendages called pyloric caeca. The digestive organs include a liver, gall bladder and spleen. Digestion continues in the intestine and undigested material is discharged from the anal opening as faeces. The fish have a kidney situated along the underside of the back-bone. The kidney not only eliminates waste products but also serves an important osmo-regulatory function, controlling the salt to water balance in the fish's body fluids.

The swim-bladder is a specialized organ of balance situated in the body cavity below the kidney and above the gut. In some species it can be filled either by gulping air at the surface or through absorption from the bloodstream. The extraction of air from the blood can take place as an automatic reaction to adjust the specific weight of the fish in relation to the pressure at the swimming depth.

The gonads or sex organs are also contained in the body cavity. The cell structures giving rise to eggs or sperm are not initially differentiated in the larval fish. On the approach of sexual maturity the developing gonads occupy an increasing proportion of the body cavity and in the later stages of development fill the space to an extent which impedes the intake of food to the stomach and partially inhibits the digestive processes.

Respiration

An exchange of dissolved oxygen and carbon dioxide between the water and the fish's blood takes place through the gills of salmonids. The gill filaments are carried on branchial arches in cavities on either side of the head which are open to the oesophagus on the inside and covered by a gill cover or operculum on the outside. A uni-directional flow of water over the gills is maintained by the branchial pump. With the gills closed, the mouth of the fish opens and water is sucked in, filling the mouth and the buccal cavity which is formed by the forward end of the oesophagus. The mouth is then closed and water is passed through the gills and out of the opening gill covers. The movements of the parts of the branchial pump are continuous but the rate of opening and closing varies with the fish's demand for oxygen. This in turn can depend on whether it is stressed in any way or is stimulated to greater activity. An increase in breathing movements in farm fish is often an indication of stress and is most usually due to lack of oxygen in the water.

The gill filaments are densely supplied with blood vessels. Carbon dioxide is released to the water at the same time as the oxygen is extracted which is then transported in the red cells through the fish's body. The main source of oxygen in water is the atmosphere but the photosynthesis of green water plants can be of great importance to fish and to the fish farmer. The production of oxygen by plant metabolism makes a considerable contribution to the total of dissolved oxygen in the water. This ceases at night and can cause a significant fall in the oxygen content of the water.

The oxygen content of water is measured in milligrams per litre. A level of 6mg/1 can, for practical purposes, be taken as the lower limit for salmonids. A level of 8-10 mg/1 is satisfactory for on-growing and 10-12 mg/1 for hatcheries and fry or smolt production. Cold water can take up and hold more oxygen and the amount which remains in solution becomes progressively less as the temperature rises. The percentage of saturation is also a way of representing oxygen content. Fast-flowing, cold water can be super-saturated with oxygen to more than 100% of saturation. The lethal level of oxygen depends to some extent on the level in the environment to which the fish have become acclimatized. This is most likely due to an increased ability to extract oxygen from water with a low concentration. The oxygen content of water can be measured quite simply in practice using an electric meter. This is a small, portable piece of apparatus which can either be read directly or connected to a continuous recorder.

Oxygen demand

The fish's need for oxygen varies with activity, temperature and food intake. Fat fish in good condition need more oxygen than thin fish. Young fish (fry, parr and smolt) need proportionately more oxygen while growing than when they are approaching maturity.

An ample supply of oxygen is particularly important during the incubation of eggs. The metabolism of the developing embryo is very demanding of oxygen and growth may be slowed down or the embryo suffocate if oxygen intake is inadequate. The enhanced need for oxygen continues during the alevin stage while the larval fish remains dependent on the yolk-sac. The most dangerous time, when oxygen demand is greatest, is just before hatching. One of the dangers of artificially increasing the water temperature in a hatchery, in order to accelerate development and reduce incubation time, is that the developing embryo may be unable to meet the increased demand for oxygen at the higher temperature, because insufficient oxygen can pass through the egg membrane.

The increase in oxygen consumption due to activity resulting from swimming in order to maintain position in a current of water or to capture food is directly proportional to the swimming speed, and is approximately similar for all salmonids of interest to fish farmers. For example, the oxygen consumption in rainbow trout cruising at a speed of 30 cm per second is about half that for trout swimming at a speed of 75 cm per second, or a fish having to maintain station against a flow of water of the same speed. This is important for fish farmers to understand as it affects not only the amount of oxygen the fish will need in tanks or raceways with fast-flowing water, but also their consumption of energy in the form of food.

Increasing temperature not only reduces the amount of

oxygen which is carried in the water, but also increases the demand for oxygen in the fish. This is primarily due to spontaneous metabolic activity in response to increasing temperature. The oxygen requirement is approximately five times greater at 20°C than it is at 5°C. This is of vital concern to the fish farmer as it means that the density at which their fish can safely be kept becomes progressively lower as the water temperature increases. The increase in the fish's demand for oxygen due to spontaneous activity is almost linear between 5°C and 20°C in the fish farmer's salmonids and it is possible to work out the proportional density at which the fish can safely be kept at a given water temperature. If the fish start to feed, this induces an additional, temporary demand for oxygen. This is not of any great significance at temperatures below 15°C but at higher temperatures the density at which the fish are kept determines the maximum temperature at which they can safely be fed.

In sea water of oceanic salinity and a temperature range of 5°C – 15°C, the density at which fish can be safely kept decreases by approximately 25% for each 2·8°C rise in temperature. For example, a cage containing on-growing Atlantic salmon in the sea at a density of 10 kg per cubic metre at 15°C could safely hold about double that weight of fish at 5°C. In practice, the density at which on-growing fish should be kept is the weight per cubic metre corresponding to the optimum temperature for growth. Less food or no food should be given at times when the water exceeds this temperature. The density can be proportionately increased when fish are over-wintered at lower temperatures.

Circulation

In the circulation of fish, blood is pumped by the heart, which has four chambers connected in series separated by valves, to the gills where the exchange of respiratory gases takes place. It then flows back to the heart through the systemic arteries and veins serving the parts of the body and the separate organs.

The heart rate accelerates when the fish are stressed. It also increases with rising temperature as part of a general spontaneous increase in metabolic activity. This can be particularly damaging to the developing embryo or to alevins in the yolk-sac stage when the pulse rate can double if the temperature rises from 5°C to 12°C.

The volume of blood is relatively low (about 2·5% of body weight) and much lower than in mammals. It contains white cells (lymphocytes and leucocytes) and red cells (erythrocytes). The red cells are fewer in number and larger than those in mammalian blood, and contain less haemoglobin.

Digestion and Excretion

The digestive tract of salmonids can be separated into two main regions. The forward part which is made up of the mouth and buccal cavity, and the oesophagus, stomach including the pyloric caeca, and the intestine, together with their associated ducts to the liver, pancreas and gall bladder. The prey is caught and held by oral teeth and is often swallowed whole. The oesophagus is a short, thick-walled tube which may serve to reject as well as accept food before it is passed into the stomach. The function of the stomach is to break down food into soluble particles which can then be absorbed through the gut walls. The secretion from the gastric mucosa is acid and contains pepsin as well as other enzymes. The nutrients enter the bloodstream as soluble proteins and fats together with a proportion of carbohydrates.

The time taken for the food to pass through the body and for undigested matter to reach the anal opening and be excreted varies with the water temperature. The metabolic rate increases as the temperature rises to the optimum for food conversion. The excretion of waste materials from the gut takes place through the anus in the form of faeces.

Gill cells also play a part in the uptake and removal of salts and the elimination of waste products. They function with the kidney in maintaining osmotic equilibrium between the body fluids and the environment. The kidney tubules act as filters. Urine is formed by glomerular filtration and the renal excretion is passed from the body by ducts near the anus.

Osmotic Regulation

The blood of fish in either fresh or saltwater must undergo continuous changes in order to maintain a balance between the salts in solution in the body fluids and the surrounding water. The process by which this is carried out is known as osmosis. When solutions of different concentration are separated by a semi-permeable membrane, water will pass through the membrane from the dilute to the more concentrated solution until the concentration on both sides of the membrane is the same. The body fluids of fish in freshwater are more saline than the environment. The gills, the gut and to a lesser extent the skin, are semi-permeable membranes. Water enters the bloodstream through these membranes and must be constantly discharged through the kidney to maintain the correct saline balance in the body fluids.

In a marine environment, the sea water is a more concentrated salt solution than the body fluids and water passes out through the semi-permeable membranes and is lost to the body. The fish must drink sea water to compensate for this loss and in doing so take in water that already contains more salt than their own body fluids. The marine teleost fish are adapted to cope with having to swallow sea water to prevent de-hydration caused by the osmotic loss of body fluids.

Salmon and other anadromous, sea-going salmonids undergo a special metaphormosis known as smoltification which enables them to adapt without undue stress to the change from fresh to saltwater. The few species and races of salmonids which do not naturally migrate to the sea at some stage during their life cycle are not truly stenohaline, which means that they can only tolerate small changes in the salinity of their environment, but can adapt by acclimatization to life in saltwater.

Fish in a freshwater environment have no special need to retain water in order to maintain a stable hypertonic solution in their body fluids. Water containing a relatively small amount of dissolved salts is taken into the body fluids through the skin. Water and salts are excreted in the urine and a very

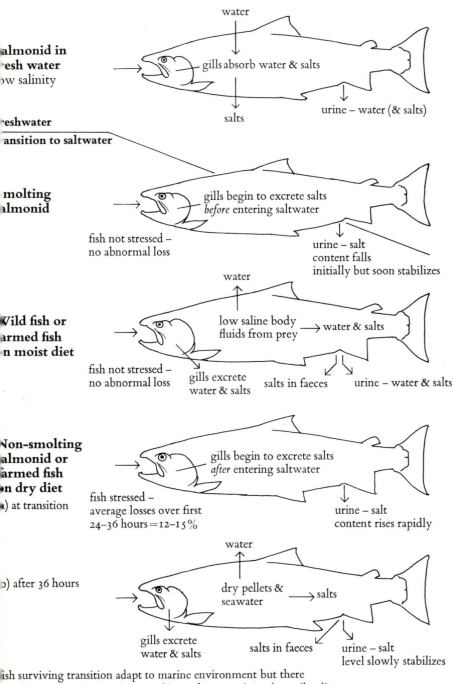

Salmonid in fresh water — low salinity

water ↓
gills absorb water & salts
salts ↓
urine – water (& salts)

Freshwater transition to saltwater

Smolting salmonid

gills begin to excrete salts *before* entering saltwater

fish not stressed – no abnormal loss

urine – salt content falls initially but soon stabilizes

Wild fish or farmed fish on moist diet

water ↑
low saline body fluids from prey → water & salts

fish not stressed – no abnormal loss

gills excrete water & salts

salts in faeces

urine – water & salts

Non-smolting salmonid or farmed fish on dry diet

a) at transition

gills begin to excrete salts *after* entering saltwater

fish stressed – average losses over first 24–36 hours = 12–15%

urine – salt content rises rapidly

b) after 36 hours

water ↑
dry pellets & seawater → salts

gills excrete water & salts

salts in faeces

urine – salt level slowly stabilizes

Fish surviving transition adapt to marine environment but there may be some continuing losses and irregular growth on dry pellet diet

Fig. 8 Osmotic regulation

small amount of salts through the skin.

Fish in the sea must retain water and excrete salts to maintain the hypertonic balance. They take in saltwater and excrete salts (and the minimum of water) through the gill cells. Salts also enter the body fluids from the gut and water passes out through the skin. The saline balance of the body fluids is principally maintained by the salt-excreting activity of gill cells assisted by excretion of salts in the faeces. The urine contains less water and more concentrated salts and less water is lost through the skin. Carnivorous fish also obtain significant quantities of water of low salinity in the hypertonic body fluids of their prey.

The most obvious of the physiological changes which are undergone by smoltifying anadromous salmonids is the silvery coating of guanin which is laid down in the skin. A function of this crystalline deposit appears to be to act as a barrier to osmotic exchange and to prevent the loss of water through the skin. At the same time, prior to the fish entering the sea, the specialized basal cells in the gills proliferate and increase the fish's ability to excrete salt.

It is possible for non-smolting salmonids belonging to races which do not migrate to the sea to adapt to life in full oceanic salinity (30 – 35‰) but they cannot make the transfer without considerable stress and consequent loss. The coastal races which are not fully anadromous acclimatize gradually to saltwater and seldom move out from inshore areas where average salinities are not greater than 15 – 20‰.

Fish farmers have frequently had problems when trying to grow-on non-smoltifying salmonids in cages in the sea, when the stocks they have used have been of mixed origin and not of a sea-going race. Their difficulties have been complicated by the use of dry, pelletted fish food which has only a small water content of about 12% compared to 70–80% in wet or moist food mixtures. The fish are then deprived of an additional source of water and one which they would have obtained naturally from their carnivorous diet.

Various ways have been tried to overcome the initial stress of transferring non-smolting salmonids to sea water. One method which has had some success is the use of a high-salt diet for a period prior to transferring the fish to the sea. The trout are fed a diet containing 10% by weight of salt for two weeks before being moved into saltwater. The high-salt diet is based on research carried out at the Dunstaffnage Marine Laboratory at Oban in Scotland. The fish used were non-smolting rainbow trout of mixed racial origin. The fish maintained on a standard diet prior to transfer to saltwater had an average mortality of 40% compared to an average mortality of 23·7% in fish which had been fed a high-salt diet. This represents a significant saving in fish but the relevent fact remains that even with a high-salt diet a loss of 23·7% occurred on transfer to water of 33 – 35‰ salinity. Such a loss is not tolerable in practice and these experimental results demonstrate the need to use an anadromous, smoltifying salmonid for marine culture in fully saline water. Non-smolting salmonids seem likely to do better in saltwater of less than oceanic salinity, but in any event should undergo a period of acclimatization in water of gradually increasing salt content.

Reproduction

Sexual maturity in fish involves the mobilization of large quantities of material for building specialized tissue and food to store in the developing eggs. In the male fish the collection of tissue-building material is not only needed for the developing gonads but also to form the structural sex characteristics such as the kype or protrusion on the lower jaw and the hump on the back of pink salmon. Anadromous salmonids all undergo a period of starvation before they reach their spawning grounds and must store sufficient fats, protein and carbohydrates not only to create eggs and milt but also to survive until they are ripe to spawn. The greatest demand is for fats, and the fat content of some species of salmon is reduced by 85% between the start of spawning migration in the sea and arrival on spawning grounds in the head-water of a river. The body fats carry the carotenoids which colour the tissues pink or red and as they are used up the flesh becomes pale, watery and tasteless. It is this loss of stored nutrients which renders sexually maturing or mature salmonids worthless to the sea farmer who must either stave off maturity in his fish or slaughter them before it destroys their value.

The process by which eggs develop in the ovary of the female fish is known as oogenesis. Maturation of the gonads is stimulated by hormonal activity and may take place over a variable period governed by racial factors as well as being characteristic of a particular species . The eggs develop in a pair of ovaries and when ripe are released and collected in the abdomenal cavity. The eggs are covered by a soft shell in which there is a small opening or micropyle below which is a

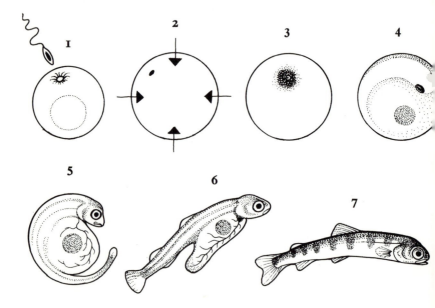

Fig. 9 Development: green egg to fry   **1** Fertilization   **2** Egg swells **3** Cell division starts   **4** Eyed stage   **5** Hatching   **6** Yolk sac alevin **7** Feeding fry

spot of protoplasm surrounding the nucleus. The male testes are also paired and in them the process of spermatogenesis produces the mobile, free-swimming sperm cells. The sperm must find and enter the micropyle in an egg in order for fertilization to take place.

Salmonid eggs and sperm are shed together by the male

and female fish. Fertilization takes place at once because the micropyle starts to close as soon as the eggs enter the water and begin to swell and harden. Sperm can only penetrate the eggs for a very short time before it is too late and the micropyle is closed. Initially the eggs are slightly adhesive and this continues during the period water is taken up and the eggs swell and harden completely. The cell cleavage begins during this period.

The developing embryo subsists on protein, fats and carbohydrates stored in the yolk. The egg shell or chorion has the ability to pass in oxygen and some essential nutrient salts from the water and to excrete waste materials. The time taken for embryonic growth varies with species and with water temperature. The demand for oxygen is high throughout incubation and highest just before hatching. The characteristic orange, oily fat globule remains in the yolk-sac after the larval fish have hatched and continues more or less unaltered through the alevin stage being finally used up just before the fry begin to feed.

Life in the Water

Good husbandry in fish farming depends to a great extent on appreciating that fish are aquatic not terrestrial animals. They are poikilothermic (having a variable body temperature) and depend for their well-being on a relatively stable thermal environment, which is quite unlike that shared by human beings with their other domestic animals. It is necessary to know and understand something of the special behavioural adaptations that equip fish for their life in the water.

Sight and Visual Stimulation

The large eyes of fish differ from those of mammals and in some ways are more efficient. The mammalian eye focuses by muscles altering the shape of the lens. The whole lens in the fish eye moves backwards and forwards like the lens in a camera. The cornea has the same refractive index as the water and the pupil bulges outwards taking in a wide visual field in both the horizontal and vertical planes. Although the eyes are set on the sides of the head, the field of vision overlaps in a forward direction giving stereoscopic sight over a cone of about 25 degrees. Theoretically, in completely still water, upward vision through the surface is restricted to a cone of a little less than 100 degrees. The size of this circular porthole varies with the depth, and beyond the periphery the fish sees only a reflection of the bottom. In reality, water is seldom motionless and fish swimming near the surface get glimpses in many directions through the waves.

Salmonids are thought to see fairly well in air and also appear to have good vision in semi-darkness. The response to visual stimulus is immediate. The reaction to sudden changes in light intensity and to observed movement is much more violent when the fish are in a confined area from which they are unable to escape. The stress suffered can seriously interfere with the normal metabolic processes. Most of the salmonids used for fish farming are still half-wild and it may be necessary to protect them from stress resulting from visual stimulus. Domesticated stocks need no protection as they learn to respond positively to land movements which they associate with the delivery of food. Young Atlantic salmon, on the other hand, are highly sensitive to visual stimulii and are easily stressed during their freshwater life. Rearing tanks should be kept shaded and food given by automatic feeders.

Lateral Line

The division which can be seen along each side of the body of salmonids and most other fish is a slime-filled pipeline, passing through holes in a row of specialized scales. The pipeline has branches opening to the surface between each scale and a group of nerve-endings connected to a nerve running along below the scale pockets. It is thought that changing pressures resulting from the fish's own movements, either when swimming or at rest, register a basic pattern in the central nervous system. Any additional changes in pressure, even though very small, upset this pattern and inform the fish of the shape and direction of the disturbance. The lateral line openings are thought to be a means by which the fish can maintain their position, avoid danger and search for prey in conditions when they are deprived of vision. Farmed salmonids may react positively to splashes on the surface and learn to associate this with the arrival of food, but it is probably more important to avoid, as far as possible, any disturbance in the water as this could be a source of stress.

Hearing and Balance

The salmonid ear is similar to that of other vertebrates and is made up of an inner ear and labyrinth which function as organs of balance as well as hearing. The labyrinth consists of three fluid-filled, semi-circular canals, each with a separate ampulla. Below the semi-circular canals are capsules containing otoliths made of hard calcium carbonate whose main function is the perception of gravity and the maintenance of the fish's equilibrium.

Research carried out on minnows and some other species of freshwater fish indicates that they respond to sounds with a frequency of about 6,000–7,000 hertz (1 hertz = one wave per second). Sound travels more quickly in water than in air and has been used as a means of attracting fish, free-swimming in a large area of water, to a central point for artificial feeding. The sound used is within the ordinary, musical range and is neither extra high or low frequency. Farmed fish do not appear to be stressed by sound within the human auditory range, but waves of low frequency in a range of 5–25 hertz may be sensed by the lateral line, causing stress and an endeavour to escape.

Swimming and Resting

Fish in a current of water are obliged to swim in order to maintain station. In static water, they only require to swim voluntarily in the pursuit of prey, to avoid predators and to keep contact with other fish of their own species. Salmonids use only the caudal or tail fin for swimming which is flexed in a sculling motion by the blocks of muscles along the sides and so

Fig. 10 Salmonid swimming movements

propels the fish through the water. The dorsal and anal fins are mainly used for vertical balance, and the pectoral and pelvic fins for lateral balance and when resting.

The swimming speed of salmonids is proportional to their length, but it is very difficult to determine accurately either the idling or maximum speed of any size or species of fish. Several different salmonids, both adult and juvenile, have been tested in flow channels where the opposing current can be progressively increased but it is impossible to tell if it is fatigue which causes the fish to fall back or turn and swim downstream. Certainly anadromous salmonids are capable of rapid acceleration over short distances but it is doubtful how long or for how far these bursts can be sustained.

Farmed fish kept in raceways or tanks with a concentric flow must swim to maintain station. In so doing they are using up energy sources which would otherwise have been stored in growing body tissues. Farmed salmonids do better in terms of good conversion and growth rate in static water where there is no directional flow, but they need a greater volume as living space in order to obtain sufficient oxygen and have to be kept at a reduced density. Where the available area is limited, fish are better kept in tanks or raceways with the minimum speed of flow necessary to supply sufficient oxygen. Given sufficient, level, non-porous ground which can be easily excavated, ponds may prove to be a better economic proposition. The best and most profitable system of on-growing salmonids is to use floating cages or tidal enclosures where an interchange of water takes place without the fish having to swim actively against a current.

Chapter 5

The Fish Farmers' Fish

The descriptions of the salmons, trouts and charrs in the wild provides a guide to their advantages and disadvantages to the fish farmer. So far, apart from rainbow trout, the salmonids artificially bred and reared as human food have not been in captivity long enough to develop domestic traits. The survival of any species or race of fish used for farming does not yet depend on close association with human beings and they can be self-supporting in the wild, given a compatible environment.

Fish farmers are still in much the same position with regard to choice of species as the earliest and most primitive farmers of terrestrial animals. Aquacultural science may now be able to telescope the process of aquisition of knowledge, but it has taken many thousands of years of selective breeding to produce the present domestic stocks of birds and mammals. Similarly efficient breeds of fish cannot be expected overnight.

For the time being the selection of a salmonid species which can be profitably farmed in a given set of circumstances depends upon ad hoc experience gained through growing fish from eggs taken from wild fish or stocks bred in captivity but retaining all or most of their wild attributes. This narrows the field and limits the number of species which it is useful to look at in detail from the point of view of the commercial fish farmer. The salmonids which have already been, or are in the process of being developed for farming as table-market fish are, in order of present importance, rainbow trout, Atlantic salmon, coho salmon, pink salmon and American brook charr. Other species of Pacific salmon have been farmed experimentally but they are generally stripped of their eggs which are hatched artificially and the young fish released to migrate to sea in order to enhance wild stocks, or more recently for sea ranching.

Basically the farmed salmonids all require much the same techniques in fish husbandry but practical experience has shown that some individual species have particular needs which must be understood and met if farming is to prove successful. Most of these are evident in the behaviour of the species in the wild, others have come to light as a result of years of practical experience.

Rainbow Trout

The races used for fish farming in most parts of the world outside North America are of the coastal type. Occasionally there is a mixture of coastal and lacustrine stocks but pure steelhead or kamloops types are very rare. The fish on nearly all commercial farms are now a domesticated strain of very mixed racial origin. Some of the best qualities of the species have been lost or submerged in this process. It is time to look again at the special characteristics of the pure races as a step towards stock improvement and the cultivation of varieties best suited to a given environment.

The traits which promoted the initial choice of rainbow trout as the prime species for salmonid farming were the ease with which the fish took to domesticated life in close contact with human beings and quick growth. They are relatively tolerant of a wide range of environments and freely adapt to life in saltwater up to full oceanic salinity. They will grow to market size on comparatively low-grade food containing as little as 30% protein and do not demand a specialized diet.★

Any simple hatchery will suffice to incubate rainbow trout eggs although the upward flow California-type system is still the best. They can be grown-on equally well in earth ponds, tanks, raceways and floating cages or enclosures in freshwater and in the sea.

The strains of rainbow trout available to most fish farmers are so mixed that it is only by a lengthy process of

★The practical cultivation of rainbow trout for the table market is covered in detail in my *Trout Farming Handbook*.

selection that stocks can be established which all spawn at more or less the same time. Generally the fish will ripen over a fairly long period. This can be a problem as it greatly prolongs the working time that has to be allocated to stripping fish. The female fish have to be frequently tested as maximum fertility does not last for more than a few days. On the whole it is usually a better economic proposition for the table-market farmer to buy-in fingerling trout for on-growing and leave egg and fry production to a specialist.

If a farmer is particularly keen to develop his own brood stock and has a suitable water supply, it is essential to start with brood stock of known parentage and established spawning time. Rainbow trout eggs are sensitive to the slightest shock within a few seconds of fertilization. They can either be placed at once under water in the hatchery troughs or water can be added to the eggs in a bucket, but in either case they must remain perfectly still for a minimum period of ninety minutes, otherwise an abnormal number of dead eggs will show up during incubation. In this respect the technique for stripping rainbow trout differs from that required for the other salmonids where the eggs are a good deal less sensitive to shock immediately after fertilization although they become so following a longer lapse of time at a later stage of cell-division.

Atlantic Salmon

Salmon eggs have been stripped from wild fish and incubated in hatcheries for enhancement of natural stocks in rivers for more than one hundred years. It was not until after the 1939-45 war that Atlantic salmon smolt of the Baltic race were first cultured on a large scale. This was in Sweden where artificially reared smolt were needed to replace wild stocks in rivers that had been regulated for hydro-electric generation and were no longer accessible to returning adults. Many years of research and practical experience have gone into the development of the specialized equipment, fish foods and skilled husbandry needed to produce viable smolt. It was not until the early 1960s that the successful culture of rainbow trout in saltwater led in Norway to the beginning of true Atlantic salmon farming.

The first and most important stage was and still is the production of healthy smolt that will transfer to saltwater with small losses.

A study of the life history of *Salmo salar* in the wild gives an indication of the difficulties that have been encountered and overcome before farming this species could be undertaken commercially. Many problems still remain to be solved and the farm stocks are still either derived directly from wild parents or from fish which have only been bred in captivity for a few generations. The species, however, has real possibilities for future domestication. What appear to be genetically distinct races have developed in different rivers. This provides a basis for stock improvement lacking in some other salmonids with more homogeneous characteristics.

The handling of gravid salmon, stripping and fertilizing eggs, incubation and hatching of alevins presents little difficulty using standard techniques. It is after hatching that high percentage survival at a later stage can depend upon the use of specialized equipment. Atlantic salmon alevins in the wild rest more or less inert in a space between the stones of the redd without having to expend any energy on maintaining position. If they are forced to swim against a current or to undertake unnecessary movement they can burn up the food supply in their yolk-sacs too quickly and fail to reach the proper stage of development before it is exhausted. They will never recover from this condition and large losses can occur either then or later on in the fry stage. Similarly, Atlantic salmon fry during the initial feeding period are sheltered from having to swim against a current of water by a hollow in the gravel on the bed of a river. Losses can be high if the fish are kept in a constant flow, over a smooth surface, where they have to expend too much energy in maintaining station.

Once the fish have started to feed actively by pursuing food, rather than waiting until food particles are brought to them by the current, rearing to the smolt stage presents no difficulties in clean, cool water. The best type of tank to use at this stage is one in which the flow encourages the fish to move off the bottom and feed through the whole water column. When the parr are 5 grams in weight they can be successfully grown-on to smolt in floating cages.

Satisfactory food mixtures for young Atlantic salmon are now fully developed, largely due to Swedish research. High-salt diets have been formulated to assist physiological adaptation to saltwater but smolt are not difficult to transfer provided they are carefully handled and not stressed.

Feeding on-growing salmon in water of full oceanic salinity still presents some problems if only dry pellets are used. Fish in the sea require an intake of water in order that their kidney can function properly and maintain normal metabolism. Salmon in the sea get water with a comparatively low saline content from the body fluids of the marine animals they eat. The metabolism of the fish can be stressed if they are deprived of this source of water and are forced to extract an abnormal quantity from their high-salinity environment.

It is evident that the most successful Norwegian salmon farmers working with salmon in water with a salinity over 30‰ are those able to use fresh fish or crustacea to make up at least part of the diet of their fish. Light also plays an important part. Atlantic salmon go north to feed in sea areas where in summer there are twenty-four hours of daylight. One of the most successful farms is inside the Arctic Circle.

There is much still to be learned of how best to farm the oceanic race of Atlantic salmon. Other races, including fish derived from sea-going parents, will adapt to live out their life cycle in freshwater. There is no reason why Atlantic salmon cannot be farmed in freshwater given the correct diet. This would overcome many of the difficulties and dangers facing sea farmers such as storm damage, marine fouling, parasites and dietary deficiencies due to the difficulty of obtaining fresh food.

Coho Salmon

This species has been cultivated with varying success in North America and to a lesser extent in Europe. On the Pacific coast it may prove more useful as a fish for ranching rather than for domestication. Cage culture in the sea has been the method generally adopted for on-growing although seawater is pumped to shore-based tanks and raceways in some farms, notably in Nova Scotia. Initially, the farmers intended to grow these fish on to maximum size prior to sexual maturity. More recently interest has increased in producing smaller fish of what is called 'pan size'.

Coho seem to have many advantages as a farm fish. They are easy to handle and are resistant to a number of common virus fish diseases. They are also hardy in saltwater when held in sea cages or in shore tanks. The water temperature during incubation should be 4°-11°C. After hatching, the optimum range is 13°-17°C. The fish will die if exposed for more than a short period to a temperature higher than 20°-23°C.

Freshwater growth is rapid at optimum water temperature and some fish will smoltify at the end of the first summer. The most successful time for transfer to saltwater is in early spring when the fish have reached a length of 20 cm. Fish can be transferred to the sea in the previous September or October if they show signs of smoltification and will grow more rapidly than fish of the same age over-wintered in freshwater. Young coho will tolerate sea water of full oceanic salinity (30-35‰) on direct transfer.

The species in the wild may feed in deep water where the temperatures range from 0°-10°C or close to the surface in temperatures up to 15°C. The diet given to captive stocks is high in fats and similar to that needed for Atlantic salmon. Moist pellets are generally used in North America rather than the dry type used in freshwater and for sea feeding in Scotland and Ireland. Young fish transferred to relatively warm sea water six months after hatching will reach weights of 130-300 gm following six to eight months in the sea. This is the stage at which they are harvested as 'pan size'.

There seems little to choose in taste or appearance between 'pan size' coho and sea-farmed rainbow trout and the only real advantage of farming coho to this size seems to lie in the legitimate use of the name 'salmon' as a selling feature. If grown-on, the fish will mature at weights of 1·3-14 kg. Early sexual maturity in the 'grilse' year is the main reason for premature slaughter at 'pan size'.

Pink Salmon

The principle research into the use of pink salmon as a farm opposed to a ranched fish has taken place in Norway but culture is still largely experimental. The Norwegians were obliged to take some interest in this species because of ranching developments carried out by the USSR in rivers running into the Barents Sea to the east and west of the Gub. Kolskaya in Murmansk. Wanderers from these plantings invaded Norwegian rivers and have established a number of self-sustaining colonies, particularly in Finnmark and Troms.

The fish appear relatively easy to grow-on to market size in sea cages but initial cultivation needs special equipment. The fry in the wild go to sea almost as soon as the yolk-sacs are absorbed and a dual salt and freshwater supply to a shore-based fry unit is essential. The salinity of the mixture should be controllable within fairly fine limits and artificially warmed if the sea or freshwater sources are naturally less than 8°-10°C.

One notable advantage of pink salmon to a fish farmer is that they grow very rapidly and have a short, fixed life span. They do not grow large in comparison with some of the other Pacific species but they reach 2-3 kg in two years from the time of hatching. This compares favourably with other salmon which have to spend at least some months or years in freshwater before transferring to the sea and consequently require a larger water supply, more space and a greater input of labour.

The Charrs

Some table-market farming of charr has been tried out in North America, mainly using *S. fontinalis* and *S. namaycush*, and a hybrid between these species. In Europe the same species have been tried as well as the lacustrine and sea-going races of *S. alpinus*. Trout farmers in Denmark have successfully crossed Arctic charr with rainbow trout producing a hybrid know as *bröding* which is a good-looking fish.

None of the charrs or their hybrids seem to have had much attraction for commercial farmers, possibly because they do not grow as fast and are not as easily domesticated as rainbow trout. The races of *S. alpinus* seem to have the best possibilities as farm fish in Northern Europe, including Scotland, where their relatively rapid growth in cold water could be an advantage.

Chapter 6

A Choice of Species

The most valuable species making up the salmon family belong respectively to the genera *Salmo, Salvelinus* and *Oncorynchus*. The different, individual species in the salmon family which may be of interest to fish farmers can be grouped according to their behaviour into those which must go to sea at some stage in order to survive; those which prefer to go to sea but maintain land-locked races that spend their whole life cycle in freshwater; those which have a migratory, sea-going race and a sedentary, freshwater or lacustrine race; and those which prefer to remain in freshwater throughout their growing life but have races that can adapt to life in estuaries or in the sea. Every sea-going member of the salmon family must return to breed in freshwater.

Adaptation to Saltwater

The first consideration in reviewing the salmon family to find the right species to farm in the sea must be their ability to transfer to saltwater without complications resulting in stress and immediate or subsequent losses. It is obviously good sense to select a species or a race that is naturally sea-going. The preference of different species to migrate to the sea is shown in Fig. 11.

The truly anadromous races in the wild have a mechanism which triggers the need to migrate downstream to the sea. The fish realize this but it can be difficult for the fish farmer to recognize the right moment when they have been reared in captivity. Large losses can occur if transfer is attemped either too early or too late. The period immediately before and after migration from fresh to saltwater is accompanied by radical physiological changes. In some species, these changes make

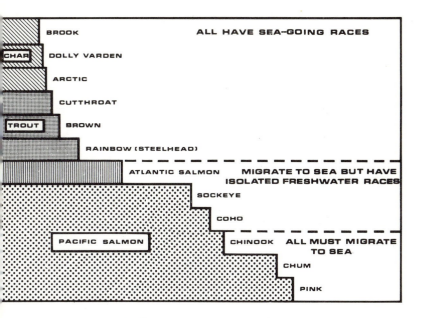

Fig. 11 The urge to migrate to the sea

the fish particularly difficult to handle. They can easily suffer fatal physical damage due to loss of scales or the after-effects of stress.

If other essential criteria have been met, the most useful species for the sea farmer are those which give a clearly recognizable indication of being ready to move into saltwater, have the greatest tolerance in the length of time over which the transfer can safely be made and are most easily handled and resistant to stress.

Natural Population Density

A factor in commercial fish farming which has received insufficient attention in the past is the ability of the species to tolerate high population densities in its captive environment. Most methods of salmonid production are intensive. They have to be, otherwise they would not be economic in terms of space or water. Some species are naturally more territorial than others. They can also be more or less demanding of territory at different periods of their life cycle. For example, Atlantic salmon and sea trout (sea-going races of *Salmo trutta*) are strongly territorial from the time they start to feed as fry. The Pacific salmon species, on the other hand, are generally school fish and remain in large, homogeneous groups throughout their lives in both freshwater and the sea.

A species which is naturally adapted to schooling and whose individuals remain in close proximity to each other is likely to react more favourably to the conditions of intensive culture in net cages or enclosures.

Response to External Stimulae

This subject obviously covers a very wide field. What is of importance to the fish farmer is not the natural reactions of the fish in the wild but the ability of the particular species to inhibit some reactions, particularly those due to fear, and to replace these with others such as the recognition of a source of food. This is the vital factor which predetermines the degree of domestication that can be achieved in any particular species. It is also important that in any response to an external stimulus the fish should exhibit a school response rather than react individually.

Domestication

The eventual aim of the farmer rearing fish to market as human food must be to breed stock that is fully domesticated; creatures that have been modified to lend themselves to animal husbandry, in a similar way to that achieved with certain species of terrestrial mammals and birds. Complete domestication, in the sense that the animals are entirely dependent for survival on their association with human beings, is unlikely with the wild species or races of fish at present being farmed in captivity.

The probability of achieving the full domestication of a

salmon species in the near future could depend on successful selective breeding or hybridization. In the meantime the most important characteristic to look for in wild races must be the qualities of their tameness and trainability. These indicate the degree in which their total behaviour patterns can be adapted to enable them to live a profitable life in an artificial environment.

Fish Food and Food Conversion

The fish species which are most attractive as food to people living in Western Europe and North America are generally carnivorous. Their basic food requirement is for a diet with an approximately 50% minimum protein content. The main practical consideration for salmonid farmers is to select a species which not only has an ability to convert the minimum food intake into the maximum body weight, but also to do this with the lowest-cost food available.

In fact there is not much to choose between the salmonids. Some species are, however, more selective than others and take less kindly to 'dry' pelleted diets containing a high proportion of vegetable protein. In saltwater they do best on a fresh, wet mixture with an all-animal protein base and the most valuable species in monetary terms are those requiring fresh diets, which are either difficult or expensive to obtain and which consequently restrict the areas in which the fish can be economically farmed.

It is vital and funadamental to the successful farming of any salmonid in the sea that a balanced judgement be made in selecting a species for farming for which a suitable food supply is available at economic cost.

Growth Rate and Environment

The time taken by fish to grow to market size is relatively less important than food content and conversion. It does, however, merit very serious consideration in the selection of a particular species or race for on-growing in an available sea-site or saltwater supply. For example, if the salinity is low or variable, the sea–going races of basically freshwater species will usually do better than species which must migrate to the sea in order to complete their life cycles.

Growth rate is important in the sense that a rapid turnover results in a more economic use of labour and investment, but concentrating culture on a quick-growing race of fish will not necessarily result in the best end-product in terms of quality and palatibility.

It should always be possible to design fish-holding units in such a way as to provide the best environment for the species selected for culture. If this for some reason proves impossible, culture should be confined to a species of fish which can be successfully grown to market size in the available facility.

Size at Maturity

The growth which can be achieved before the fish reach sexual maturity is of great importance but it is not simply a question of choosing the species which grows largest and matures latest. Most members of the salmon family cease to make economically useful growth after they have reached sexual maturity. Some species die after spawning. Others may spawn a number of times and continue to grow between spawning seasons but their condition deteriorates. It is seldom worthwhile to continue feeding table-market fish beyond the first onset of sexual maturity, except as brood stock.

The species selected must be one which can be economically grown to the marketable size for that particular variety of fish before it becomes sexually mature.

Resistance to Disease

Fish diseases are nearly all endemic in the piscine environment. Salmonids in the wild are resistant to most epizootics because they are seldom stressed. It is stress in fish culture which is the prime cause of serious, large-scale loss from disease. The more densely fish have to be kept and the more widely their life in captivity differs from that they enjoyed in their natural state, the more liable they are to succumb in an epizootic outbreak of disease. This rule can be applied not only to infectious diseases of bacterial or virus origin but also to pathogenic symptoms induced by dietary deficiencies and infestation with parasites.

The best prophylactic for fish diseases is to try as far as possible to select a species for culture that is adaptable to life in the environmental conditions imposed by the available water supply. The type of unit in which the fish are to be kept and the methods of husbandry used must be designed to avoid stressing the particular species selected for culture.

Processing and Marketing

The selection of a salmonid for farming must finally depend on the profitable sale of the finished product in the available markets. This is a matter of demand in relation to price and quality. The members of the salmon family are high-price fish and the most important market factors are taste and appearance. Some species taste better than others but not necessarily to the same group of customers. Some retain carotin better which results in a red flesh-colour. Pink or red flesh is essential in marketing sea-farmed salmonids and can be an advantage with fish farmed in freshwater.

It is likely that eventually the bulk of farmed fish, certainly fish of the salmon family, will be processed in some way prior to retail sale. Market considerations govern the form of processing. Some species can be more profitably processed in particular ways. Salmon or other large salmonids can be sold fresh, whole and in the round, but they can also be gutted and deep-frozen, cut into steaks and packaged, or cold-smoked and sold in the side or sliced. In most circumstances it will be more profitable to process at the farm.

Trout and charr can also be sold fresh and in the round but the comparatively rapid decomposition of farmed fish after slaughter requires quick dispersal. Much better quality is achieved by immediate processing.

The selection of a species for farming must therefore depend on the distance from the available market or the facilities that can be set up for processing at or near the farm site.

Chapter 7

Oceans, Seas and Lakes

The greater part of the surface of the world is covered by water. Mankind must eventually cease hunting wild fish and farm the waters as the land is farmed. Rational aquaculture will then require the cultivation of plants and animals far lower down the food chain than the fish at present reared for human food. Salmonids are near the top of the food chain. When kept in captivity they have to be fed mainly on animal protein which is already in short supply. For the time being, however, they offer the best, and in many areas, the only economic return to fish farmers who farm fish in the colder seas and lakes of the higher latitudes.

Oceanography

Currents in the Sea

Oceanic currents in both hemispheres flow from the warm water near the equator round the ocean basins towards the poles. The rotation of the earth directs the currents clockwise in the northern and anti-clockwise in the southern hemispheres. In the north, where the warm currents meet the cold arctic water are the rich feeding grounds of the Atlantic and Pacific salmon.

In the north-west Atlantic there is no temperate zone in the sea and in winter the eastern coast of the North American continent as far south as Cape Hatteras is in the icy grip of the Labrador current. Ships are coated in ice in the harbour of Halifax, Nova Scotia, which is on the same latitude as the South of France. The Gulf Stream warms the eastern Atlantic as far north as the Norwegian Sea where the surface water temperature seldom falls below 4°C. The same pattern of sea

78

temperature and climate is repeated in the Pacific, where the warm ocean currents moving northwards flow away from the coasts of Japan and north-east Asia and cross over to the shores of British Columbia, which has a climate similar to the coastal areas of Europe which are warmed by the Gulf Stream.

Coastal Currents

Where large rivers run into the sea, currents of lighter, less saline water form and flow along the coast inshore and usually in the opposite direction to the ocean currents. Coastal currents in the northern hemisphere flow generally north in Europe and on the western seaboard of North America, and south along the American Atlantic coast and the northern Pacific coast of Asia. The boundary between oceanic and coastal currents is indicated by changes in the temperature and salinity of the water.

The intensity of coastal currents varies with the seasons. They are of importance to fish farmers not only because of the flow of water through a farm site but also because of the changes they may produce in salinity and water temperatures. These may be detrimental to fish held in cages or promote dangerous growths of poisonous or suffocating plankton.

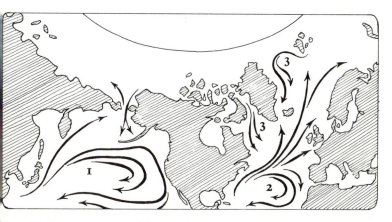

Fig. 12 Ocean currents of the northern hemisphere: **1** Japan Current **2** Gulf Stream **3** Arctic Current

Tides and Tidal Currents

The moon takes twenty-four hours and fifty-two minutes to rotate round the earth and its passage is followed by two tides which become later by fifty-two minutes each day. The sun also causes two much weaker tides during each rotation of the earth. At full moon, the sun and the moon are on opposite sides of the earth and at the new moon they are both on the same side. Their gravitational forces then act together and produce the extra high and extra low 'spring' tides. At half moon, the sun and moon are at right angles and counteract each other's gravitational pull. This results in the small 'neap' tides. The succession of 'spring' and 'neap' tides progresses through the lunar months of twenty-nine days.

A continuous tidal wave cannot follow round the earth's surface in the wake of the moon because of the intervening land masses. The oceanic tides flow round the ocean basins leaving central zones with very little tidal rise and fall and causing progressively greater tides on the more distant shores. The mechanics of the tides may be of academic interest but tidal movements in coastal waters are a vital factor in the selection of sites for sea farming. The deep ocean tides cause little lateral movement, but in shallower areas the water is shifted by tidal currents and changed at least twice daily in bays and inlets. Without this movement and interchange, cage sites for fish enclosures would become low in oxygen and fouled with waste products.

Salinity

The water of the open oceans and seas holds between 3 and 3·5% of salts. Salt content is usually measured in parts per thousand and oceanic water has a normal salinity of 30–35‰. It is peculiar that the composition of sea salts remains the same in all the seas and oceans. Only the concentration varies from brackish such as in parts of the Baltic Sea to the strongly saline water of the Mediterranean. The principle sea salts in sea water are (milligrams per litre = mg/1):

Sodium chloride	27·13
Magnesium chloride	3·85
Magnesium sulphate	1·66
Calcium sulphate	1·26
Potassium sulphate	0·86
Calcium carbonate	0·12
Magnesium bromide	0·074
Trace elements	0·0035

Alkalinity

All marine animals are highly sensitive to changes in alkalinity. The carbon dioxide that enters the water from the air, or is produced by the respiration of marine animals and photosynthesis by plants, forms carbonic acid and bi-carbonates in sea water which have a buffering action. This prevents rapid changes in the carbonate equilibrium and maintains a stable pH, and is one of the benefits gained by on-growing salmonids in the sea, provided the salinity remains constant in cages or enclosures.

Aeration

The life of fish in the sea and in large lakes depends mainly upon the mixing of air and water at the surface by the wind and waves. In summer, during periods of calm weather, plants in the depths reached by sunlight also make a significant contribution to the oxygen content of the water.

Temperature

The water temperature of the surface layer in temperate climates and in the north where coastal waters are warmed by ocean currents seldom drops below 3°-4°C. In summer the water temperatures do not rise much above 10°-15°C. By contrast, surface water in the Arctic and Antarctic can remain close to 1°C all the year round and summer temperatures rise to 30°C in the Red Sea.

Freezing

As ice forms, the frozen water loses salt and the salinity below the ice increases. When the ice melts, the freshwater floats over the surface layers and salinity falls rapidly. Ice formation on the surface of waters used for cage culture is not necessarily fatal to the fish but when the ice breaks up wind-driven ice-floes can wreck fish cages or enclosures.

The freezing point (T) of sea water depends on its salinity and can be found by the equation:

$$T = -0.054 \times S \text{ (where S = the salt content in parts per 1,000).}$$

For example, brackish water with a salinity of 10 parts per 1,000 would freeze at $-0.54°C$, but sea water with full oceanic salinity of 35‰ freezes at $-1.89°C$ and water with a salinity of 20‰ would freeze at $-1.1°C$. Very cold water induces increasing passivity in salmonids and it is reckoned that they can only withstand temperatures down to about $-0.5°C$. It is therefore possible to get critically low temperatures which could be lethal without ice being formed. In some northern waters, where in winter the sea water temperature is maintained above freezing point by warm ocean currents, snow in blizzards over rough seas can mix with surface water causing temporary super-cooling. This can be fatal to fish held in cages where they cannot escape to deeper water.

Pollution

The blueness of the sea is not an indication that it is either clear or clean. Ocean waters are a mirror for the sky although they can contain some colouring matter. Inshore waters can be coloured by plants or animals and by detritus washed down by rivers or disturbed from the sea bed in stormy weather.

Pollution of the sea in coastal areas is becoming an increasing problem and can limit the choice of sites for sea farming. The effect of man-made pollution can be either directly poisonous to fish life or can change the water chemistry in such a way as to encourage the growth of poisonous or suffocating plankton. The risk of oil pollution is now an ever present menace to the sea farmer.

Location of Sea Farms

Some basic hydrographic features are common to all cooler waters in the northern hemisphere that could prove suitable for salmonid farming in the sea. Atlantic oceanic water is distinguished by a stable salinity in the region of 35‰ and a small, stable temperature range. Coastal waters in areas where they are influenced by the influx of freshwater or the intrusion of Arctic currents usually have a variable and generally lower salinity and a more variable temperature range than the open ocean. A high salinity generally indicates stable salinity while low salinity is usually variable.

Marine conditions in coastal water are governed by the overall behaviour of currents and the average movement of inshore water masses resulting from meteorological factors and the effect of tides. Variation can be short–term over a few months, annual or medium-term, and long-term, taking place slowly over a period of years. Short-term changes are indicated by sudden local alterations in water temperature and salinity, and in the speed and direction of currents. They result from the effects of radiation, evaporation or the rapid influx of freshwater. Such changes are often brought about by an alteration in local tides caused by gale-force winds.

In the northern hemisphere surface water is pushed offshore at right angles to the wind direction. This means that on coastlines running north and south a northerly wind forces surface water away from the shore which is then replaced by colder water from greater depth. A prolonged period of strong northerly winds during the summer months can lead to a rapid drop in coastal water temperature of as much as 5°-7°C. Southerly winds tend to produce the opposite result. The general effect of wind on coastal water conditions can be modified to a great extent by the geography of a particular area and local water temperatures may not conform to the expected pattern. A discrepancy is most likely in the confined waters of fjords and sea lochs, particularly where there is a substantial inflow of freshwater.

Some fjords and most sea lochs have a well-defined threshold between open sea and the deeper water on the landward side. This can result in the strongly saline water from outside the threshold forming a steeply sloping boundary surface with the over-lying, less saline water in the sea loch. Interchange of water between the sea loch and the open sea can be prevented, particularly during the summer months, by the formation of a boundary surface at a threshold, and stale water of lower oxygen content and salinity then circulates back and forth inside the enclosed area. The effect of the formation of a boundary surface is likely to be less noticeable in places where the tidal range is greatest.

There is a wide variation in the average ranges of tides on those parts of the European and North American coasts suitable for farming salmonids in cages or enclosures. An indented coastline with off-shore islands can result in large local differences. Where there are eddies and confused currents, neutral zones can occur with practically no tidal flow. The strongest flow in sea lochs usually occurs at half tide.

Site Exploration

The essential factors governing the selection of a sea site can be summarized as follows:

prevailing wind and weather	bottom formation
local geography	tidal flows and currents
exposure	water temperature, salinity
water depth	and chemistry

The initial sources of information are maps and charts. All relevant reference books should be consulted. Marine sailing directions can give a good deal of information on the local geography and hydrography of inshore waters. The broad characteristics of weather systems may be of less importance in the selection of a sea–site location than local modifications and the protection afforded by nearby land. Exposure to wind and wave action is a basic factor for consideration in site selection. Maximum 'fetch' (distance to the nearest land) should not exceed approximately 3 km in the direction of the prevailing wind. A longer fetch can sometimes be tolerated in otherwise well–sheltered waters but a site should remain workable in any force of wind from any direction.

When a sea area has been found which is sufficiently sheltered to provide a safe anchorage for cages, it must be surveyed to establish the depth and bottom formation. There should be a depth of at least 10 metres below the cages at neap tides. This is essential to avoid the risk of accumulated excreta and waste food contaminating the water in which the cages are suspended or promoting eutrophication and abnormal plankton growth.

A bottom survey should include a wide enough area to cover the entrance to any bay or sound in order to make sure that a threshold will not interfere with the interchange of water from the open sea. The type of bottom is a useful indication of deep currents. A muddy bottom usually indicates a poor interchange of water at depth. The converse is indicated by a clean bottom. An absence of bottom fauna, such as crustacea, often indicates a stagnant area and should be avoided. Sites in channels with sufficient depth, close to large shallow, muddy or sandy areas should be avoided as the water may become turbid in winter gales.

Tidal Flows and Currents

Currents close to the surface are essential in order to bring clean, well-oxygenated water to suspended cages or enclosures. In shallower water, currents near to the bottom may be needed to prevent accumulation of waste products, otherwise the cages may soon have to be moved to a new anchorage. The average current over a site should be greater than 100 mm per second and not more than 500 mm per second, otherwise net cages may be distorted and damaged. Beware of sites between islands or off peninsulas and avoid deep channels away from rocky areas as there are likely to be strong, scouring currents and cages cannot be safely anchored.

Salmonids in sea cages suspended in clean, well-oxygenated water, will tolerate a nil flow for about one hour over dead low water, but the fish should not be fed during this period when sea temperatures are high during the summer months. The movement of fish held at fairly high density in small cages will cause a direct interchange of water which is sufficient to keep them alive, provided the cages are not too close together.

Temperature

Little is known of the most favourable temperature for growing salmon in cages in the sea. In the wild, the water temperature over their feeding areas is likely to be in the region of 8°-10°C during the summer. The optimum temperature for on-growing some members of the salmon family is known from experience to be 15°-16°C. Pacific salmon will tolerate comparatively high sea water temperatures and appear to do reasonably well in water up to 15°C. No experience has yet been gained with sea-going charr in captivity in the sea. Arctic charr (*Salvelinus alpinus*) in north Norway feed in coastal waters where the summer temperature is in the region of 10°C. The temperature range is greatest in confined sea lochs where the salinity is relatively low. The surface water in an enclosed area with a narrow opening may have a considerably higher temperature in summer and lower temperature in winter than more open waters, even if the salinity remains relatively high and stable.

Salinity

It is evident that the salinity of the environment has some direct effect on the growth rate of the sea-going races of salmonids and that racial characteristics are the dominant factor in salt water tolerance. Races or species which migrate to the open sea and spend their period of most rapid growth in water where the salinity is 33-35‰ would be expected to make optimum growth if kept under similar conditions in captivity.

Fully anadromous species or races appear to be stressed by changes in salinity. Very little is known on this subject and research so far carried out has not provided any clear-cut information.

Oxygen

The oxygen content of sea water varies over the year and is at a maximum in early summer and a minimum in early winter.

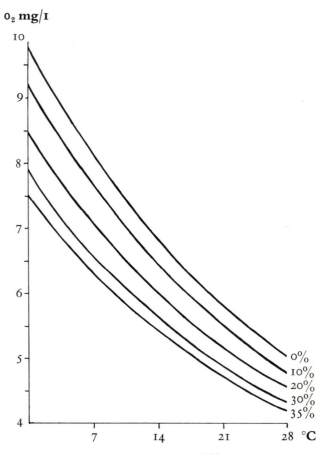

Fig. 13 Dissolved oxygen in seawater at different water temperatures and salinities

The amount of oxygen in sea water depends upon the water temperature, the salinity and atmospheric pressure. For practical purposes, at an atmospheric pressure of 760 mm of mercury the amount of oxygen can be determined by the following equation (Truesdale and Gameson 1956):

$$\text{Oxygen in mg/1} = \frac{475 - (2.83 - 0.011\ T) \times S}{1.38 \times (33.5 + T)}$$

Where T = Temperature and S = Salinity in parts per thousand.

The amount of oxygen that fish need depends mainly on water temperature and their degree of activity. The amount needed increases when fish are feeding and rather unexpectedly decreases in proportion to their size. This means that the density at which the salmonids can be kept in sea cages increases as they become larger. The presence of free carbon dioxide in the water is also known to increase the demand for oxygen in fish.

Acidity and Alkalinity

The pH of sea water in northern coastal waters, where photosynthesis is taking place, is generally between 7·5 and 8·5. The pH tends to rise in summer when photosynthesis is at a maximum and to fall in winter. The pH in a sea-cage site area should not exceed 9·0 or fall below 5·0. There is little risk of the pH rising to a lethal level but the decay of waste products accumulated below cages and in enclosures, or held in the site area by a threshold at the outlet to a fjord or sea loch, could cause the pH to fall to a dangerously low level.

Water Quality

The main risk of pollution is from the accumulation of waste products from the fish themselves. It stands to reason that a site would not be chosen in the first place if there was any risk of pollution from outside sources, either as a result of human activity or the natural decay of organic matter. The danger following the breakdown of accumulated faeces and un-consumed food is from free ammonia being released at a level that becomes actively poisonous to the fish which are held in a cage or enclosure and cannot escape to clean waters. It is as well never to lose sight of the fact that it is easy for an otherwise attractive site for a sea farm to become a self-polluting death-trap if there is an insufficient depth of water below the cages or no current at the sea bed to disperse rotting waste-matter collecting on the bottom.

Surveying a Site

Measuring Wind and Wave Forces

An anemometer is the accurate way of measuring wind speeds but time may not permit sufficiently long-term recording for the results to be of any real use. A guide to wind force over a

Fig. 14 Exploration equipment: **1** and **2** Sampling bottles **3** Hydrometer **4** Current measuring drogue

period can be obtained from 'tatter flags' which are pieces of material fixed to a staff that shred at given wind speeds. Wave formation and the height and length of the sea are more important than wind strength. These are a consequence of 'fetch' as well as wind force and the relationship between fetch, wind speed and wave height can be plotted.

The Meteorological Office can be a useful source of information but inshore fishermen or other people who use the sea in the general area of the proposed sea-farm site are the best sources of information. A safe anchorage for small boats is a safe anchorage for sea cages as far as wind and wave forces are concerned but is usually too shallow.

Depth and Bottom Formation

The general depth of water and some idea of the formation of the sea bed can be read from the chart. A more detailed, local survey, using a depth meter should be made and checked by sounding. The appearance of the shore-line will give some indication of what the bed is likely to be and this can be checked from local sources of information. The best way to examine the sea bed in shallower water is by skin-diving.

Tidal Flow Measurement

There are various ways of measuring the speed of tidal currents. A simple flow-measuring drogue consists of a buoy on the surface which supports cross-shaped plates moved along with the current. Its speed of travel can be measured over a given distance from an anchored boat.

Net cages can be weighted to prevent their being pulled out of shape in stronger currents but the angle of the net to the perpendicular should not exceed 15 degrees or there will be damage to gear. The angle likely to be made by a net in a current can be roughly checked using a drogue adjusted to hand at a depth equal to the bottom of the net cage and suspended from an anchored boat.

Measuring Temperature and Salinity

The water temperature at the surface is easy to take but the thermometer must be given time to stabilize and should preferably be read in the water. The specific gravity of sea water depends upon temperature and salinity. The salinity at the surface can be measured by taking the temperature of the water and using a hydrometer to measure the specific gravity. Samples of water below the surface can be taken using a weighted flask sunk to the required depth. A cord is jerked to pull out the cork. The flask is then given time to fill and drawn up. The water in the neck is thrown out and a thermometer put in to take the temperature. The sample is poured into a measuring cylinder and the specific gravity read off with a hydrometer.

In practice, it is seldom necessary to measure salinity with an accuracy of more than ± 2 parts per thousand. The difference in specific gravity produced by changes of ± 5°C above and below an average sea water temperature of 10°C is so small that for practical purposes it can be disregarded and the salinity can be estimated from a hydrometer which can be directly graduated for salinity.

Sites for Enclosures

There are three basic types of enclosure used for salmonid culture in saltwater. Siting any type of enclosure is governed by the tides. All enclosures require the erection of a fish-proof barrier from the surface to the bed of the sea which has to withstand wind and wave action. It is impracticable and uneconomic to put up a barrier high enough to operate over a large range in tidal rise and fall. In practice the difference in water level between high and low tide should not exceed about 1 metre at ordinary 'springs'. Although the tidal ebb and flow must be small, there must still be sufficient flow to change the water inside the enclosure and to carry away waste.

The tidal current through large enclosures made between islands or in open-ended channels may prove insufficient and

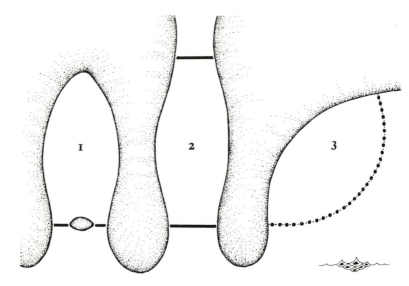

Fig. 15 Outline of typical farm sites: **1** Inlet   **2** Closed channel
3 Enclosure

have to be supplemented by pumping. This method can still be profitable for a big-scale development. It is difficult to find a satisfactory site for an enclosure to be made by erecting a barrier across the seaward end of the inlet as there has to be a good tidal current through the site if fish are to be kept at a worthwhile density. Both these types of enclosure need a clean bottom, free from rocky outcrops and from places of attachment for weeds.

The third variety of enclosure is a simple structure consisting of a double barrier of net carried on supports round an area of sloping shore. The beach should be stable, clean, free from boulders and slope seawards at about 20 degrees to the horizontal.

Sites in Fjord Lakes

This type of large lake is only to be found in relatively few locations usually where fjords, filled with sea ice during the last ice age, have risen as the ice melted so that their original 'threshold' has now separated them from the sea. The fjord-like shape remains and the lakes are of great depth, with their beds often below present sea level.

The particular interest of these lakes to fish farmers is that they never freeze. The great mass of deep water maintains a stable temperature gradient at the surface which does not fall below about 4°C in winter or rise to more than 14°C in summer. Such lakes offer nearly all the advantages of farming fish in the sea, without the disadvantages of storm damage, marine fouling and infestation of the fish with marine parasites. The physical criteria for the siting of floating cages in a fjord lake are similar to those of sea sites. Much of the shoreline of this type of lake consists of a fairly narrow shelf of gently sloping bed close inshore which suddenly gives way to water which may be over 100 metres deep. The place to anchor cages is just beyond the edge of the inshore shelf where the surface water temperature remains stable and waste matter slips away into the depths.

The dangerous wind is the one which blows towards the land and can drive cages ashore if anchor cables break or anchors shift. A large lake can become very rough with short, steep seas. The length of open water in the direction of the prevailing wind should be similar to that for sea-cage anchorages.

Freshwater Enclosures

Enclosures have not been seriously tried out for commercial salmonid culture in freshwater lakes. There is no reason that they should not function well provided barriers can be made properly fish-tight on the lake bed. A drawback is that the water would have to be fairly shallow, not more than about 5-6 metres in depth on a level bed, if net barriers were to be mounted and held in place at economic cost. The lake would have to be very well sheltered if there was any risk of ice forming on the surface. Fish could only be kept at low density, otherwise the enclosed area would soon become foul. Enclosures in a freshwater lake would, in fact, only be an extension of the principle of feeding free-ranging fish in large ponds, mainly used for on-growing warm-water species. It would seem to have some application to salmonid culture in temperate waters.

Other Factors in Site Location

Easy access is vital by both water and land. There must be a satisfactory area for a landing stage with an access road from which cages and enclosures can be serviced and where fish can be landed and equipment brought ashore for repairs. The nearer the landing stage is to shore-based stores and fish processing premises the better. The cost in time of transporting staff, fish food and fish over unnecessarily long distances, either by sea or land, can make any sea farm unprofitable to operate.

No matter how much hydrographic or other investigation is carried out in advance of selecting and commencing operations on a sea farm, some of the potentials of the site, good and bad, will only be properly appreciated when it is being worked and begins to rear fish. Sea cages are generally portable and can be moved to another site. It is therefore prudent not to make any large investment in either fixed marine or inshore facilities until a pilot project has been carried out and the results have been assessed.

Chapter 8

Planning Salmon Farms

Farming sea-going salmonids involves the three steps of egg production and incubation (which includes the handling of brood stock), rearing parr and smolt, and on-growing table-market fish. The first two processes are often undertaken by specialists. A decision to buy-in eggs, fingerlings or smolt depends mainly on site considerations and the availability of fresh water. Where possible it is certainly more profitable to carry out all stages of rearing, with the possible exception of maintaining a brood stock for a supply of eggs. It is evident in the case of Atlantic salmon that stocks of certain races from particular rivers have advantages as farm fish. In the longer term, a large-scale salmon farm should establish its own lines of brood stock best suited to local conditions. At present many farmers purchase eyed eggs for hatching taken from fish of known parentage, if they can find a reliable source. Those farmers who lack an adequate freshwater supply must buy-in smolt for direct transfer to the sea.

Rearing Young Fish in Freshwater

The techniques of hatchery work and fingerling or parr rearing are basically the same for all non-smoltifying salmonids. These are old-established and generally well-known. A number of special modifications have been developed for species which smoltify or which go to sea soon after hatching.

Water Supply and Siting

It is usually difficult to find a site with an adequate supply of freshwater close to a salmon farm in the sea, or one using pumped sea water. It is possible to use a system which recycles the main flow and only requires a relatively small volume of make-up water.

The water supply for a smolt rearing unit producing sufficient fish to service a salmon farm with an annual production of 100 tons is approximately 1·0 million gallons per day. The water must be saturated with oxygen and completely free from any source of pollution. It should also remain clear and free from suspended solids. Slightly acid water with a pH between 6 and 7 is better than alkaline water as it is not such a good medium for the growth of either bacteria or fungi. Surface water is preferable to borehole or well-water, which is frequently supersaturated with air, causing gas-bubble disease in the fish, or contains free carbon dioxide and sometimes poisonous metal salts. Spring water drawn from close to the spring often has the same drawbacks.

The best sources of surface water are the headwater of streams, which may contain stocks of wild salmonids, but are inaccessible to anadromous fish. Water drawn from the outfall to a clean, cool lake, on high ground, is probably the best supply that can be found for a smolt rearing unit.

Hatcheries

In its simplest form, the artificial hatching of salmonid eggs involves immersing them in clean, well-oxygenated water during incubation and larval development. During this period the eggs and alevins of wild fish remain in the gravel of the redd or nest, where they are not only protected but rest undisturbed in the spaces between the stones. The ideal artificial method is one which reproduces as closely as possible the natural environment. A complete approximation is not a practical proposition but certain conditions are essential and should be provided in any hatchery system.

The flow of water in which the eggs are immersed should come, at least partly, from below. The old 'California' system in which egg baskets with a perforated base are arranged to fit behind one another in a trough has never been improved upon for general use in salmonid hatcheries. Water flowing down the trough is forced up through the bottom of the first basket. It then flows out through perforations close to the top of the downstream end of the basket, down between the baskets and up through the bottom of the next basket and so on down the line.

Troughs and California baskets will work satisfactorily for any salmonid eggs but the need for alevins to be kept in an environment in which they do not have to expend energy on maintaining their position in the water has led to modifications of this principle. Research carried out in the 1960s on Atlantic salmon alevins showed that if they rested quietly during the yolk-sac stage this resulted in a significantly higher survival rate and better growth during the subsequent fry stage. Developing alevins have to have a plentiful supply of oxygen. The difficulty is to provide a sufficient flow of water without disturbing the larval fish and forcing them to burn energy, and consume stored food which should be used for development. The simplest way to do this is to put clean, even-sized stones about 5 cm in diameter in the bottom of the hatchery trough, and to make sure that the water flows along the bottom of the trough through the stones. This method works well enough but it is wasteful of space and the stones are heavy and have to be taken out, cleaned and stored. One advantage of this simple system is that the alevins, which disappear into the chinks between the stones, appear again above them as soon as they are ready to feed, giving the best indication of when feeding should start.

Many methods have been tried for providing a protecting substrate for young salmon during the alevin stage. These include the use of different kinds of plastic mats and mouldings with indentations, studs or bristles. The best system so far is that devised by Don Marr in his original experiments and simply consists of a basket with a corrugated base made of perforated metal. The eggs, and subsequently the alevins, lie quietly in the corrugations.

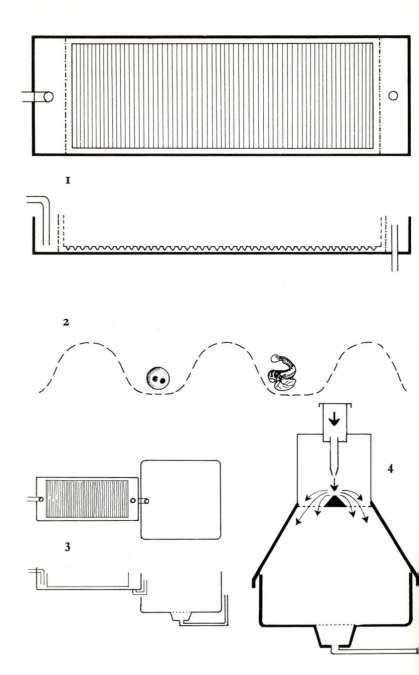

Fig. 16 Special hatcheries for genetic control: **1** Hatchery trough **2** Corrugated inner tray **3** Trough with attached fry-tank **4** Fry feeder over tank

Salmon Hatching and First Feeding

The following design is for a simple trough and tray system with a capacity of seven to ten thousand salmon eggs.

Trough	Constructed in g.r.p. Interior dimensions (approx.) 150 cm x 50 cm x 20 cm deep. Sloping guides for fish screens about 10 – 12 cm from each end. A baffle is either built-in or fixed in position across the intake end of the trough extending from the top of the sides to within about 2 cm of the bottom. The intake pipe is controlled by a screw valve. The outlet is a stand-pipe (45 mm i.d. approx.) passing as press fit through a flange in the bottom of the trough. This controls the water level in the trough.
Inner tray	Welded aluminium frame, holding perforated aluminium sides and a corrugated perforated aluminium base, standing on legs 2 – 3 cm in length. The aluminium must be zinc-free. The perforations should be 1·5 mm in diameter with the maximum open area consistent with strength. The corrugations extend across the width of the trays and are rounded. Each corrugation is about 1·6 cm measured from the top of the next. Either one or two trays can be made up to fit each trough.

After hatching, the alevins remain in the trays until they are ready to feed. The egg shells have to be removed by siphon or suction pipe. Feeding can begin when the larval fish start to swim up from the corrugations, either initially in the baskets or after they have been emptied into the trough (with the end-screens in position).

An adaptation of the simple trough and corrugated tray has been developed for use in connection with stock improvement, where it is necessary to keep separate the progeny of particular pairs of brood fish. The trough is somewhat smaller and the corrugated-base tray empties directly down a pipe leading into a 1 metre square Swedish type tank, with rounded corners and a central drain covered by a flat screen. The water level in the tank is controlled by an outside elbow-pipe. The fry are released into this tank before initial feeding starts and fed there for the first three to four weeks.

Some commercial producers hatch their salmon eggs in trays either mounted over or in the tanks in which fry will be initially fed, and the fish grown-on for the first summer. Incubation and initial feeding in separate, smaller tanks is probably a better procedure, likely to produce stronger fry with a higher survival rate.

Smolt Rearing

The methods described are applicable to Atlantic salmon but can be applied to any salmonid intended for on-growing in cages or enclosures in the sea. The first and most essential step is that the fry should be encouraged to feed up through the water column as soon as possible. This produces a far better use of water space and a better distribution of food. It is much easier with some salmonids than with others and Atlantic salmon can be difficult to shift off the bottom. The type of tank used is not so important as the way the water supply is delivered.

The standard shape and size of tank for this stage of production is either rectangular 2 m x 2 m with rounded corners or circular 2 m in diameter. Round tanks are preferable for salmon. Both types have a screened, central drain. Water level in the tanks is controlled either by a stand-pipe inside the tank or an outside elbow-pipe. The water supply should be delivered by a vertical pipe, controlled by a valve, entering the water at the periphery of the tank. The pipe should be perforated by a line of holes one above the other below the water-line, and articulated so that it can be turned to direct the flow round the tank in a series of jets at different depths.

Larger, circular tanks of 4–7 m in diameter can be used for over-wintering, and on-growing to the stage at which the fish are moved to saltwater. These tanks will need at least two

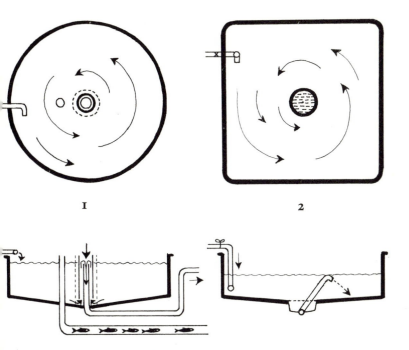

Fig. 17 Small fish tanks: **1** Circular tank with cross-section showing fish pipe for central grading   **2** Rectangular tank with cross-section showing elbow pipe outlet for water level control

peripheral water intakes, which should be of the same type as those described for the 2 m tanks. G.r.p. tanks are recommended as they are relatively trouble-free compared to concrete or steel. They should be bought from a reputable manufacturer and should be designed for the particular purpose for which they are intended. The free-standing type which does not require to be set on a concrete base is the most satisfactory in practice.

Tank Covers

Most young salmonids, particularly Atlantic salmon, show a strong nervous response to any movement above the water. Stress resulting from visually perceived disturbances outside a tank can cause fish to stop feeding and slow down growth rate. The simple way to avoid this is to cover the tanks (and to use automatic feeders).

Tank covers should not exclude light and the best, low-cost material is a loosely woven mesh of about 2–3 mm, in a strong artificial fibre which is treated to resist the effects of sunlight. The covers can be stretched over rectangular tanks and holding hooks should be built-in at corners. The covers can give trouble if there is a fall of snow as they tend to sag into the water and have to be kept clean.

Covers for round tanks should be supported on a simple hemispherical frame. This is made up like an umbrella, with the spokes coming down from a central junction point to fix on the side of the tank. Narrow openings should be left in the cover for servicing automatic feeders and operating water-supply valves and distributors. This type of dome-shaped cover will shed or support a fall of snow without having to be continuously cleaned.

Buildings

One of the commonest causes of hatchery loss is the water freezing in the supply pipes or in the troughs. In practice a frost-free building is essential. The water supply main should rise inside the building and be buried below the frost level in the ground outside.

Some smolt rearing units continue to rear in tanks inside a building for several months after the fish start to feed, but it is more usual to have only the smaller, initial feeding tanks under cover. The fish are moved out of doors as soon as the weather warms up and the ambient water temperature in the outside tanks rises to about 10°C. Both systems work equally well but the choice depends on the local climate and the hatching system in use on the farm. If the spring is late and the farm uses recycled, heated water in the hatchery, the fish may have to be kept indoors until well into the summer.

Winter-housing

Some of the original Scandinavian units, rearing Atlantic salmon smolt, constructed indoor and outdoor tanks so that the fish could be over-wintered in the buildings. This principle effectively overcomes the problems associated with very cold, snowy winters but is also very expensive. Some smolt producers in the far north have found it essential to keep their fish under cover throughout their freshwater life-period, in an artificially lighted building which can be heated in winter. This system has obvious advantages from the point of view of improved working conditions, but it is not necessary if the water outside is warm enough for a sufficiently long period during the first summer and autumn to promote growth to smoltification in the following spring or early summer.

Artificial Lighting

The feeding period of parr can be lengthened and growth accelerated by artificially prolonging the daylight hours. This can be done either by lighting individual tanks or by flood-lighting a large area. The light source used should be one which provides the closest approximation to sunlight. A number of different light regimes have been tried with varying success. The one which seems to work fairly well in latitudes between 55° and 60° is to allow the hours of daylight to increase naturally until mid-summer without any additional lighting, then to artificially prolong the daylight hours into the autumn until the water temperature falls significantly.

Filtration

Filtration methods used in fish culture are basically the same as those used for domestic water supply and sewage treatment. Initial filtration may be needed to remove suspended solids in the raw water supply to a hatchery or smolt rearing unit. The fish-farm effluent may require to be treated to comply with the stipulations of authorities concerned with the control of pollution, or for recycling inside the farm.

The simple way to remove matter in suspension is settlement, but the water has to remain for sufficiently long in a large tank or pond to allow this to take place. Raw water which is dirty enough to need settlement is of no use for salmonid farming, but a simple filter may be essential for the water used in a hatchery or fry-rearing unit particularly if it contains peat fragments or other finely divided particles which can settle on eggs or alevins.

The simplest type of water filter is a container filled with a filter medium, which can be either coarse or fine, and consists of a variety of different materials. The filter most commonly used is graded sand or gravel. The water may pass through progressively finer grades of filter material in the same container, or through a series of inter-connected containers. The basic flow systems are upward, with the water entering at the bottom, or horizontal, from side-to-side (in open-channel filter beds from end-to-end). All filters should have a method of cleaning by back-washing. This usually consists of an arrangement by which the flow can be reversed through the filter, either by gravity or pumping, and discharged by a separate drain.

Other types of more complex filtration involve the use of pressure and vacuum in a closed container, and multiple re-circulation. Some are fast, others are slow. Some provide a cleaner effluent than others. The choice of a system depends on the flow requirement of the hatchery or rearing unit, the space available and the cost of filtration.

There are two basic types of sand filter, slow and fast. Slow filters give a cleaner effluent but pass too little water in a given time to be of any use in fish farming. The flow through a rapid sand filter depends on the grades of filter medium. Material used in the filter can range from about 0·5–1·5 mm in particle size and pass between 40–140 litres per minute for each square metre of filter surface area.

Rapid flow sand filters have to be cleaned by back-washing. The volume flow required means that 30–35 cubic metres of water per day, for each square metre of surface area on the filter, will have to be retained and returned through the filter. One or more header tanks at a higher level will have to be constructed to hold sufficient filtered water for back-washing and to supply the hatchery or rearing unit while this is taking place. In practice, a compromise has to be made between the required cleanliness of the water after filtration, and the time required for back-washing the filter.

Full biological treatment in a filter system involves the breakdown of organic pollutants in solution as well as the removal of solids. The filter medium must provide for the attachment and growth of micro-organisms which, in the presence of air or oxygen, can break down organic waste and convert ammonia, first to nitrite and then to comparatively harmless nitrate. The amount of oxygen needed in the process is used as a measure of the polluting strength of the organic waste matter in solution and is termed the B.O.D. (biological oxygen demand) of the effluent. The strength of fish-farm effluents varies according to the method employed and is likely to be greatest in a re-circulation system. The B.O.D. can be greater than 10 mg/1 which means that it will require at least 10 mg of oxygen to purify each litre of polluted water.

The systems developed for the treatment of recycled water in fish farms, with or without initial settlement, have biological filters usually containing a filter medium composed of limestone or crushed shell, mixed with a neutral material such as gravel or silica. The proportion of water recycled in these systems is usually 90-95% of the total flow. The flow rate achieved, in relation to the size of the filter, may range from about 35-60 litres per minute for each cubic metre of filter medium, but biological filter systems with a higher rate of flow have been designed.

Heated Water

The results of hatching and rearing young salmon in artificially warmed water can be dramatic. It is possible to reduce the normal incubation period by as much as two to three months and subsequently produce fry approximately three times heavier than those hatched and reared in cold water. This represents a great advantage as a large proportion of the under yearling parr will then become 1 + (S1) smolt in the following spring.

The economic benefit that can be derived from artificially warmed water depends on the natural water temperature. It will be of greatest value in areas where the average annual temperature is relatively low, resulting in a short growing time, where a substantial proportion of parr will not smoltify until they are two plus years old (S 2). Some fortunate salmonid farmers may have a source of clean, sun-warmed surface water available for six months of the year and sufficient spring water at an ambient temperature of 9° – 10°C to supply an over-wintering unit. They will probably produce a sufficiently high proportion of one plus smolt (S 1) to make any artificial water-warming unnecessary or of no significant economic benefit. They are exceptional and most smolt rearing units would benefit from a source of heated water in winter, provided it is not too expensive.

The supply of warmed water must be sufficient to maintain the artificial increase in temperature until the natural water temperature has reached 9°–10°C. No advantage can be gained from merely reducing the incubation time, and this by itself can be dangerous. The fish must be in water of a temperature sufficiently high (8°-10°C) to induce feeding when their yolk-sacs have been absorbed. They should then be maintained in an environment where the water temperature is steadily increasing towards the optimum for growth.

It is essential to continuously monitor the water temperature when it is warmed artificially. A failure of the warm water supply is not likely to cause serious losses during the incubation period or early on in the yolk-sac stage, provided that there is no sudden fall in water temperature, and the overall reduction does not exceed 5°-6°C. A prolonged drop in water temperature due to the loss of the source of warmed water can be very damaging if it happens when the alevins have almost completed absorption of their yolk-sacs or shortly after absorption is complete and the fish have started to feed. The previous artificial acceleration of their metabolism can result in the fish starving to death before they can be induced to start or recommence feeding.

The period taken for incubation of salmonid eggs and for the absorption of the yolk-sac is directly dependent on temperature. Consequently, each stage can be separately controlled to be completed at pre-determined times. The selected time schedule should be planned according to the natural temperature changes of the primary water supply.

A flow of approximately 5 litres per minute of water saturated with oxygen is needed for each ten thousand eggs under incubation. The flow has to be increased to 15 litres per minute during hatching and after the alevins have hatched. Eggs stripped in November and kept in water at an average ambient temperature of 3°C will hatch in about 145 days. In water heated to 10°-12°C they will hatch in about forty days. Care must be taken not to over-accelerate development during the final incubation and the larval, alevin stage. It may therefore be safer to incubate at 8°-9°C and maintain this temperature until the fish are ready to feed. After feeding starts, the temperature can again be raised to 12°C. The fry should not be transferred to unheated water, or the source of heat turned off, until the natural ambient water temperature has reached 10°-12°C.

The cost will become progressively greater the longer the fish have to be fed in artificially heated water. The temperature of the incoming water supply should be continuously measured by a sensor and the heat input required to raise the temperature to the pre-determined level adjusted and controlled electronically. The alternative is to use a heat exchanger to heat the water in a separate circuit and to control the temperature by adding cold water in a mixing tank. In either system the heated water should not be piped direct to the hatching troughs or fry tanks but to a header tank. A sensor should be fitted to the inlet pipe before it reaches the header tank which can activate a switch to turn off the heaters and sound an alarm if the temperature rises above the safe level (allowing for some heat loss during delivery). An additional sensor and alarm should be fitted as a fail-safe in the header tank which operates a solenoid and turns on a supply of cold water into the tank. The initial use of heated water to accelerate growth could still be profitable in Atlantic salmon smolt culture even if the natural water temperature is not high enough for the heat to be turned off until late May or early June.

Aeration

Artificial aeration of the water to maintain the dissolved oxygen content at a safe level is a useful adjunct in freshwater fish culture and can also be used to supplement the oxygen in seawater pumped to shore-based tanks. It is essential in all re-circulation systems, not only to keep the fish alive and well, but for the processes of biological filtration.

Aeration can be achieved in various ways. The simplest system is by pumping in compressed air through distributors such as porous bricks or perforated pipes. An alternative method is by sucking in air with the water supply through a venturi. Oxygen can also be introduced directly into the water as a gas from a cylinder or a liquid storage tank.

Re-circulation

The economics of re-circulation at present only makes sense if the comparatively high cost is justified by the value of the fish produced. In salmonid farming it has so far proved profitable for Atlantic salmon culture in cold climates, in order to produce S 1 smolts. Further south, where there is an ample supply of relatively warm water and a long growing season, it is not difficult to produce a satisfactory proportion of S 1 smolt (just over a year after hatching) in water at ambient temperatures.

A re-circulation system for smolt rearing on a salmon farm in Arctic Norway uses round tanks arranged in groups of four. Each group has its own, separate re-cycled water supply. The recycled flow is approximately 200 litre/minute for each group of four tanks with 10 litres per minute added as make-up water.

The water supply to each group of four tanks is by gravity from a 30 cm plastic pipe at a higher level. The recycled water, filtered, re-oxygenated and heated, is pumped up into the large-bore high-level pipe, which is not under pressure. The make-up water is added in this pipe. It can be either freshwater from a shallow well in river gravel below the site or seawater of 33–35‰ pumped from the nearby fjord. The top of the main

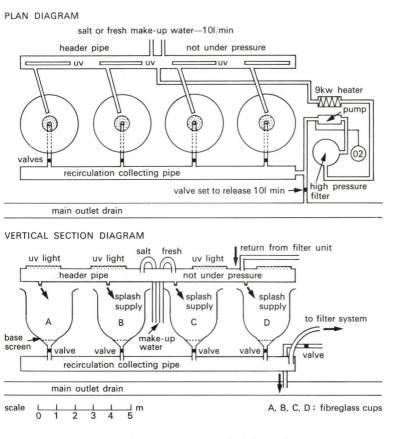

PLAN DIAGRAM

VERTICAL SECTION DIAGRAM

Fig. 18 Smolt rearing in recycled, heated water

supply pipe is slotted to hold a line of ultra-violet lamps
directed into the water in order to kill bacteria and parasites.

The flow to each tank is distributed by a spray-bar, which
is a pipe perforated to spray the water in one direction, fixed
over the surface. There is no air-sucking venturi on the intake
pipes to the individual tanks, although this could be an
advantage. The central drains have flat screens and the outflow
is controlled by gate-valves on the drain-pipes below the
tanks. Simple, articulated elbow-pipes would be a better

method of controlling the water level in the tanks.

The drains discharge by gravity into a large-bore, plastic collecting pipe. A certain amount of settlement takes place in this pipe and a valve at one end allows for periodic cleaning. The water is pumped from this pipe into the recycling system. On the way a by-pass valve is set to release 10 litres/minute to a main drain running at a lower level taking the surplus make-up water from all the groups of tanks.

The recycling system consists of a pump which forces the water into a sealed pressure-vacuum biological filter. A high-pressure gas hose connected directly to a cylinder delivers oxygen to the water on the intake side of the pump. The filtered water passes through a 9 kw heater before being returned to the high-level main header-pipe. The temperature and oxygen content of the out-going water are electronically monitored and controlled.

The Norwegian system is obviously expensive, not only in terms of capital investment, but also in running costs. It is evidently profitable but this may be in part due to the low cost of electricity for industrial use in Norway. There are many variations on the theme of re-circulation but they all work in much the same way. The difficult parts of any unit, which require expert professional design, are the filter, oxygen input and electronic control system.

Cages for Parr in Freshwater

Salmon and other smoltifying salmonids can be grown-on in floating cages in static water. They can be transferred to suitable cages as soon as they reach a length of about 5 cm and are sufficiently large not to pass through a small-mesh net. A net for parr cages should have a mesh which measures 6 mm along each side. It should be woven without knots and hung so that the mesh openings are square, not diamond-shaped. The floatation gear can be circular or rectangular but should preferably have a walkway all round. The joints can be inflexible but if the site is at all exposed a flexible linkage between walkway sections is likely to remain serviceable for a longer period. Useful dimensions for parr cages are sides (or diameter) of 5-6 m, depth 4-5 m and capacity about 140 cubic metres.

Experiments have been made in growing fry in cages during the first summer but very small mesh nets have to be used, woven with extra-fine twine, which are very easily torn. The idea is perhaps worth pursuing as it would avoid the use of expensive fixed tanks, and water supply and drainage systems. Sites would have to be very carefully selected where there was a continuous flow of clean water, such as at the mouths of streams entering lakes. The necessity for a fairly complex system of automatic feeding would require the use of stable walkways, preferably connected to the shore.

Acclimatization

Anadromous salmonids, even when fully smoltified, are more safely transferred to seawater if they are given a period of acclimatization in gradually increasing salinity. If the smolt rearing unit is close enough to the sea, a saltwater supply can be laid-on directly to the large parr tanks. This is the best system. The seawater intake should be similar to that described for shore-based on-growing tanks. Pumping from beach wells is preferable to using un-filtered surface water but this may be impracticable if a large volume is needed.

Pink salmon fry, which naturally migrate to saltwater as soon as their yolk-sacs are absorbed, need a seawater supply laid-on to the initial feeding tanks. They have to be grown-on in shore-based tanks until they are large enough to be transferred to sea cages, depending on the minimum practical mesh size that can be used. The saltwater supply to the shore unit has to be in the ratio of about 20 to 1 to the freshwater supply.

The arrangement of acclimatization tanks will depend on the site but the water supply should be by gravity from reservoirs at the highest level which can be kept full by pumping. There should be at least two separate reservoir tanks for both salt and freshwater. Mixing can be done in an intermediate reservoir but a better system is to have separate fresh and saltwater mains providing a gravity flow to a line of

4-5 m diameter g.r.p. tanks, 1·25 m deep, each with a separate intake and mixer valve.

Easy vehicle access is essential to the acclimatization tanks in order that smolt can be transferred from a tanker truck with the minimum of stress. The smolt tanks should be free-standing and have large-bore, elbow-pipe drains so that the acclimatized smolt can be run-out into containers for transfer to sea cages or on-growing tanks.

Some of the most successful salmon farms have dual fresh and saltwater supplies to their smolt rearing units. The parr are gradually acclimatized to an increasing degree of salinity over a period of several months prior to smoltification. They can then be transferred directly to seawater of 30-35‰ without stress or loss.

Saltwater tolerance and required periods of acclimatization for different salmonids suitable for sea farming are discussed in the chapter on fish husbandry.

Transportation

Fully-developed smolt are extremely delicate and difficult to transport without physical damage or stress. It is imperative that they should not be netted or handled in any way. The tanks used for over-wintering and the final period of parr rearing should have a drainage system which allows the smolt or pre-smolt parr to be run-out through the outlet system. The simplest way is to use free-standing tanks with outside elbow-pipes of sufficiently large bore for the smolt to pass through them easily and be collected in a container for transfer to the tanker truck. It is possible to use a fish suction pump to lift the fish directly into a tank on the truck but this can stress the fish and cause a loss of scales.

Tanks, even for comparatively short distance transport (100-200 miles), should preferably be insulated. The fish are safe to travel in water at the ambient temperature of the supply to the rearing unit in cool weather. The water temperatures in the transportation tanks should be evened up with the tanks at the delivery-end before the fish are transferred. The tanks on the truck should have a supply of pure oxygen (spare cylinders

Top A hen salmon ripe for stripping. The eggs are loose in the body cavity and fall towards the head when the fish is held up. *Bottom* A cock salmon large enough to fertilize the eggs from several females.

Top 'Stripping' a hen fish. *Bottom* Running in the milt from a male salmon.

Top Eyed eggs after 'shocking' stage showing infertile and weak eggs which have died and turned white. *Bottom* Salmon parr in automatic feeder for dry food.

A salmon farm in South Norway.

Top An experimental salmon sea cage farm in Norway. *Bottom* Large salmon cage under repair.

Salmon counting and fishing fence with gantry crane on rails over a fish trap.

Top Live salmon swimming in the trap over the false floor. *Centre* Dead salmon having been killed instantaneously by high voltage electric shock (see electrodes centre and bottom right). *Bottom* Fresh ranched salmon ready for packing.

should always be carried) and air from a petrol-driven compressor. A water pump is also essential on longer journeys where the water may have to be changed.

The fish tanks on trucks used for long distance transport should not only be insulated but also have a thermostatically controlled cooling system. The fish are put into the water in the transporter tanks at the same temperature as that in their rearing tanks. The water temperature is then slowly reduced to 4°-5°C and kept at that temperature during the journey. A re-circulation system incorporating a filter may also be necessary for long deliveries. Some losses through stress may be inevitable even when every precaution has been taken. These may occur on the journey or in the forty-eight hours following delivery. They should not exceed 10%.

Sea Farms on Shore

The attraction of building a saltwater salmon farm on the shore, rather than using cages or enclosures in the sea, is that it can be easily serviced and is not open to damage or put out of reach by wind or weather. The principle disadvantages are the high capital cost of construction, the problems of corrosion and marine fouling in pumps and pipelines, the risk of pump failure, and above all the cost of continuously pumping a very large flow of water. The height to which the saltwater has to be pumped is the most important factor in deciding whether a project of this kind is likely to prove worthwhile on a particular site. A place with a tidal range at spring tides of more than about 2 m at the sea intake is unlikely to be worthwhile developing.

Saltwater Supply

The seawater intake is the most important part of the unit. This must be kept as simple as possible. If the sea area is well-sheltered, a floating intake is possible. This consists of an anchored raft connected to the shore by a flexible, armoured hose supported on floats. The seaward end of the hose passes

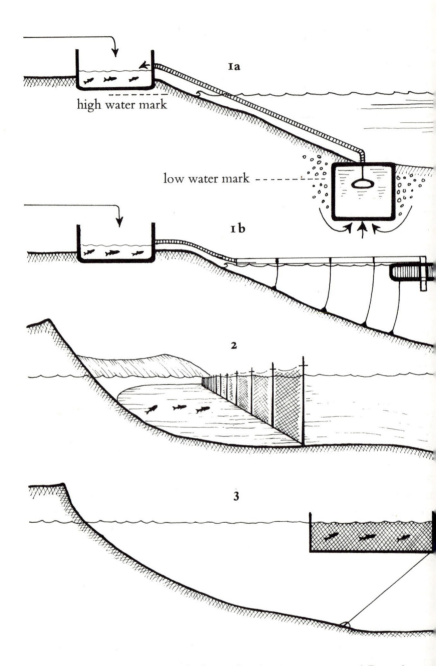

high water mark

low water mark - - - - - -

1a

1b

2

3

Fig. 19 Basic systems of salmon farming in seawater: **1** Pumping to shore tanks **(a)** from beach well **(b)** from floating intake **2** Shore enclosure **3** Floating cage

down through the raft and is screened by a large rose or a tubular screen attached to the underside of the raft. Screens or roses must be removable for cleaning and be replaceable by duplicates. Pumps are electric, either submersible on the end of the hose below the raft or sited on the shore. In either case, a diesel stand-by generator with automatic switching is essential.

An alternative system is to construct a fixed sump on the sea bed, supporting a platform above the surface. The water intake can either be through side-screens above the bottom or downwards through a flat screen on the top of the sump. A number of separate smaller intakes is a much safer arrangement than a single large intake. A stand-by intake should be provided to allow for shutdown during maintenance. The piping is laid on the sea bed or preferably buried in a trench. This type of intake is more expensive than the floating type but is essential in an exposed sea site.

Beach Pumping

This is a low-cost method of saltwater salmon farming which has so far only proved workable on a small-scale. The system is based on pumping the main seawater supply from a shallow well on the beach, between the high and low water marks. The beach acts as a filter sufficiently fine to exclude the sporophyte and gametophyte generations of marine algae and the free-swimming, veliger larvae of mussels. The well is lined and is about 1 m in diameter and 2 m deep. It fills from the bottom upwards with water drawn in from the surrounding sand and gravel. The surface of the beach round the sealed well-head is kept clean by the ebb and flow of the tide and if properly constructed the well and filter area does not need back-washing.

The well-cover carries a 700–1,000 w submersible pump suspended in the well which delivers water to a 7 m diameter x 1·5 m deep g.r.p. tank on the shore. The tank is capable of producing about 1 tonne of salmon a year.

The fish are bought-in as smolt and acclimatization has proved relatively simple. This was carried out by filling the shore tank with freshwater before the smolt were delivered. Oxygen is supplied from a cylinder to the static water in the tank through a distributor on the bottom. The smolt are transported at night and delivery made at first light. The water temperature is checked and evened up. The fish are transferred to the tank and allowed to settle down for three to four hours in freshwater. The pumped seawater supply is then turned on at 250 litres/minute and gradually replaces the freshwater over the next three to four hours.

Saltwater Tanks and Ponds

The basic designs are much the same as those used for salmonids in freshwater. The cheapest and simplest systems in Scandinavia consist of large ponds which usually have concrete sides. The dimensions are approximately 30 m long by 10 m wide and 2 m deep. The bottom should slope from the long sides to the centre and towards the seaward end. The ponds should be capable of being drained dry. More than one intake should be provided to prevent the formation of 'dead' areas with no interchange of water. This type of tank will hold up to 20 kg of sea-going rainbow trout (Av. wt. 1 – 3 kg) per cubic metre of water and requires a flow of about 300 litres per minute.

Other methods include circular ponds and tanks in

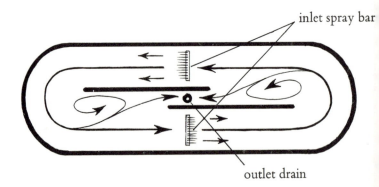

inlet spray bar

outlet drain

Fig. 20 Foster–Lucas tank

concrete or g.r.p., concrete raceways, round-ended circulating raceways of the Foster-Lucas type or rectangular circulating raceways of the type originally designed by Burrows and Chenoweth. The decision as to the type to use depends on the following factors:

1 The site area, the tidal range and the seawater intake.
2 The required flow of water and pumping costs.
3 The weight of fish per cubic metre of water which
  can be grown-on and the rate at which they will grow.
4 Husbandry. Is it easy to distribute fish food, keep
  the tanks clean and catch the fish for grading?
5 Maintaining the health of the fish.

A comparison of the various tanks and raceway systems made by Burrows and Chenoweth showed that the rectangular circulating raceway gave the best results on all counts. In selecting or designing any circulating tank or raceway it should be borne in mind that the fish will burn-off energy and not put on weight so quickly in a fast flow.

Tank Construction

The materials used for making shore tanks should have the greatest possible resistance to the corrosive effects of seawater. They should also provide a surface on which it is difficult for marine plants and animals to find attachment. Concrete, reinforced with either steel or glass-fibre is not a particularly good material. Even when very well finished it still offers a relatively rough surface. A better material for tanks is either g.r.p. or a tough plastic which is strong enough to be used without reinforcement.

Enclosures in the Sea

Beach Net Enclosures

A method which has proved profitable for small units in Norway, where there is a good tidal interchange, uses

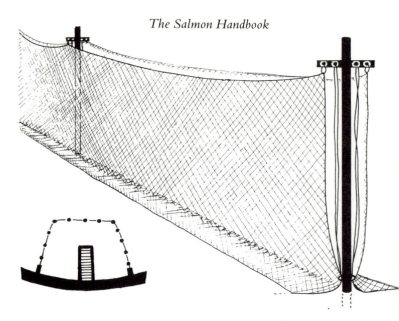

Fig. 21 Beach enclosure showing double net wall

enclosures made of net, on a sloping shore, consisting of a double barrier made of two walls of netting supported on poles driven into the beach. The shore must slope fairly steeply (1 : 2·5). Pressure-treated wood posts are driven into the beach at intervals of about 3 m enclosing a semi–circular area which must extend well beyond the low water mark of spring tides. Each post has a T-shaped cross–bar at the top at right angles to the shore. The ends of the cross-bars carry a stretcher rope which supports a wall of net. A second stretcher rope is bound to the net near the bottom and attaches the net to the base of the poles. The nets then extend for a distance of about 1 m along the bottom on each side of the barrier and are kept down by weights. The shore side of the enclosure should be lined with a concrete wall and there should be walkways extending seaward for fish feeding.

Enclosures of this kind have not been used for salmon but with a good tidal interchange, they will carry 8 – 10 kg of sea-going rainbow trout (Av. wt. 1 – 3 kg) per cubic metre of water, averaged over a tidal range which changes the water one and a half times in each cycle. Several enclosures are needed along a stretch of shore for different ages and sizes of fish, surrounded by nets of the appropriate mesh.

Permanent Enclosures

An arm of the sea, or channel between the shore and an island, is closed off by solid, fish-proof barriers. These are usually made of steel-bar screens supported between reinforced concrete piers. The barriers must extend at least 1·5 m above the surface at high water on spring tides and it is unlikely to be economically worthwhile to plan an enclosure of this kind in a place where there is a maximum tidal range of more than 1-2 m.

The tidal flow through a fixed enclosure may be insufficient to maintain the oxygen content of the water or to remove waste matter. In these circumstances, it is necessary to use impeller pumps to supplement the tide and draw water through the enclosure, if it is to hold a high enough density of fish.

This system has been successfully developed for Atlantic salmon culture in Norway. Two enclosures are needed to cover a sea-feeding cycle of about eighteen months from smolt to market size. The density of salmon (Av. wt. 1·5-6 kg) held in the Norwegian permanent enclosures (1·2 hectares in area) is about $0·5$ kg/m^3 without pumping, and 2-3 kg/m^3 with pumping. The fish are fed by piping a wet food mixture into the water and are recaptured for market by putting a net round the feeding area. A problem is that once smolt are released into a large enclosure of the permanent type the fish cannot be properly checked or treated for disease. An enclosure may hold salmon worth up to £500,000 which is too many 'eggs in one basket'.

Sea Cages

Salmonid sea farming in both Europe and North America has in recent years turned increasingly towards the use of floating cages anchored in sheltered water. The majority of the new generation of sea farms are of this type. The principle advantage of cages over any kind of static enclosure, either on land or in the sea, is their versatility. They can be of the shape and size to suit the scale of a project and, if necessary, moved to a new site without incurring large capital losses.

A wide variety of materials have been employed to construct floating fish cages. Some earlier types were made of metal mesh panels fixed in rigid frames which had to be supported by large floatation collars. Modern cages all basically consist of a simple bag of net suspended from the surface. Cages can be anchored separately to the sea bed or attached together in groups to form flotillas. They can be arranged round a fixed raft or working 'island', or alongside floating pontoons forming a walkway from the shore. Floatation gear can consist of plastic floats or blocks of polystyrene encased in g.r.p., wood or concrete. In one type of circular cage the frame holding the net is made of large diameter PVC piping filled with plastic foam and sealed at the joints to form a floatation ring.

Different types of cages for salmonid sea farming can be bought ready-made. Most of these designs have been developed and fully tried-out in commercial farms by the manufacturers. They are all generally capable of functioning well, provided they are operated in waters similar to those for which they were developed, but they can prove very unsatisfactory in different conditions. The cages at present being manufactured for sale fall into three main groups:

1 Comparatively small, inflexible rectangular cages with floatation collars sufficiently wide and stable to form working platforms. This type of cage is usually joined to others to make up a flotilla.
2 Large, multi-sided cages with floating walkways, flexibly linked together to form hexagonal or octagonal enclosures. This is the type of cage most commonly used for farming salmon in the sea.
3 Cages available in a variety of sizes and shapes with nets mounted on light flexible frames attached to plastic floats. These cages have no working area and have to be serviced

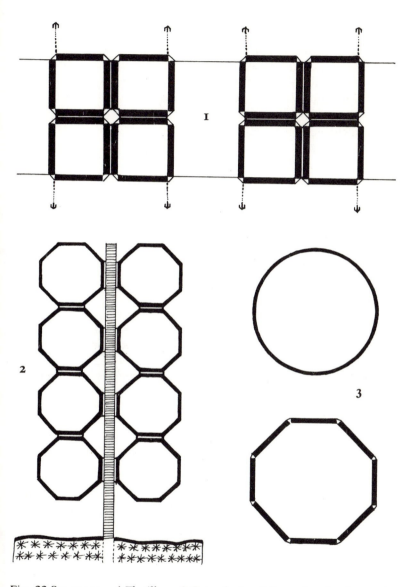

Fig. 22 Sea cages: **1** Flotillas **2** Cage dock **3** Round and polygonal cages for individual anchoring

from a boat. They are too flimsy to anchor close to a pontoon or fixed platform.

Some fish farmers make their own cages. Occasionally these are based on original ideas but are more usually copies of well-tried standard types. Before deciding to make cages it is as well to bear in mind that a large cage can hold fish worth more than £20,000 which is a great deal of money to lose through a basic fault in the design.

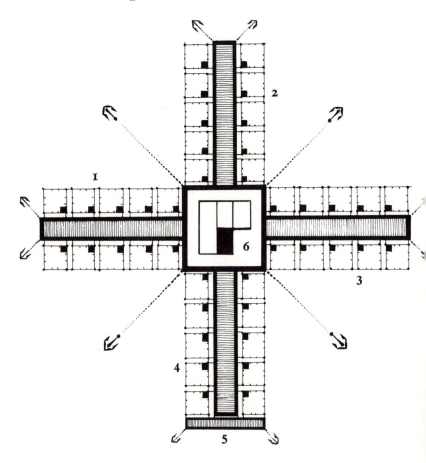

Fig. 23 Plan of floating sea or freshwater cage fish farm (annual production 120-150 tonnes per year) Scale: 1 : 1000 **1, 2, 3** and **4** Service walkways with moored fish cages and compressed air fish feeders **5** Landing stage for work boat **6** Central service raft with guard house, generator and compressor and stores for fish food and fuel.

Small Inflexible Cages

The most common type is rectangular and consists of four walkways which are joined together rigidly to form a floatation collar. The sections of walkway consist of pressure-cured wood frames, enclosing polystyrene floats, fixed rigidly together at the corners by galvanized steel plates. Vertical stanchions, joined by horizontal members are bolted to the inside of the walkways, to act as hand-rails and support the net. Average overall dimensions for a cage of this type are 6 m x 6 m with a net which may be 4 – 6 m deep.

Large Rigid Floatation Collars

A good collar of this type is a hexagon made up of H-section steel bars with two large, air-filled buoys at each corner. The collar supports a net of approximately 300 m^3 capacity. A serious drawback to this kind of collar is that it provides no satisfactory walkway or working platform. Floatation collars that allow workers to balance on a narrow beam or tube without secure foot and hand holds can be extremely hazardous in rough weather.

A circular cage made of tubing has been developed in Norway and is appropriately known as the Polar Circle. This is a continuous tube of heavy PVC about 30 cm in diameter, filled with polyurethane foam, to which upright PVC tubes about 7 cm in diameter are welded at intervals of 2 m. The tops of the uprights are joined by a second continuous circle of 7 cm diameter PVC tubing. The sections of the collars have to be welded up on site. The floatation ring supports a net of 300-350 m^3 capacity. This type of cage seems to work well in sheltered Norwegian waters, but it has no walkways and workers have to balance on the slippery round collar.

Flexible, Multi-sided Cages

The most versatile floatation gear, which can be used in exposed as well as more sheltered sites, consists of walkway sections flexibly linked at the ends to form polygons. The walkways carry vertical stanchions which hold nets to prevent the fish leaping out of the cages as well as supporting the main cage net. The best type of walkways are made from blocks of polystyrene covered in g.r.p., with a non–slip surface on the upper side. Each walkway, with or without galvanized iron stanchions, is a complete unit which can be linked in a variety of ways to form any shape of polygonal floatation collar or working platform. They are built like boats and are intended to last a long time in the sea. The sections are 6 m long and when made up to a hexagon will carry a net cage of approximately 300-350 m^3 capacity.

The average density of Atlantic salmon which can safely be held in floating cages is 10 kg/m^3. The weight per m^3 can be increased during the winter when the water temperature is below 6°-7°C.

Nets and Net Mesh

Nets used for floating fish cages or enclosures should be woven of a strong, artificial fibre which is not affected by saltwater. The netting should preferably be woven with a square mesh as opposed to the diamond mesh used for fishing nets, as it is hung as a flat wall not a loose curtain. Smaller mesh cages can be made up of knotless netting because it offers a greater open area for the passage of water, but cages to hold large fish are better made of ordinary knotted netting as this is easier to repair.

The mesh of nets and the twine size used depend upon the size of fish to be kept in the cages or enclosures. The largest mesh capable of preventing the escape of fish is not only the cheapest but also offers the least barrier to the interchange of water. The possibility of the fish either being gilled in the net or caught by their teeth is a limiting factor which must be taken into consideration in determining mesh size. The minimum mesh for salmonids at the stage they will tolerate average marine salinity is approximately 12 mm measured knot-to-knot.

Many different methods have been devised for mounting cage nets. The first consideration is to enclose the maximum volume of water within the depth of hanging net. Salmonids in floating cages tend to swim round the enclosed area. Their turning circle is a factor of their size. Large fish in square or rectangular cages can waste the water space in the corners. There is also a risk of abrasion causing skin damage and disease when the turning fish brush against the flat sides of the net. This is an important reason for using multi-sided or round floatation collars, particularly for cages holding larger fish.

The nets supported by either round or multi-sided collars are in fact round as they hang. They can either be made up as a cup, or with a vertical side and a flat bottom. The cup is less expensive, and rather easier to handle and keep clean, but the flat-bottomed net holds more fish. All mounting points have to be designed to avoid abrasion and keep the net from rubbing on floats, walkways or linkages.

The vertical stanchions mounted on a floatation collar above the water carry a ring of net round the cage to prevent fish from leaping out. This net need not be so strong as the cage net but should be of a mesh small enough to prevent the fish from catching in it if they strike it when jumping. The net should stand 1-1·5 m above the water.

Sea nets must all be treated with an anti-fouling dip or paint. Most anti-fouling material contains copper salts or other poisons intended to prevent the attachment of marine plants and animals. These can also be poisonous to fish. Even the best paints or dips are still only a compromise and any which are used must be guaranteed as non-poisonous to the fish enclosed by the treated nets. Nets mounted just below or above the surface of the water will deteriorate in sunlight and have to be renewed fairly frequently. They should be made as a separate detachable skirt and the twine should be dyed a dark colour. There is no evidence that the colour of cage nets has any effect on the fish enclosed but generally dark colours or black are preferred.

The panels forming the large nets used in multi-sided cages must have bags filled with 2-3 kg of stones or metal sinkers attached at the bottom corners. Weights are also attached to the bottom corners of small rectangular nets to help them stay in shape and to reduce their tendency to stream sideways in a current.

125

Cages in Rafts

A complex system of walkways and cages joined together to form rafts is commonly used for fish culture on the Pacific coast of North America. A typical arrangement consists of flat-topped pontoons, made of polystyrene coated with a skin of reinforced concrete, linked in a pattern to form rectangles or open-ended berths in which the fish nets are suspended. The whole unit forms a large, stable working area while at the same time remaining relatively flexible. It may incorporate a landing-stage for boats or be directly accessible from the shore over a pontoon bridge. The principle drawback to a development of this kind is that it represents a large investment in a static system which leaves little room for modification in the light of experience gained on the site. There is also a danger of the cages becoming self-polluting if there are no strong currents to dispose of waste matter. Raft units are better kept small and anchored separately in deep water where advantage can be taken of their stability while retaining some room for manoeuvre. Dispersal also reduces the risk of the spread of disease.

Other Methods

The possibility of submersible cages has been one that has attracted specialist engineers interested in fish farming. The main advantage of such a system would be that the cages could be submerged to avoid wind and wave action or ice formation. An alternative to a cage which can be submerged when required is one where the cages are permanently suspended below the surface, or an enclosure is made on the sea bed. Fish enclosures below the surface of the sea, which escape the limitations of the litoral zone and the restrictions imposed by the need to shelter from bad weather, are natural developments in the progressive exploitation of the farming potential of the sea. This will, however, require full submarine installation and management by divers who will have to be trained to new techniques in fish husbandry in an alien environment.

Chapter 9

Fish Feeding and Nutrition

The food originally provided for members of the salmon family, hatched to supplement wild populations or grown-on to re-stock angling waters, was either the same or resembled as closely as possible what the fish took naturally. The increasing domestication of salmonids as a result of their being farmed for the table market has led to the investigation of a whole new range of nutritional needs. Carnivorous fish require a diet very different from the mammals and birds that have been farmed in the past, in terms of proteins, fats, carbohydrates, vitamins and minerals.

The formulation of diets and their development as a part of the animal-feeding industry has taken place comparatively recently, but dry crumb or pelleted fish foods, first produced in the USA, are now a commonplace item which can be prepared in any mill with a pelleting machine that obtains a satisfactory formula and the right ingredients. Good quality dry fish feeds are now completely successful for all stages of the freshwater culture of salmonids. They are not so successful by themselves for feeding salmon and trout at sea, although a milled meal with added vitamins is now generally regarded as an essential constituent of the moist diets used for sea-feeding.

The protein in a fish diet contains the essential amino-acids which have to be present in the correct proportions to promote the vital physiological functions of the body. Fats of low melting point, usually fish oils, are the main sources of energy. The essential poly-unsaturated fatty acids are linoleic, linolenic, and arachidonic. High-fat diets are essential for sea-going salmonids in saltwater and for the production of S1 smolts in freshwater. Some carbohydrates, in small quantities, can be digested by salmonids to provide an additional source of energy.

A good deal is now known of the vitamin needs of salmonids and vitamins are added to all dry diets and to the meals combined with wet food mixtures. Vitamin deficiencies cause symptoms that can be mistaken for those produced by some bacterial and virus diseases. The calcium and phosphorous needed for bone formation must form part of the diet. Traces of other minerals are needed to promote catalytic processes in the body.

Animal protein which is the main constituent of all good quality fish diets is expensive. Other proteins such as soya and feather meal are also used in commercial food formulation. The single-cell proteins have proved a satisfactory alternative, particularly the variety derived from methanol by the action of methylophilis bacteria. In the longer term, algal protein may prove to be the solution to feeding domestic carnivorous fish. This represents the rational progression which has taken place in husbandry on land where plant crops are grown, harvested and processed to feed terrestrial farm animals.

TABLE I
Basic Constituents of Commercial Dry Fish Feeds
(Percentage of total weight excluding ash and fibre)

Materials	Juvenile Fish in Freshwater		Growers in Saltwater	
	Trout	Salmon	Trout	Salmon
Protein	40 – 45	50 – 55	35 – 40	45
Fats	15	17	17	16 – 18
Carbo-hydrate	20	11	25	18
Water	8 – 9	8 – 9	8 – 9	8 – 9

Dry Feeds

Commercial fish food manufacturers have their own formulations, usually based to some extent on local availability of ingredients. Table I shows the basic proportions of the constituents in high quality dry feeds made up for feeding juvenile anadromous salmonids in freshwater and for growing-on the fish in saltwater. Vitamins and minerals are added to the dry food mixtures.

Special, fat-reduced formulations are made up for feeding brood fish. Feeds containing carotenoids can be obtained to pigment the flesh of fish prior to slaughter. Medical feeds for the treatment of bacterial diseases are also available, either directly from the food manufacturers in some countries or under veterinary prescription in others. Binder meals for mixing with wet foods contain a cellulose or alginate binding agent and additional vitamins. The added vitamins include thiamin (vitamin B1) to replace that destroyed by the anti-vitamin thiaminase in minced fish belonging to the herring family.

Wet or Dry Feeds

There is no argument about the economy and general superiority of dry feeds over wet feeds for salmonids in freshwater. They score on all counts not least of which is reduced pollution, although even in freshwater there is some evidence that salmonids make better use of the protein in wet rather than dry diets. The only real problem with dry feeds used for young fish is the formation of dust during transportation and storage. This can enter the gills of the fish and promote bacterial gill disease. The best high-fat diets avoid the problem because they are slightly tacky and do not form dust.

The main controversy over the use of all dry feeds for feeding fish in saltwater is whether or not their exclusive use causes osmotic stress. The osmo-regulatory process has been discussed in some detail in another section. The concentration of salts in the body of anadromous fish in fresh or saltwater has to remain within certain prescribed limits in order for them to survive. In the sea, fish which have to drink seawater must get rid of the excess salts. This is an active process demanding the use of energy.

A Norwegian experiment was carried out in 1972 – 1973 by S. Ugletveit at the Havforskningsinstitutt in Bergen.

Rainbow trout in seawater were fed on dry pellets. The pellets were not completely dry as water had been added in a gelatine coating. The dry pellets initially contained approximately 8% of water and the added gelatine solution was adjusted to vary the final moisture content between 20% and 80%. The pellets were crumbled before the gelatine was added so that the food was in fact given as a form of moist pellet and not as a true dry feed.

No significant differences in food consumption were observed in the various groups under test. It was concluded that a food mixture containing 20% water does not cause osmotic stress resulting in a diminished growth rate.

The results of this Norwegian experiment are interesting in that they show osmotic stress appears to be prevented if rainbow trout in the sea are fed a diet with a minimum water content of 20%. The experiments do not provide any information about possible osmotic stress when the fish are fed commercial dry pellets with a moisture content of only 8-9%. In experimental work carried out in Japan feeding rainbow trout a dry diet in seawater, it was then found that no osmotic stress was apparent in water of a salinity less than 20-23‰

Improved Dry Feeds for Seawater

It may not be possible for fish farmers to obtain supplies of fresh industrial fish or fish offal in many places where there are excellent sites for salmon farms. Usually this is not because suitable industrial fish species are not present in nearby waters, but because there is no industrial fishing on conservation grounds or for some other reason. It is not an economic proposition to transport and store wet trash fish or fish-offal deep-frozen because of the large water content. Sea farmers have been forced to feed dry pellets in these circumstances, sometimes with less than satisfactory results. What is needed is a new commerical pellet diet. Pellets should be transported and stored dry but should be hygroscopic. Freshwater sprayed on them before they are fed to the fish would be absorbed to make up at least 30% of their weight, without causing the pellets to disintegrate.

Essential Amino-Acids in Diets

The following amino-acids are thought to be essential in the protein content of salmonid diets. The quantities expressed as a percentage of the total protein in the food are as follows:

Argenine	6·0	per cent	Methionine	1·3	per cent
Cystine	2·5	" "	Phenylaline	3·0	" "
Histidine	1·7	" "	Threonine	2·3	" "
Isoleucine	2·5	" "	Tryptophane	0·5	" "
Leucine	3·9	" "	Tyrosine	2·0	" "
Lysine	5·0	" "	Valine	3·2	" "

There are often considerable differences in the amino-acid make-up of the various proteins used in the commercial preparation of dry feeds or wet food supplements. An analysis of the amino-acids in a typical sample of a high-quality dry feed, expressed as a percentage of the total protein in the diet, is approximately as follows:

Alanine	3·2	per cent	Lysine	3·4	per cent
Argenine	2·7	" "	Methionine	1·3	" "
Aspartic acid	4·2	" "	Phenylaline	2·1	" "
Glutamic acid	6·8	" "	Proline	2·7	" "
Glycine	3·0	" "	Serine	2·1	" "
Histidine	1·6	" "	Threonine	2·0	" "
Isoleucine	1·6	" "	Tyrosine	1·4	" "
Leucine	4·0	" "	Valine	2·7	" "

Vitamins in Fish Diets

The quantities of the different essential vitamins that are added to dry food mixtures depend on the amounts naturally present and retained in the ingredients after processing and storage.

Salmonid water-soluble vitamin requirements in mg per kg of the dry weight of food are approximately as follows:

Vitamins	mg	Vitamins	mg
Thiamin (B1)	10 – 12	Folic acid	6 – 10
Riboflavine (B2)	20 – 30	Inositol	200 – 300
Pyridoxine (B6)	10 – 15	Choline	500 – 600
Pantothenic acid	40 – 50	Cyanobalamine	a trace
Nicotinic acid	120 – 150	(B12)	
Biotin	1 – 1.2	Ascorbic acid (C)	150 – 450

Salmonids also need the fat-soluble vitamins (A, D, E and K). These differ from the water–soluble vitamins because they can accumulate in the body and cause vitamin poisoning or hypervitaminosis. The quantities of these vitamins given in a dry food mixture or supplement must therefore be adjusted to the quantity and the type of fats in the original mixture. The following are average amounts per kg of fish food.

Vitamin A	8 – 10,000	I U
Vitamin D	1,000	"
Vitamin E	125	"
Vitamin K3	15 – 20	mg

Minerals

Wild salmonids obtain the essential minerals they need for healthy growth from ingesting the water in which they live and from the tissues of their prey. Minerals are added to commercial dry feeds and wet food supplements. Calcium and phosphorus must be available in unrestricted quantities. Dry fish meal contains about 26·0 gm of calcium and 21·0 gm of phosphorus per Kg which is ample for the diet. If one of the single-cell proteins and soya is the main source of protein in the diet there will be too little calcium and phosphorus and more will have to be added as calcium carbonate and di calcium phosphate. The minerals added to proprietory mixtures are shown in the example of a commercial diet.

Fats

High-fat diets are now considered essential to promote quick growth in freshwater, early smolting and for on-growing in the sea. The amount of supplementary fats which may have to be added in the form of fish oils depends on the fats in the dry constituents of the mixture. The make-up of various dry meals is shown in Table II.

It can be seen from Table II that in dry feeds where fish meal and soya are the main ingredients, assuming that the proportion is constant and bearing in mind that the fat content of different sóya meals can vary considerably, the amount of fat in the initial mixture will depend on the original fat content of the industrial fish in the fish meal. For example, if capelin (*Mallotus villosus*) in pre-spawning condition were used to make the fish meal and the proportion of the other ingredients remined the same, the fat content of the pellets would be four to five times greater than if the fish meal had been made from white fish.

The fat content of a dry food mixture will also be raised considerably by using a high-fat soya or by increasng the proportion of dry milk solids. Meat/bone meal is not a good source of additonal fat as it contains saturated fatty-acids. The utilization of fats in salmonid diets is improved by the addition of lecithin to the dry food mixture. Final adjustment of the fat content by the addition of fish oils is only possible within certain limits as the mixture can become too moist to form a good pellet.

If the components of salmonid diets lack the essential fatty sources of energy for balanced nutrition this is, in practice, made up by adding digestible oils directly to the other constituents. The presence of linolenic acid is essential and fish oils contain an average of 30% compared to only 6-8% in soya oil. Fish oils are therefore the preferred source of supplementary unsaturated fatty-acids.

Preservation of Fats in Salmonid Diets

Rancidity in the oils used to formulate dry feeds or as additives in wet food mixtures can be particularly dangerous and result in serious, permanent damage to the digestive system of the fish, even if fed for only a short time. The fats used in diets

TABLE II
Raw Materials that may be used in Dry Pellets and Meals
(all these components are not used in every formula and others
may be substituted by manufacturers)

Nutrient Components (Crude Protein 40 – 55%)	Minerals (not more than 3% of total wt.)
Fish Meal	Calcium carbonate
Meat bone meal	Di-calcium phosphate
Blood meal	Manganese sulphate
Hydrolized feathers	Magnesium sulphate
Soya meal	Iron sulphate
Wheat meal	Iron carbonate
Cane molasses	Iron oxide
Fish oils	Copper carbonate
Soya oils	Zinc sulphate
Lecithin	Zinc oxide
Vitamins	Potassium iodide
Anti-oxidants	Sodium carbonate
	Sodium chloride
	Cobalt sulphate
	Cobalt carbonate

should be as fresh as possible and treated with an anti-oxidant
such as Ethoxyquin, a solution which should be incorporated
in fish oils at the rate of 2 gm per litre. Vitamin C is also a useful
anti-oxidant.

The Vitamin E (*alpha-tocopherol*) content of high-fat diets
is of importance in hindering the oxidation of fats during
storage. Approximately 0·4 gm of Vitamin E should be added
per 100 gm of fat in each kg of the mixed food (i.e. a food
mixture with 10% fat content will require 0·4 gm Vitamin E
per kg and pro rata).

Manufactured Dry Feeds

The constituents of commercial pellets and meals vary widely, due mainly to the availability and cost of raw materials. The essential factors in a good dry feed are that its composition should be consistent and its manufacture carefully controlled so that it is fully up to the manufacturer's specification. Basic raw materials commonly used to manufacture dry, pelleted fish foods are given in Table II.

Adequate vitamins are normally present in commercial dry feeds. Thiamin may be added as an additional precaution against thiaminase if the pellets have been stored for several weeks and it is suspected that the main source of crude protein was fish meal derived from fish of the herring family. The thiamin should be made up in a 1-2% aqueous solution and sprayed on the pellets at a rate of 2 litres per 100 kg.

Energy in Dry and Wet Foods

The energy consumption of fish is measured in kilo-calories (Kcal), or mega-calories (Mcal) (1 Mcal = 1000 Kcal). The total available energy in fish foods is measured in usable or metabolizable energy (ME), which includes the energy remaining in the body's waste products. The sources of energy in fish feeds are proteins, fats and carbohydrates. The digestability of a particular diet will vary according to its components.

In dry feeds the average digestibility of protein in pellets and meals is about 80%. That is to say the fish can digest about 80 gm out of every 100 gm of protein they eat. The digestibility of the fat content in the form of fish oil is about 85%.

Simple, usable carbohydrate mixtures consisting of the monosaccarides (fructose, glucose and galactose) and disaccarides (lactose, maltose and molasses) have a digestibility of about 60%. Salmonids can only tolerate about 12% by weight of digestible carbohydrate in any diet. More carbohydrate is often included in food mixtures but this is safe if it is indigestible and serves no useful purpose except as a filler

TABLE III
Average Content of Meals used in Dry Feeds
(Gm per kg of total dry weight)

Raw Material	Dry Matter	Protein	Fat	Ash	Cellulose
Fish Meal (Vacuum dried)	960	740	100	120	—
Meat/Bone meal	930	560	80	260	—
Skimmed Milk Solids	940	130	15 – 20	90	—
Soya Meal	900	460	20	60	40
Soya Protein	920	625	10	56	56
Fulfat Soya	929	412	172	54	27
Wheat Meal	875	155	50	30	40
Dried Yeast	895	477	7	75	2

together with the ash and fibre contents of the feed.

The metabolizable energy yields for the main groups of components in the average dry feed are as follows:

Material	Kcal M E per gm
Protein	3·5
Fats	8·0
Carbohydrate	2·3

Fresh Wet Feeds

In practice sea farmers have found they get an improved economic return by feeding minced raw or deep-frozen industrial fish and crustacea mixed with a vitaminized meal and binding agent to form a thick porridge.

The average energy content of diets composed of minced industrial fish or fish offal, with the addition of a source of carbohydrate in the binding agent, are as follows:

Material	*Kcal M E per gm*
Protein	3·9
Fats	8·0
Carbohydrate	1·6

Food Value

The nutritional quality of commercial dry feeds is nearly always given as a conversion factor or ratio. This simply means the amount of food in kg it takes to produce 1 kg of fish (usually ignoring the not-inconsiderable amount which is wasted). It is not this simple ratio which decides the economic value of a fish food but the metabolizable energy (M E) which it provides to the fish. This is why it is often essential to incorporate comparatively large amounts of digestible fats in the form of fish oil in the diets of salmonids as these are their main source of M E. A low energy content in fish food is the explanation for poor growth in fish although they have been fed what is apparently a high-protein diet.

Wet Fish Food Mixtures

Table IV shows how the protein and fat components of different wet fish food sources vary due to the fish species available and the time of year when they are caught. The fat content has the greatest range and this produces a wide range in the M E per kg of raw food. This can vary from about 1000 Kcal to more than 1900 Kcal per kg. This means that at least double the quantity of low-energy food will be needed to produce the same growth as from a high-energy food. The main source of energy is the metabolizable fat in the food or food mixture. It is this which may have to be maintained at the desired level by the addition of fish oils.

The total fat requirement of salmonids is thought to depend on water temperature ranging from about 7-8% of the diet in winter to 18-20% in summer.

The use of any particular fish or shell-fish as the main component of the diet of salmonids will depend upon

TABLE IV
Marine Animal Tissue in Wet Diets   B.F. = Before Spawning
(gm and ME Kcal per kg of feed)   A.F. = After Spawning

Species and Feed	Dry Wt.	Protein	Fat	Kcal	Fat energy %
Capelin (B.F.)	290	130	140	1630	70
(Mallotus villosus)(A.F.)	200	130	40	830	58
Sprat or Brisling (B.F.)	310	160	130	1650	63
(Sprattus sprattus) (A.F.)	285	160	105	1480	53
Other Clupeids (Herring family)	300	160	130	1650	62
Herring offal	230	150	40	1000	50
Blue Whiting (B.F.) (Micromesistius	260	165	75	1243	48
poutassou) (A.F.)	240	165	35	950	30
Saithe (whole) (Pollachius virens)	250	175	50	1120	40
(offal)	235	165	30	990	30
Norway Pont (B.F.) (Boreogadus esmarkii)	300	165	120	1608	60
(A.F.)	220	165	20	820	20
Sandeels (Ammodytes spp)	270	180	60	1320	52
White Fish Offal	200	160	25	965	24

availability and price. Given that there is some element of choice, the fat content can be adjusted either by choosing a fatty fish or by the addition of the right amount of oil to bring up the calorific value to the desired level.

The digestible material in food mixtures (D M) to form a satisfactory wet diet should result in a balance between the energy (Kcal M E) derived from protein and from fats. If this cannot be achieved from the available raw materials the fat energy source must be artificially increased by adding fish oil. The final mixture should have a total weight to dry-weight ratio of about 3 : 1 to give the right consistency. Moist, rather than wet, foods can be made by increasing the dry content to include more nutrients in addition to the binding agent, but mixtures of this kind fall more into the category of moist pellets.

High-quality raw materials usually contain adequate amounts of the essential vitamins but when fat fish of the herring family are used as the main source of protein, thiamin should be added in the proportion of 0·2 gm per kg of total weight.

Wet Feeds, Raw Materials and Costs

The factors to be taken into consideration in producing a wet food mixture for on-growing salmonids in the sea are total protein, total fat, ME balance between protein and fat energy sources and cost. The following diets illustrate the results in terms of nutrient value of different mixtures.

The mixture has added shrimp waste as a source of astaxanthin to pigment the flesh red. An artificial substitute could be used for this purpose. The ash content is not included in the figures.

et 1. Ingredients per 100 kg of Wet Food Mixture.

ed Mix.	Total Wt. kg	Dry Wt. kg	Prot. kg	Fat kg	Carbohyd. kg	M.E. Mcal
ue Whiting	40	10·4	6·6	3·0	—	49·7
iite Fish Offal	40	8·9	6·4	1·6	—	37·8
wn Waste	10	2·4	1·3	0·2	—	6·8
:amin Meal	10	8·8	0·9	0·3	7·0	22·0
tals	100	30·5	15·2	5·1	7·0	116·3
itrient %	—	—	49·8	16·7	22·9	—
ergy %	—	—	50·0	35·1	31·5	—

This diet is rather low in calories as it only contains 1163 Kcal per kg. It has adequate protein but too little fat. If 20 gm fish oil and 10 gm of lecithin per kg is added to the mixture this would increase the total calories to about 1400 Kcal per kg. It would also bring the fat energy level up to 59·1% which would then be in balance with the protein energy.

Diet 1 is basically a lean, low–fat mixture. It is better to produce a balance between the energy sources without having to add extra fats.

Diet 2. Ingredients per 100 kg of Wet Food Mixture.

Feed Mix.	Total Wt. kg	Dry Wt. kg	Prot. kg	Fat kg	Carbohyd. kg	M.E. Mcal
Industrial Clupeid	45	13·5	7·2	5·9	—	74·3
Saithe Offal	25	5·9	4·1	0·8	—	24·8
White Fish Offal	20	4·0	3·2	0·5	—	19·3
Vitamin Meal (added thiamin)	10	8·0	0·9	0·3	7·0	22·0
Totals	100	32·2	15·4	7·5	7·0	140·4
Nutrient %	—	—	47·8	23·3	21·7	—
Energy %	—	—	42·8	42·7	8·0	—

This is a much better mixture than Diet 1. The ME Kcal is 1404 per kg. There is adequate protein and a good balance between the protein and fat energy.

It is quite possible to use only a combination of locally available industrial fish or fish offal provided that the protein and fat contents are known. It is also possible to add up to 30–35% of the total weight of the mixture in the form of dry vitamin meal, based on good–quality fish meal. The mixture will still remain sufficiently liquid to be easily distributed.

Binding Agents for Wet and Moist Food Mixtures

The binder most commonly used which gives good results is Methyl-cellulose (Carboxymethylcellulose = CMC or

Hydroxypropylmethylcellulose = HPMC). This substance quickly absorbs water to form a stable, water-soluble gel. Approximately 1% may be added directly to the ingredients of the mixture but for wet feeds the binding agent usually forms part of the vitaminized meal which contributes about 10% by weight of whole feed.

Alginates may be used as binding agents in the preparation of moist pellets. Their binding efficiency depends upon their degree of polymerization in the presence of free calcium ions. A source of calcium ion has to be provided in the food mixture. Approximately 30 mg of calcium ion is needed per gm of alginate. If calcium hydrogen phosphate (CaH Po4 2H$_2$0) is used as a source of ion, 130 mg should be added per gm of alginate. A small quantity of NaCl may also be added, depending on the salt content of the ingredients in the food mixture and whether the feed is being given in seawater.

Moist Pellets

The moisture content of wet feeds usually averages about 70%. Moist pellets have a moisture content of 20-50% of their total weight. The pellet mixture consists of the following basic components:

Fresh industrial fish and fish offal.

Fish and other protein meals, including some carbohydrate.

Fat in the form of fish oils and milk concentrates.

Vitamins, minerals, anti-oxidant and binding agent.

The advantage of moist pellets is that they do not disintegrate to the same extent as wet feeds and can be auto-fed. At the same time they contain sufficient water to be fed exclusively to salmonids in the sea without causing the problems associated with an all-dry pellet diet. It is a comparatively straightforward operation to manufacture moist pellets using a modified industrial mincing machine, fitted with a revolving blade. The blade cuts off the 'worms' of pre-mixed food in short lengths as they come out of the perforations on the face-plate of the mincer.

TABLE V

Abernethy Moist Pellets (Salmon-Cultural Laboratory, Longview, Washington, USA)

Feed mix	%	Derivation	Vitamins	Mix % of each vita- min
Fish meal	30·0	High-fat fish	Thiamin	0·26
Dried Whey	17·5	Max. 52% lactose	Riboflavine	1·21
Cottonseed meal	10·5	Min. 50% protein	Pyridoxine	0·53
Vitamin mix	1·0	—	Niacin	8·36
Soybean oil	4·4	—	Ca pantothenate	2·39
Water	25·9	—	Inositol	23·92
CMC binder	1·0	High viscosity	Biotin	0·05
			Folic acid	0·18
			Vitamin (E)	18·40
			Vitamin (C)	44·69

TABLE VI

Solberg Moist Pellets (Research Trout Farm, Brøns, Denmark)

Feed mix	%	Derivation
Fresh fish	50·0	Raw minced industrial fish
Fish meal	21·2	High-fat
Soya meal	22·2	Low-fat. Carbohydrate 69 gm per kg.
Fish oil	3·0	2gm per litre Raloquin added as anti–oxidant
Lecithin	2·0	—
Potassium iodide	0·2	—
Sodium chloride	0·24	—
Di-calcium phosphate	0·136	—
Thiamin (B1)	0·02	—
Vitamin (E)	0·004	—
Alginate H120 Binder	1·0	—

Moist pellets were originally developed in North America. The pellet formula in Table V was produced in the USA and that in Table VI was developed in Denmark. The American formulation used all-dry components with added water. The moisture in the Danish mixture is derived from fresh industrial fish and added oils.

Pigmentation of Salmonid Tissues

The pink or red flesh-colour is an essential characteristic of sea-going members of the salmon family that should be produced in farm fish. The natural pigment is a carotenoid called astaxanthin which occurs in marine animals such as prawns, shrimps, krill and certain plankton copepods. The fact that a fish species feeds on these animals does not necessarily mean that it has pigmented flesh. The red or pink muscle colour depends on the ability of the cells in particular fish species to retain the carotenoid pigment. Some salmonids are better at this than others and will develop deep red flesh by ingesting a smaller amount of carotenoid for a shorter period than others.

Natural sources of astaxanthin used by European fish farmers to form part of fresh-food mixtures are as follows:

Species of Crustacea	Astaxanthin mg per kg
Prawn waste (Pandalus borealis)	97 – 128
Plankton Red Copepod	76 – 84
Krill	73 – 98

The artificial carotenoid, canthaxanthin, is also used to pigment salmonid muscle. It produces an attractive colour more quickly than most natural sources of astaxanthin. A concentration in the tissue of 4 mg per kg of carotenoid pigment is needed to produce pigmentation in salmonid muscle. Canthaxanthin fed at a rate of 100 mg per kg in a high-fat diet will pigment rainbow trout in about eight weeks.

Salmon take longer to pigment when fed the same amount of canthaxanthin and the muscle will not attain a satisfactory colour until the fish have been fed with the carotenoid for about six months prior to slaughter. It is possible to reduce the time taken to pigment the flesh by increasing the dose. A concentration of 450 mg per kg in the food is needed to produce the deep red colour that is naturally attained by some species of Pacific salmon.

A relatively new source of dietary pigments for salmonids is the red yeast *Phaffia rhodozyma*. This contains astaxanthin as its main carotenoid pigment. The yeast can contain 500–800 micrograms of astaxanthin per gm, dependent on the growth conditions and the strain used. This concentration is about ten times higher than that in prawn or shrimp waste. *Phaffia rhodozyma* has the same properties as ordinary brewer's yeast and can be used as a supplementary nutrient to salmonid diets, as well as a source of red pigment. Incorporated in the diet of rainbow trout at 15% of the total weight it pigmented the muscle in about six weeks.

Mechanical Fish Feeding with Wet Food Mixtures

A machine capable of automatically dispensing wet food mixtures was devised for feeding Atlantic salmon fry on Swedish rearing stations in the early 1950s. This was a relatively easy proposition as the fry were in tanks arranged in regular lines and the feeder could be mounted on a track. A mechanically operated piston forced out a measured amount of food through a nozzle as the feeder passed each tank. Salmonids in freshwater are now fed dry food pellets or crumb so the problem does not arise. A modification of this type of feeder, constructed in a larger size, might be of considerable value as an automatic feeder for salmonids on-grown in saltwater in shore-based tanks.

Machines developed for wet food feeding consist of a large container with an air-tight lid, a compressor and an air receiver to create pressure in the food tank, which is connected to an articulated pipe with a trigger-operated mechanism to eject the food. Experiments made in Denmark have demonstrated that machine feeding with wet food produces at least as good growth in the fish as hand-feeding and is more economical. There is a considerable saving in man-power (it takes about one fifth the time to feed by machine that it does by hand). The fish also consume more of the food and there is less waste and consequently less pollution of the water or fouling of ponds or enclosures.

Saltwater farmers using separate off-shore cages have not made much use of machine feeding. It has been used for fish in cages anchored to the shore and in enclosures. The machine feeders and food pumps so far developed for wet food eject a single jet of food and the amount fed depends on the bore of the food-pipe. An improvement would be to devise an ejector-head with multiple openings that could deliver a number of smaller jets at the same time.

Automatic Feeders for Dry Food

A wide variety of machine feeders capable of distributing dry feed are available from manufacturers of fish farming equipment. They have control mechanisms capable of sensing light intensity and water temperature, as well as distributing the food at pre-determined intervals.

The use of high-fat dry foods has caused problems with some automatic feeders as the tacky food tends to clog the mechanism. The most satisfactory of all types of automatic feeders for dry feed are those operated by compressed air. A blast of air drives a quantity of food from a pipe fixed to a hopper, out over the fish tank or enclosure. The source of compressed air can be either from small, individual compressors or from a central unit through pipe-lines. The delivery of food is controlled by sensory devices and time clocks. This system has been satisfactorily adapted to feed salmon and rainbow trout at most stages of growth, even when in small 2 m x 2 m tanks. Another type of feeder may be needed for initial feeding in very small tanks or troughs.

Fish Feeding

The manufacturers of commercial dry pellet or crumb feeds for salmonids provide tables showing the amount of their feed fish of different species require at any given age or weight, according to water temperature, and the intervals at which they should be fed.

Sea farmers generally have their own ideas as to when and how their fish should be fed to give the best results. The basic principles are as follows:

1   It is generally considered that salmonids in seawater of 30 – 35‰ will continue to grow satisfactorily if up to 20% of their total diet is given as dry pellet food.

2   Salmonids cultured in saltwater are usually given as much food as they will eat at the prevailing water temperature. The daily requirement varies with the Kcal of the food as well as with the water temperature. Fish in water at 15°C will need three to four times as much food as they need in water at 5°C. A rough average of the daily food intake, allowing for waste, is about 7-9% of the body weight of the fish.

3   Allowing for waste, about 4,500 Kcal ME is needed to produce 1 kg of fish.

4   The food must be properly distributed to a large surface area, but it should be directed towards the middle of cages or enclosures where there is not much tidal flow, in order to avoid waste.

Fish Foods – Raw Materials and Storage

1   Rancidity or putrefaction is particularly dangerous. The wet fish and fish oils used in wet diets or to make moist pellets, must be fresh. The best test is to look for any smell of ammonia as a first indication of decay.

2   Whole industrial fish or fish offal in cold-store should be held at below minus 40°C.

3   Freezing can cause deterioration in fats and vitamins in raw food materials. Fresh food should not be stored deep-frozen unless this is strictly necessary.

4   It is essential to make sure that dry components in food mixtures are up to specification, particularly vitamin meals and mineral supplements. Their contents should be checked periodically by an independent laboratory.

Deficiencies in Salmonid Diets

The most likely cause of poor growth, and generally lean fish do not do well when fed on a wet food mixture, is that the protein-fat content is out of balance, usually with too much protein and too little fat. The use of indigestible fats of high melting-point containing saturated fatty-acids causes degeneration of the liver. Rancid fish-oil can cause pancreatic damage with symptoms not unlike those produced by the virus disease known as IPN.

Serious digestive disorders, the effects of which are usually irreversible, are caused by feeding dry or wet diets containing putrid ingredients which have deteriorated in storage. Dry food which has become mouldy or smells musty can be actively toxic to fish.

The majority of dietary deficiencies are due to a lack of essential vitamins or minerals in the food mixture, caused either by deterioration or by partial destruction in preparation. Commercial dry foods and vitaminized meals may not always be up to the manufacturers' specifications. Some of the following symptoms attributed to particular vitamin deficiencies have only been observed in the laboratory:

Thiamin (B1). Loss of appetite and impaired equilibrium; convulsive movements in advanced stages.
Riboflavine (B2). Loss of appetite; fish seek shade or darkness and swim deep; eye lenses may be clouded and eyes blood-shot; skin darkens.
Pyridoxine (B6). Loss of appetite; hyper-activity; rapid breathing and gasping; quivering of gill covers; fluid collects in the body cavity; anaemia; skin darkens; early rigor mortis.
Biotin (H). Loss of appetite; muscular atrophy and convulsive movements; skin darkens; intestinal lesions.

Nicotinic acid. Loss of appetite; jerky movements; fluid collects in stomach and intestine.

Pantothenic acid. Loss of appetite; gill filaments clogged with mucus; skin lesions.

Folic acid. Poor growth; sluggish movements; anaemia; skin darkens; fraying of fins.

Inositol. Poor growth; distended stomach.

Choline. Poor growth; fatty degeneration of the liver bleeding in kidney and intestine.

Alpha-tocopherol (E). Poor growth; skin darkens; pancreatic damage which can be mistaken for IPN.

Ascorbic acid (C). Loss of appetite; lethargy; resting on the bottom. Symptoms may not appear for about twenty weeks of feeding at 15°C. The normal recommended quantity in the diet should be increased if the fish are stressed in any way such as by transport, grading or handling for anaesthesia and external medication.

Fish Food Supplies

Freshwater fish farmers in most developed countries have no problems in obtaining dry fish foods and some choice is usually available in terms of quality and price. Supplies of fresh or deep-frozen industrial fish for making up wet feeds or moist pellets for feeding salmonids in saltwater can be difficult and even impossible at present for some sea farmers in countries where there is little or no fishing for industrial fish.

There is no doubt that some of the most successful salmon farmers are those who operate their own fishing boats and catch their own supplies of fresh food fish. This is a course of action strongly to be recommended as it makes the farmer independent of outside economic pressures and difficulties of supply. Surplus fish can be sold for fish meal or cold stored. Fishing can be on a co-operative basis between a group of sea farmers. Non-industrial species captured can be marketed for human consumption.

Chapter 10

Fish Husbandry

Some confusion has arisen in the past over the status of commercial fish culture in relation to marine biology. The breeding and growing of fish as human food is a form of animal husbandry and more specifically fish husbandry. It is not a department of marine biology which is a discipline concerned with the study and conservation of wild fish stocks. Similarly the diagnosis and treatment of fish diseases should be the concern of veterinarians.

The best and only way to learn how to look after animals of any kind is through practical experience. A book on the subject is no substitute for apprenticeship but should be a useful source of reference and a guide to practice.

Stock Selection and Improvement

Salmonid farming is still at the stage in which wild races of the different species are being tested to determine those suited to domestication. The 'homing' of anadromous salmonids has led to the development of separate populations with a gene pool corresponding to the environment to which they constantly return on spawning migration. The physical separation of different stocks resident in freshwater has also produced distinct racial characteristics. Blood-typing of salmonids has demonstrated genetic differentiation. The second stage, which is yet to be generally explored, is genetic engineering designed to improve the quality of the selected, cultivated species.

The most sought-after features in sea-going salmonids are as follows:

1   Unstressed tolerance of an artificial environment.
2   Short freshwater life period before smoltification. Production of S1 smolts in Atlantic salmon.
3   Resistance to disease.
4   Ease of acclimatization to seawater.
5   Good food conversion and rapid growth to market size.
6   Delayed gonad development and delayed onset of sexual maturity. In Atlantic salmon, the minimum of fish which mature in the grilse year (after about fourteen months in the sea).
7   Marketability. Flesh quality and colour. Body shape for processing.

The Norwegians are the leaders in the field of selection and the testing of various races of Atlantic salmon. They have a very wide range of rivers to draw upon for wild stocks, most of which have distinct racial characteristics. Considerable variation in resistance to disease has been found as well as differences in marine growth rate.

Strains of Atlantic salmon from fourteen different rivers in Norway and Sweden (Baltic Sea salmon) were hatched, reared separately and transferred to sea cages as S1 smolts. At a total age of three years, the average weight of fish belonging to stocks hailing originally from the Norwegian river Jordalsgrendea was 5·1 kg. Strains from other rivers in Norway averaged between 4·1-4·9 kg. The fish from the Swedish rivers did not grow as large as those from Norway and the races which grew more slowly in the sea tended to produce a higher proportion of fish which matured as grilse.

Hybridization (See Table VII)

The purpose of experimental attempts to create hybrids between the species of salmonids has been firstly to produce more useful characteristics and secondly to induce sterility. It is possible to cross-fertilize the eggs of most salmonids but survival during the alevin and fry stages is very variable and can be virtually nil. In the majority of cases it is too small to be of any practical use and many of the hybrids are only of scientific interest and not at present of any value to fish farmers.

Francis Day in *British and Irish Salmonidae*, published in 1887, describes a number of hybrids produced at the Howietoun Fisheries at Bannockburn near Stirling in Scotland in the latter half of the nineteenth century. The most successful were between American brook charr (*Salvelinus fontinalis*) male and brown trout (*Salmo trutta*) female. The cross between brook charr and brown trout has been frequently repeated with the sexes reversed in either direction. The progeny is the well-known tiger trout which is of little interest to fish farmers. Rainbow trout x brook charr is not successful but, in Denmark, rainbow trout have been successfully crossed with Arctic charr to produce the hybrid known as 'bröding' which has good appearance and vigour.

Atlantic salmon have been successfully crossed with brown trout and sea trout (*Salmo trutta*) but the hybrid does not seem to have any particular advantage over the parent species. The most successful hybridization so far achieved in Norway has been between Arctic charr (*Salvelinus alpinus*) and Atlantic salmon (*Salmo salar*).

Hybrids have been produced between most of the Pacific species. Sockeye, pink and chum salmon have all been crossed successfully in either sex direction, with the exception of male pink x female sockeye which proved unsuccessful. Spring or chinook will cross with all the other North American species of Pacific salmon in either sex direction except female spring with male pink. In some cases the hybrids proved fertile.

TABLE VII
Norwegian Hybrid Salmonids

Percentage hatch of fertile eggs

Male		*Female*	*%*
Atlantic salmon	x	Arctic charr	59
(*Salmo salar*)		(*Salvelinus alpinus*)	
Arctic charr	x	Atlantic salmon	89
sea trout	x	Arctic charr	48
(*Salmo trutta*)			

Average weight after eleven months in freshwater

Male		Female	grams
Atlantic salmon	x	Arctic charr	70·7
Arctic charr	x	Atlantic salmon	96·5
sea trout	x	Arctic charr	58·3
Atlantic salmon	x	Atlantic salmon	30·0

Average weight after fourteen months in the sea

Male		Female	grams
Atlantic salmon	x	Arctic charr	1525
Arctic charr	x	Atlantic salmon	1256
sea trout	x	Arctic charr	1222
Atlantic salmon	x	Atlantic salmon	1524
Arctic charr	x	Arctic charr	500
sea trout	x	sea trout	686

Sex Reversal and Sterilization

The physiological changes which take place as salmonids approach sexual maturity greatly reduce their market value. Various ways have been experimentally sought to delay or prevent gonad development. It has proved possible to surgically sterilize the fish when they reach a length of about 20 cm. The operation takes three to four minutes and has a relatively high success rate. It has to be carried out by a skilled operative and the fish have to be anaesthetized. The cost, however, not only in monetary terms but in stress to the fish, is likely to rule out the procedure as a practical technique in fish farming.

The production of sterile fish by inducing polyploidy through manipulating the number of chromosomes in the cells of the fish has been experimentally tried out with some success, but difficulties have been encountered with salmonids. The production of sterile hybrids has also been attempted.

It is possible to reverse the sex of some members of the

salmon family by hormone treatment and so far this is the only practical course open to the fish farmer. Female salmonids grow rather more slowly than males but take longer to reach sexual maturity. Female survival is much greater and recovery more rapid in those species which do not die after spawning. Re-absorption of unshed eggs also takes place so that further economically useful growth can be made after the fish have reached sexual maturity.

In salmonids, gonadal development in primary germ cells is initiated in the embryo about six days before hatching. Differentiation of the gonads (male or female) takes place during the period of initial feeding which commences shortly after the yolk-sacs have been absorbed and is complete about sixty days after hatching at 10°C. The experimentally developed method which has proved useful in practice consists of immersing the eyed eggs in an aqueous solution of 17 beta-oestradiol at a strength of 250 micrograms/litre for two periods of two hours each during the eyed stage of incubation, and again immersing the alevins in a similar solution for similar periods. The fry are then fed 17 beta-oestradiol, 20 mg mixed with each kg of food, during the first feeding period. Automatic feeders were used and fish were fed at the standard rate. Aeration was available in the tanks. In field tests, 100% sex reversal to female was obtained for both Atlantic salmon and rainbow trout, in twenty-one days and thirty days respectively after the commencement of feeding.

The hormone was dissolved in ethanol and released to a static volume of water containing the eggs or alevins to produce the required concentration. The steroids were fed to the fish in a special fat-reduced diet to avoid possible degradation of the hormone. Field testing showed that the steroid diet was sufficient by itself to induce sex reversal in rainbow trout if fed for a period of thirty days. Atlantic salmon fed with the hormone diet for a period of eighty days in fish from one hatch and thirty days (after being fed on an ordinary diet for the first fifteen days) from another hatch, showed 100% sex reversal to female, without previous immersion in the hormone solution as eyed eggs or alevins.

Controls from the same hatches averaged approximately

fifty/fifty males and females. Treated fish did not initially grow as rapidly as untreated fish, probably due to the fat-reduced diet. Sex reversal to male can also be achieved by the oral administration of 17 beta-methyltestosterone. There is, of course, absolutely no trace of the steroids remaining in the fish when they reach market size.

Brood Fish

The selection and keeping of brood stock is not necessarily a job for specialists and all fish farmers should know something of the basic procedures. The initial step is simple selection. The best fish are graded out, which in practical terms means those that grow to largest size in the shortest time at each stage in freshwater and in the sea. A stockman soon learns to spot the good 'doers' in the animals he tends. These are the ones to select and keep back as brood stock.

Aspects of nutrition, hygiene and disease prevention are dealt with elsewhere. The holding arrangements for brood fish are not different to those for fish intended for market but they should be kept at a reduced density.

The treatment of salmonids approaching spawning time differs according to species. Female trout and charr will probably be retained to be spawned again in successive seasons. Some of the males may also be worth retaining for marketing, although they are seldom worth the trouble of restoring in condition to use again as brood stock. Atlantic salmon females may be worth keeping-on as re-conditioned kelts, but only if they belong to a particularly valuable strain or eggs are likely to be in short supply the following season. Pacific salmon all die after spawning for the first time.

Falling water temperature combined with increasing gonad development naturally reduces the fish's appetite. Salmon should cease to be given food when secondary sex characteristics become apparent and the males and females should be separated at this stage. If the fish are in sea cages (200-300 m^3 or larger) they should be moved into smaller, rectangular cages. These should be 3-4 m^2 and 3 m deep. Ropes should be attached to the nets and pass down under the cages and up on the opposite side. When these ropes are pulled up the bottom of the net cage can be raised to form two or four separate sections. The fish can then be easily checked for ripeness.

Brood stock on a shore-based unit can be kept in the ordinary large tanks until they are approaching spawning time. They should then be moved into smaller tanks and the sexes separated. At this stage it is better to provide a freshwater supply, if sufficient is available on the site. Each tank should have a 'crush' which consists of a movable grid or wall of net that can be shifted to enclose the fish in a small part of the tank for ripeness testing. The tanks should be covered and the fish kept in semi-darkness.

Hatchery Practice

Salmon and rainbow trout can be successfully stripped of their eggs after being taken directly from the sea, provided they are washed in freshwater before and after being anaesthetized. The eggs can be fertilized on the spot and removed to the hatchery when they have completely 'hardened', or sperm and eggs can be transported separately. Sperm remains viable for several hours if kept cool in a vacuum flask and is completely free from water. Unfertilized eggs also remain viable if they are in ovarian fluid and free from water. An alternative method is to bring the ripening fish ashore and store them in semi-darkened tanks until they are ready to strip. When ripening brood fish have to be stored in shore-based tanks for any length of time, they are healthier and easier to keep free from fungus attack if the tanks have a supply of both fresh and saltwater.

Anaesthetizing Fish

Before the use of anaesthetics became general it was common practice to put some form of halter on large salmonids so that they could be more easily handled for stripping their eggs. Atlantic salmon were often suspended by a noose round the body under the pectoral fins while they were stripped. Large rainbow trout were particularly difficult because their deep short bodies are hard to hold.

Some anaesthetics are cheaper than others. Some are critical and difficult to use safely. The most critical can be used as a humane means of slaughtering fish. (See Table VIII.)

The use of ethyl-aminobenzoate as a fish anaesthetic stemmed from the need to find an alternative to M.S. 222. The method to be followed is to dissolve 0·2 gm of benzoate powder in 5 cc of acetic acid (1gm in 25 cc). The solution is diluted to 40 ppm in distilled water (1 cc of the concentrated solution in 1 litre of water). Increasing the strength to 50 ppm will increase the rapidity with which the fish are immobilized (1·25 cc of concentrated solution in 1 litre of water).

Fish taken directly from sea cages for stripping should be washed in freshwater before being immersed in the anaesthetic solution (remember that if the fish are dripping water each time one is put into the anaesthetic solution it will soon become weak and need renewing or topping up).

After stripping the fish should be washed in a solution of 0·5% common salt (NaCl) if they are intended to be retained alive. Recovery should take place in a flow of clean, well-oxygenated water with the fish held facing upstream in the normal swimming position.

It is possible to make a simple 'holder' for fish during recovery. This consists of a rectangular trough divided into parallel channels along its length which are just wide enough to support the fish. Baffles at the leading end divide the flow between the channels.

Stripping Eggs

There are no hard and fast rules about the fish-stripping operation, which must be learned by demonstration. Most fishmasters have their own techniques. The main essential is to have ripe male and female fish to hand in small tanks of convenient size where they can be easily caught up with a minimum of stress. Separate tanks will be needed for holding

TABLE VIII
Fish Anaesthetics

Chemical	Dosage. (parts per million)	Immobilization Time - min.	Recovery Time - min.	Notes on Use.
Carbon dioxide Solid acid-bicarbonate	100 - 200	1 - 2	—	Used for killing fish.
M.S. 222 Tricaine methanesulphonate	40 - 80	4 - 6	4 - 6	A good general anaesthetic but now thought to be a possible carcinogenic in man.
Quinaldine 2-methyquinoline	10 - 15	2 - 4	3 - 5	Non-critical. Expensive.
M.S. 222 and Quinaldine	20 - 30 5	3	10 - 20	Slow recovery. Fish will tolerate long immersion (60 min.).
2-phenoxyethanol	40	2 - 5	5 - 10	More concentrated solutions up to 100 ppm may be needed for large fish in warmer water. Recovery time may be longer.
Ethylaminobenzoate 98% in acetic acid	See detailed instructions.	2 - 5	5 - 10	A good, cheap anaesthetic.

male fish, female fish, anaesthetizing the fish and for recovery. Various mechanical methods have been tried out for stripping eggs including air and water bags which compress the fish and squeeze out the eggs or sperm, but nothing is really as satisfactory as the human hand. Sperm intended for storage can be drawn up directly from the vent of ripe males using a pipette or a large syringe, which is easier than trying to run the sperm directly into a container. Fish of both sexes must be washed clean of anaesthetic solution and carefully dried with a cloth before they are stripped.

Fertilization

Salmon eggs are relatively easy to handle before, during and after fertilization. Trout eggs need more careful treatment if a high percentage of fertility is to be achieved. The more simple causes of loss are crushing while stripping, exposure to ultra-violet light in bright sunshine, and frost. Infertile eggs are not only a loss but are wasteful of space in the hatchery as they are difficult to detect before routine 'shocking' is carried out at the eyed stage.

Eggs and sperm carefully stripped from healthy, uninjured fish, when mixed together out of contact with water should normally result in 100% fertility. Eggs become very sensitive to disturbance for a period after water has been added and swelling starts. Losses are likely to be greatest due to movement during the first thirty minutes. Eggs take in water more quickly at higher temperatures. Swelling takes about one and a quarter hours at 6·5°C but only about twenty-five minutes at 13°C (spawning of some species of salmonids has been found to be unsuccessful at temperatures above 13°C). The commonest cause of loss during the sensitive period following fertilization is from washing off the surplus sperm. If the eggs are washed (at 8°C) between four minutes and fifteen minutes after water has been added, 40 – 50% may die over the next forty-eight hours. Losses of up to 20% can occur if the eggs are disturbed for up to one hour after being placed in water.

Fertilized eggs can be quite safely kept without washing

in a mixture of ovarian fluid and sperm for periods up to one and a half hours then put directly into the water in the hatchery troughs. The alternative safe method is to wash the eggs at once, about one to two minutes after sperm is added, then leave the fertilized eggs standing completely undisturbed in a plentiful amount of clean water for ninety minutes before they are moved.

A Practical Method

A simple stripping method is to anaesthetize a number of male and female fish (dependent on their size and the time it takes to strip one fish). When the fish are quiescent, wash them in clean running water. Dry each fish carefully with a cloth and put them into an insulated polystyrene box. Strip each female fish into a plastic bowl. When all the females are stripped, run in the sperm from two to three males and stir gently. The eggs can then be poured into a bucket and the process repeated with another group of male and female fish. When the first lot of fertilized eggs have been in the mixture of sperm and ovarian fluid for about one hour, all the eggs that have been stripped and fertilized can be transferred to the hatchery troughs. Standing eggs must be kept cool and the bucket or egg container should be in an insulated box.

Each group of hatchery troughs should have its own litre measure. The eggs are poured directly into troughs from the measure. Eggs occupy less space before swelling and this must be taken into consideration; 1 litre of swelled or 'hardened' eggs is approximately equivalent to 1·4 litres of eggs before water is added.

The Effect of Light on Eggs

Exposure to light in the blue or violet part of the spectrum can be deadly to salmonid eggs either in air or water. Eggs should be kept in the dark. When artificial light has to be provided in a hatchery this should not be from fluorescent tubes. Yellow or orange light is safe to use but ultra-violet light (UVA) can penetrate to considerable depth in water.

Disinfection

Imported eggs bought in during the eyed stage should always be disinfected. Recommended disinfectants are iodophors. These are solutions of iodine in organic solvents. The manufacturer's recommendations should be followed for trade preparations.

Wescodyne. Solution 50 ppm for ten minutes in a buffered solution with a pH of 6·0-7·5.

Betadine. Solution 100 – 200 ppm for fifteen minutes, otherwise as for Wescodyne.

Disinfectants should not be used on salmonid eggs when the eyes of the embryo are visible through the chorion (eyed stage).

The Law on the Import of Salmonid Eggs to Great Britain

It is illegal to import the eggs of any salmonid to Great Britain unless the importation is covered by a current certificate of health provided by an approved veterinary pathologist in the country of origin. The health certificate requires that the brood stock and eggs have been tested by an accepted procedure and found free from particular virus diseases. All countries in Western Europe have similar regulations which may vary slightly in their application. North American countries have their own regulations governing imports of live fish and fish eggs. It is possible to import salmonid eggs to Great Britain without a health certificate under special licence from the appropriate Department or Ministry, if the importer can provide approved quarantine arrangements.

It is illegal to import to Great Britain any live fish belonging to the salmon family under the Diseases of Fish Act 1937.

Cryopreservation of Salmonid Sperm (and Eggs)

Considerable interest has been aroused during recent years in the possibility of creating and maintaining a sperm bank for farm salmonids. This would avoid having to keep male brood

160

fish and might lead to the general use of sex reversal in both brood and market stock which would then be all-female. The problem has been to find a suitable 'extender' for fish spermatozoa. This is a chemical compatible with seminal plasma, such as a modified Cortland solution, that can be used to dilute the semen for long-term storage at very low temperatures. At the same time a compound such as dimethylsulphoxide (DMSO) has to be added to protect the sperm cells from damage during freezing and thawing.

Various methods have been tried out to obtain really rapid freezing. A technique developed by H. Stein at the University of München has proved most successful and has resulted in a high percentage of fertilization using cryopreserved sperm. The diluted and prepared semen is allowed to fall in droplets on to 'dry ice' at − 78·6°C. The frozen pellets are then stored in liquid nitrogen (LN2).

Cryopreservation of sperm from Atlantic salmon, rainbow trout, brown trout and from four species of Pacific salmon, pink, coho, chum and sockeye, has been shown to yield actively motile spermatozoa capable of fertilizing a useful percentage of eggs. The commercial development of long-term sperm storage will probably follow stock improvement and the creation of particularly valuable strains. Attempts to cryopreserve unfertilized eggs of teleost fish has not shown much promise of success, probably due to the size and complexity of the cell structure.

Egg Densities

It is common practice in rainbow trout hatcheries to put the eggs down to incubate in layers two or three deep in the hatchery baskets. The quantity of water required to incubate trout or salmon eggs is so small, much less than is needed for subsequent rearing of fry or parr, there is no real need for a farmer incubating eggs for his own use to overload his egg trays and baskets. A layer one and a half eggs deep is quite sufficient for trout. Atlantic salmon eggs should not be more than one layer deep. The eggs are then clearly visible and much easier to pick and keep clean.

The available flow of water at 100% sat. with oxygen should be 5 1/min for each ten thousand eggs in the hatchery.

Incubation

The standard incubation procedures for salmonid eggs are quite straightforward. Removal of dead eggs, which are easily recognized because they go white, is best carried out each day in smaller hatcheries producing fish for on-growing on the same unit. This can be done in various ways using a continuous siphon or a suction bulb. If not removed, the dead eggs will form a focus for fungus which will then attack surrounding healthy eggs. A continuous record of the dead eggs removed should be kept.

When the eggs under incubation have become eyed (the eyes of the embryo becoming visible as black spots through the egg shell or chorion) they should be 'shocked'. A simple way to do this is to lift the egg trays out of the water and leave them in the air for a few moments propped across the trough. The effect of 'shocking' is to show up infertile eggs, and any weak eggs, which will then go white and can be removed.

Specialist farmers using flask incubators, in which the eggs form a thick column in a vertical container with an upward flow of water, or hatcheries where very large quantities of eggs several layers thick are incubated in troughs, may have to use a fungicide bath to kill off fungus spores, without trying to remove the dead eggs.

Fungicides for Use on Fish or Fish Eggs

The fungicide commonly used in the past was a compound known as malachite green. This substance is now alleged to be dangerous to the people who use it over long periods (the hands of most freshwater fish farmers are generally stained green). A new fungicide has now been developed for the treament of eggs under incubation. This is called proflavine-hemisulphate. The eggs are immersed in a solution of this compound at a strength of 1 part in 40,000 for one hour (fish farmers using this stuff are now generally stained yellow up to the elbows).

Egg Counting

Automatic egg counters, which also extract dead eggs, have been developed for use by specialist egg producers. The eggs are put through the machine when they have eyed-up. In one type, a disc with holes corresponding to the average size of eggs is fixed in postion and then automatically loaded with eggs from a hopper as it revolves. Any dead eggs (which are opaque) intercept a beam of light as the disc in which they are held passes a light source. This causes a jet of water to blow the dead egg forward out of the hole into a container. As the disc revolves further round, the live eggs are also ejected into a separate container. The machine can not only differentiate between the dead and live eggs but counts them separately. The counting rate is approximately forty thousand eggs per hour. Other commercial machines can count and sort dead and live eggs at rates up to one million per hour. They are a useful tool for the large-scale operator and the cost, including purchase price, is less than one fifth that of manual picking.

Hatching and Alevin Development

When hatching starts, the flow of water (at 100% sat. with oxygen) to the troughs should be raised to 15 1/min for each ten thousand alevins.

Egg shells should be removed from egg baskets after the alevins have hatched out, together with eggs which have failed to hatch. The contents of the baskets may look a mess at this time and a double-bottomed egg basket which allows the alevins to drop through a removable, perforated inner-tray is an advantage. Cleaning up after hatching is more of a problem in neutral or alkaline water. Shells and other debris dissolve and disappear fairly quickly in water of a pH below 6·5.

Alevins should continue to be kept in semi-darkness on a corrugated substrate until they are ready to feed. Some salmonids give a clear indication of when feeding should start by swimming up from the bottom. It is relatively difficult to judge the right moment with Atlantic salmon. Feeding should begin when the temperature is over 8°C and the yolk-sacs are nearly absorbed. At this stage there is a small orange bulge remaining on the belly of the fish. They will be seen to have turned into the normal dorsal-ventral swimming attitude, and no longer lie partly on their sides due to the weight of the yolk-sacs.

The flow of water at 100% sat. with oxygen will have to be raised to 20 1/min for each ten thousand fry starting to feed.

Super-saturation

Saturation of water with oxygen means that the water has dissolved the total volume of the gas which it is capable of taking up at a given temperature. Water, particularly from underground sources, can become super-saturated with gas due to being subjected to pressures greater than atmospheric. Water taken from below the turbines in hydro-electric stations or from the stilling basin below the spillways in high dams can also become super-saturated. The usual gases involved in super-saturation are nitrogen (air) and carbon dioxide. The effect on fish, particularly fry, is to produce what is know as gas-bubble disease when bubbles of gas appear under the skin. Carbon dioxide can also cause a condition known as nephro-calcinosis in which calcium is deposited in the fish's kidney.

The surplus gas can be removed from the super-saturated water by exposing the water to air in a thin layer. The correct balance is maintained in fast-flowing rivers by the water running over the shallows. In a hatchery, the surplus gas can be removed by creating artificial falls or percolating the water through perforated metal plates. Mechanical de-aerators may have to be employed in large hatcheries using underground water. Blowers force great masses of air through shallow tanks. Such arrangements are fairly common in cold climates where bore-hole water is frequently used for hatcheries, initial fry rearing and over-wintering of parr.

Freshwater Rearing

Water Supply

The water requirement at 100% sat. with oxygen for each 10,000 Atlantic salmon fry and parr being reared to make S1 smolts.

First four weeks	5 gpm (22 – 23 l/min)
Second four weeks	10 gpm (45 l/min)
Up to mid–October	15 – 20 gpm (70 – 90 l/min)
Over-wintering	100 gpm (450 l/min)
Last four weeks before smolting	150 gpm (680 l/min)

Juvenile anadromous salmonids which grow more quickly, and can be transferred to saltwater younger than Atlantic

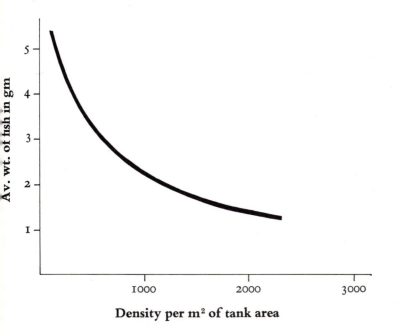

Fig. 24 First summer salmon rearing: fish density compared to average weight (4m^2 tank)

salmon, will require proportionately more water in relation to their size at a given age.

Fish Densities in Tanks

Atlantic and Pacific salmon parr $10 - 15 \, \text{kg/m}^3$
Steelhead Rainbow trout parr $20 - 25 \, \text{kg/m}^3$

Feeding of Fry and Parr

The subject is covered under the chapter on feeding and nutrition. Automatic feeding is essential and should, if possible, be used from the start, if top quality quick-growing parr are to be reared for early transfer to the sea. Automatic feeding is also important in avoiding stress in juvenile fish, as well as maintaining regularity in the nutritional regime. Automatic feeders are described in another section. Gravity or electrically operated hopper-feeders may be used initially for very small fry but once the fish are moved into larger tanks the compressed air gun-type is by far the most reliable. It is also the only type which can properly distribute the tacky, high-fat food pellets used in diets for sea-going salmonids.

Hopper-feeders may have to be used for fish over-wintered in cages unless these are anchored alongside a fixed walkway.

Grading

The after-effects of stress during grading small fish can last for about thirty days and reduce the growth rate during that period. Grading of all young, anadromous salmonids, intended for transfer to the sea, should be kept to a minimum and if possible to one or at the most two gradings before smoltification.

Atlantic salmon need to be graded only once during the first summer when the fish are transferred for on-growing or over-wintering in larger tanks or cages in freshwater. Most of the parr which reach a length of 10 cm by November of the first year will smoltify the following spring. Norwegian experience has shown that over 90% of the parr that fail to pass through the bars of a grader at 10 mm spacing will make smolt in the following May.

Smolt farmers recognize the size their fish should reach at each stage of parr growth if they are to become S1 smolt. They may wish to grade early and dispose of under-sized fish for wild-stock enhancement (or use them for ranching) to save fish food and space in tanks for over-wintering. The earlier selective grading takes place the greater will be the margin of error in the selection of potential S1 smolt. The most certain selection can be made from January onwards.

Ordinary commercial fish graders of the simple, manual type consist of a cradle holding interchangeable bar-screens of variable spacing through which the smaller fish can pass. Various types of mechanical graders are also available. The fish are either pumped or poured in with a flow of water which carries them through successive screens, with decreasing spaces between the bars. At each stage a different size range of fish is filtered off into separate pipes or tanks. Farms specializing in smolt production may need to measure as well as grade their pre-smolt parr to check growth rates. Measurement can be carried out electronically but the fish may have to be anaesthetized before passing through the counter.

All grading which involves catching the fish causes stress but it is possible to construct a simple 'crush' grader for use in round tanks which involves the minimum of fish-handling. This consists of a removable screen which fits across the diameter of the tank and is hinged at the centre. The screen should have rubber flaps along the bottom and at the ends, which make continuous contact with the sides and bottom of the tank. The screen is put in position straight across the tank and one half is then slowly turned to bring the two halves close together. The larger fish which have not been able to pass through the screen are then left in a small wedge of water, from which they can be netted or pumped directly into another tank. The 'crush' method will only work in tanks with flat-screen drains, without stand-pipes.

The system of central grading in which the fish are piped directly from the tanks to a sump has not been used for juvenile sea-going salmonids, although it has proved successful for grading rainbow trout farmed in freshwater for marketing at a size of 170-220 gm.

Over-wintering

S1 smolt production depends on maintaining growth in the fish through the winter and early spring. In cold climates it is necessary to use artificially heated water or naturally warmed water from an underground source. The fish also have to be kept under cover in a winter-house. A high proportion of S1 smolt is unlikely unless ambient water temperatures remain high enough to keep the fish feeding for most of the winter. The expected proportion of S1 Atlantic salmon smolt from parr over-wintered in unheated water, using the best techniques for growth and selection, may be as high as 70 – 80%. Without strict grading and with less-expert husbandry, the proportion is likely to be between 40-60%.

Cages for Over-wintering Parr in Freshwater

Small cages of 70-100 m^3 are better than large cages for over-wintering parr in freshwater lakes. They should be at least 4·5 m deep. The floatation collar should have walkways, preferably all round. Hopper-types of automatic feeder should be mounted to slide out along bars fixed over each cage. Feeders should be electrically operated and switch on and off daily through a light-sensing cell. More sophisticated systems can easily be made with an over-ride switch controlled by water temperature, which turns off the feeders when it becomes too cold for the fish to feed.

The density for Atlantic salmon parr over-wintered in cages in freshwater should be 15 – 16 kg per m^3.

In the spring, about four weeks before smolting, the pre-smolt parr should be removed from the cages and returned to tanks in order to give them time to recover from the stress of recapture from the cages. The cage nets should have fixed ropes to allow them to be raised so that the fish can be caught up easily in dip-nets.

Precocious Male Parr

A curse of Atlantic salmon smolt culture can be male parr whose gonads mature prematurely. These fish are not only useless to retain for on-growing in saltwater but can be a focus for fungal infection, particularly in neutral or mildly alkaline water containing wild, anadromous salmonids. They could be a serious source of loss when parr are over-wintered in cages, where they cannot be regularly inspected. If the strain of fish being cultured on the unit is known to produce significant numbers of precocious male parr they should not be over-wintered in cages. It may be worthwhile anaesthetizing the parr in December and removing any ripe males.

In Atlantic salmon about 20% of pre-smolt 1+ male parr are likely to be precocious males.

Smolt Age

The production of S1 Atlantic salmon smolt is regarded as being highly desirable by salmon farmers. It is perhaps worthwhile thinking again about the pros and cons of S1 and S2 (parr which smolt in the second as opposed to the first spring after hatching). Consideration should be given to subsequent growth in the sea or in saltwater. An S2 molt which can weigh 80-90 gm may grow to a weight of 3 kg after only one year in the sea. S1 smolt weighing only 30-40 gm may only reach a weight of 1 kg before maturing as grilse and having to be slaughtered.

Marking Fish

Some farmers may wish to mark their fish so that they can recognize individuals or groups later on in the sea. Marking should be carried out when the fish are pre-smolt parr after they have reached a length of about 10 cm. The only method so far devised which will produce an easily recognizable, external mark without stressing the fish, or attaching something to the surface of the body, is freeze-branding. Various techniques have been devised all based upon the use of liquid nitrogen, which is relatively cheap and easy to obtain.

A small reservoir is fitted into a hollow in a block of polystyrene foam, which can either be hand-held or mounted on a bench. A rod or tube which acts as a 'branding iron' extends from the reservoir and sticks out of the insulating block. The intensely cold end of the rod is used to mark the skin of the fish. Marking takes one to two seconds and lasts up to twenty months. The method has been successfully used on many species of anadromous salmonids, including those of interest to fish farmers.

Liquid nitrogen evaporates very quickly. There must be a vent in the reservoir to release evaporating gas and containers must be carefully handled with thick gloves and wearing goggles.

Smolt

The young of all anadromous fish species and races belonging to the salmon family which have to spend an appreciable part of their lives feeding and growing in freshwater (as opposed to those which migrate directly to the sea as fry), enter a period of physiological change immediately before and during their migration to saltwater. The name smolt is given to the fish at this stage of their life cycle. The origin of the word is said to be either Scandinavian or Scottish and derived from smelter which is the bright metal newly separated from ore.

The onset of the smolt stage is of vital importance to the culture of salmonids in the sea. It is the indicator that fish are ready to tolerate saltwater. Failure to recognize and interpret the signals of smoltification correctly can result in the fish being put to sea too early or too late. Serious losses can then occur as the fish cannot acclimatize properly to the new environment.

Different species and races of the same species may acclimatize more quickly than others to fully saline water. Some small rivers have no estuaries and discharge directly into the sea. Even when these rivers are in flood, the area of water with lowered salinity near the mouth is small, and smolt leaving such rivers must be able to tolerate more or less direct transfer from freshwater to water of 33-35‰.

At the other end of the scale, Swedish salmon (*Salmo salar*) and sea trout (*Salmo trutta*) from the rivers running in to the Baltic Sea move gradually from fresh to brackish water and may never experience a strongly saline environment. Similar differences in the rapidity of change from fresh to saltwater are encountered by all the migratory members of the salmon family. It is possible that the genetic characteristics of the anadromous salmonids in a river with no estuary would induce the fish to adapt to direct change from fresh to saltwater. This could be of value in selecting stock for sea farming, but only if the other genetic factors making up that particular stock were equally useful.

The morphological changes that take place during smoltification are a reflection of physiological changes within the fish. The altered appearance of the fish both externally and internally is linked to the rapid reduction in stored body-fat of sea-going salmonids. The increase in fat metabolism which takes place is accompanied by some additional storage of protein. Smolt appear to use fat to bring about changes in their internal protein structures as the balance of amino-acids can be shown to have changed after full smoltification. The natural reduction in body-fats leads to a general weakening and loss of muscle tone. This may be a factor pre-disposing wild smolts to migrate downstream.

Other changes include the appearance of large chloride-secreting cells in the gills and in the epithelium. These cells have an osmo-regulatory function. An increase in thyroid activity (possibly due to a stimulating hormone (TSH)) and changes in the pitiutuary cells have also been observed, of which the significance is not fully understood.

The combined effects of the physiological changes that take place during smoltification have important implications in the context of sea farming. In addition to weakening the fish these changes also make them very much more sensitive to traumatic injuries, particularly while they remain in freshwater. All the changes, both morphological and physiological, which have been observed to take place in young salmonids at the time of smoltification are directly related to the coming transition from a fresh to saltwater environment. Most of these changes, although essential to enable the fish to go to sea, cause stress and are temporarily detrimental to the health of the fish. The debilitating effects brought about by smoltification are probably rapidly rectified in the wild, but may continue to cause losses in cultivated fish after they have been transferred to saltwater, unless steps can be taken by which they are either avoided or counteracted.

Pre-smolt parr naturally try to store vitamins in preparation for smoltification. Fish food manufacturers make some allowance for the special needs of pre-smolt parr. These are mainly for added vitamins and fats. The A and B1 vitamin requirement is approximately doubled and for B2 can be as much as five times greater during smoltification than in pre-smolt parr. Vitamin deficiencies must be replaced in the diet. Many of the distress symptoms in smolt on transfer to saltwater may in fact be attributed to a reduction in their resistance to stress due to avitaminosis.

Atlantic Salmon (Salmo salar) Farm Smolt

The growth factor to look for in forecasting S1 smoltification in the first autumn is a weight of 14–15 gm. This is followed by growth to a weight of 15–17 gm early in the following year.

The triggers which set off smoltification are increasing daylight and rising water temperature. Parr may start to become silvery at weights of 25–30 gm when the temperature reaches 7°-10°C and smoltify completely when the water reaches 10°-12°C. The average weight at full smoltification is approximately 35–40 gm, if the fish have been over-wintered in unheated, surface water in a temperate climate.

All S1 (or S2) smolt do not smoltify at the same time. Some fish may take several weeks longer to smoltify until well into the summer. The smaller parr may not begin to smoltify until the water reaches 11°-12°C.

The changes in the appearance and behaviour of pre-smolt parr at smoltification are the essential indicators showing that the young fish are ready to be transferred to the sea. The most distinctive alteration in appearance is the silvering of the fish. This masks the finger-print parr markings and spots on the sides of the fish. In the early stages of smoltification the parr markings are still faintly visible but the fish become lighter in overall colour and finally the finger marks disappear completely.

At this stage the scales become very loose on smolt and are easily displaced. This is one of the factors which makes smolt particularly prone to injury and difficult to move without causing casualties.

There is one observable change in the behaviour of young Atlantic salmon, indicating that they will tolerate being transferred to saltwater, which is particularly useful if there are no facilities for acclimatization. The fish in round tanks, which have been swimming against the current, facing 'upstream', turn round and intermittently swim 'downstream' with the current round the tank.

Smolt Transport and Acclimatization to Seawater

Smolt are delicate and extremely sensitive to stress in freshwater. It is far better to acclimatize the fish to saltwater as pre-smolt parr and to transfer them to the sea in water of full marine salinity. The fish will then be unstressed and travel well and casualties will be insignificant. Transport in freshwater tanks inevitably leads to some degree of stress, usually due to enforced exercise and the instability of their environment. Stress can be kept to a minimum by using a method of transfer which causes the least disturbance in catching the fish or moving them between tanks. Fluctuations in water temperature and oxygen content should be avoided.

If at all possible, the final transfer of anadromous salmonids to seawater of full marine salinty (30-35‰) should take place through a period of acclimatization in water of gradually increasing salinity. The time taken for acclimatization varies not only according to species but also in relation to the practice developed by experience.

Norwegian farmers introduce parr to saltwater some time before they smoltify. The first introduction may be made

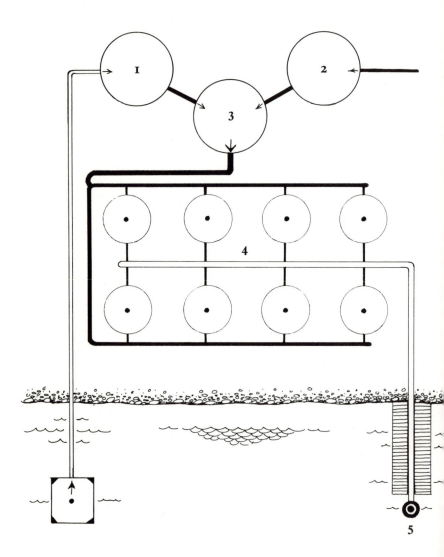

Fig. 25 Smolt acclimatization   **1** Seawater header tank   **2** Freshwater header tank   **3** Mixing tank   **4** Smolt tanks   **5** Smolt collecting point for transportation to cages

four to six weeks before any silvering is apparent on the fish. The tanks in which they are kept have dual fresh and saltwater supply. The salinity is first increased to about 10–15‰. When the parr begin to smoltify it is increased to reach full marine salinity in mid–May. No fish are transferred from the tanks until they have been in fully saline water (30–35‰) for at least a week. All transportation is carried out in tanks with fully saline seawater.

Steelhead rainbow trout and Artic charr, for either spring or autumn transfer to seawater, are acclimatized for a period of four to eight weeks in steadily increasing salinity, starting at 5–10‰. In the Norwegian fjords where the surface water is considerably less saline than water at depths of 2 m or more, the bottoms of cage nets are raised to keep the fish in the surface layer for the first two to four weeks. The bottoms of the nets are gradually lowered so that they have access to water of increasing salinity.

Scottish experience with Atlantic salmon smolt is that provided the fish are perfectly ready they can be transferred to seawater with comparatively little loss, without acclimatization. Losses can be avoided if a short period of acclimatization can be given, lasting only a few hours.

A method successfully used for rainbow trout has been to surround a sea cage, anchored alongside a jetty, with a continuous curtain of plastic sheeting, extending from above the surface to a depth of 2–3 m. Freshwater is piped from the shore into the cage and replaces the strongly saline surface water. Gradual mixing provides a period of acclimatization.

Coho Salmon Smolt (O. kisutch)

The freshwater growth of coho parr in temperate climates can be very fast. Young coho may smoltify in the autumn of the first year and can be transferred to seawater when they reach a weight of about 30 gm. Casualties have been experienced with smaller fish transferred to the sea at the end of August but later transfers during the autumn made with larger fish have resulted in insignificant losses.

Coho smolt have been successfully acclimatized by initial

introduction to water at 10‰ salinity for a period of four days. The salinity was then increased to 20–25‰ over a period of ten to twenty days, according to whether the fish showed any signs of stress. They were then transferred to sea cages in water of full marine salinity (30–35‰).

Smolts Retained in Freshwater

The morphological differences become less pronounced as time goes by and the silver coating loses its shine by early autumn. The chemical make-up of the fish returns towards the pre-smolt parr condition. The fat content increases and is regained by October.

Losses are likely to occur unless a high-fat diet with added vitamins is maintained until the de-smoltifying process is complete. Post-smolt retained in freshwater after smoltifying become less resistant to salinity and may not survive transfer to full seawater, although they can be safely released into brackish water such as that in the Baltic Sea.

Salmonids in Seawater

Although the principles are the same for fixed or floating saltwater holding systems, there are fairly wide differences in the husbandry techniques and operational cycles used in the different methods. Shore-based tanks are quite straightforward to operate. Small enclosures and cages anchored to a fixed walkway, connected to the shore, are also fairly easy to operate. Floating offshore cages provide a more secure environment for the fish because they are not open to the risk of pump failure or pollution by accumulated waste products, but they are exposed to damage by wind and wave action and are much more difficult to service.

Fish densities, water flows and fish feeding are discussed in other sections.

Shore Tanks

The handling, grading and medication of fish in shore tanks

present no problems and the husbandry is similar to that required for a freshwater farm, with a pumped water supply. Marine growth in the tanks and fouling and corrosion in pumps and pipelines are the greatest problem. They are also the most expensive to avoid or to cure. Duplicate water supply systems are essential to allow for regular cleaning.

Comparatively small, raceway-type tanks built in concrete can cause skin abrasion and add to the risk of disease, when used for holding large fish. Grp or plastic-lined tanks are more satisfactory, but on-growing salmon not only require sufficient oxygen but also adequate living-space in the water. They do not do as well when held at densities greater than 10-15 kg/m^3. Such low densities may not be economic in an expensive tank unit.

Practical experience indicates that the best type of shore-tank for on-growing large salmonids is the simple, rectangular-concrete pond holding 600-700 m^3 of water. Duplicate ponds are needed and a good supply of freshwater should be available on the site for killing and flushing-out marine growths. Grading as such is not necessary when fish are being grown-on for market in seawater. Fish-handling should be kept to the minimum needed for checking on growth, fish health and for medication.

The growth period for rainbow trout and charr grown-on in seawater in shore-based tanks, sea enclosures or floating cages is approximately one and a half years. The fish may be put to sea in the period April to June or October to December. For example, a unit with tank groups A and B will put fish into tanks in group A in April of year 1. These fish will be ready for market in October of year 2. Small fish will then be put into the tanks in group A in October of year 2 and will be ready for market in April of year 4, and so on. Tanks in group B will take in young fish and market large fish at the opposite times of year to those in group A. This system takes full advantage of the continuous growth in seawater and provides fish available for market practically throughout the year.

Small, Fixed-net Shore Enclosures

This method has been developed mainly as a low-cost system of producing large rainbow trout. It allows for a fair amount of supervision and for the fish to be recaptured so that they can be transferred through a series of enclosures and worked on the same cyclical system as that used in shore tanks.

Problems in husbandry are mainly concerned with keeping the walls of net free from fouling in order to allow an adequate exchange of water through the enclosures. The accumulation of waste can also foul the bottom of an enclosure, which may have to be abandoned for a time to allow a free flow of the tide to disperse the waste matter.

Large, Fixed Sea Enclosures

This type of enclosure has been used almost entirely for Atlantic salmon. The tidal flow through nearly all large sea enclosures must be supplemented by pumping, if the density of fish that can be kept is to be sufficient to justify the high cost of the permanent barriers. The accumulation of waste food and faeces can be a serious problem, not only by physically restricting the depth in the enclosure but also through polluting the water. Waste matter may have to be periodically removed by dredging or suction pumping.

Wet fish food is distributed by being pumped out in a pipeline which may have to be supported on floats to a considerable distance from the shore. Fish are usually re-captured by running a ring-net round the feeding area and more than one feeding point can cause confusion and make re-capture more difficult. The only alternative to ring-netting is to sweep-net, as the enclosures cannot be drained. Some fish congregate in the current near the intake and outlet screens and it is difficult to induce them to go to the feeding points. This can lead to significant differences in growth rate.

It is impracticable in most large enclosures to try to recapture the fish from the time they are released as smolt until they are netted for market. The stock in an enclosure is therefore out of reach for close inspection. Any observed disease or parasite infestation can only be treated by medicated food.

No grading for grilse is normally carried out and the stock of salmon used for culture should be one which has a very low proportion of fish which mature after only one year in the sea.

The construction of two enclosures, sited fairly close to each other, appears to offer the best chance of an economic return on a large investment. The second enclosure should be designed to be completed some time after the first enclosure has been stocked. In the stocking cycle, smolt are released into enclosure A in May of year 1, and into enclosure B in May of year 2. Cropping for market starts in enclosure A in the spring of year 3, the largest fish being taken out first, and is complete by May, when enclosure A is re-stocked with smolt. Enclosure B is stocked in May of year 2 and cropping starts in early spring of year 4, and so on. This system allows an annual crop to be taken.

Sea Cages

The husbandry is similar for both shore-anchored and offshore cages, although they are a good deal easier to work if they can be reached from a firm walkway extending from the shore. A higher degree of supervision can then be given to the fish and they can be easily recaptured for inspection and medication, if necessary in freshwater tanks.

Some farmers grade for grilse in their cages during the second summer. It is claimed that an experienced fishmaster can recognize fish that are going to mature as grilse. They are generally somewhat thinner than fish of the same age which will mature the following year as salmon, and have a more forked tail fin. The removal and sale of maturing grilse, however small they may be, is certainly an advantage as once the gonads develop the fish are virtually unsaleable. Even the females do not recover in quality or appearance, if they manage to survive the winter and re-absorb their eggs.

The hardest job is net-hauling. The cage nets are very heavy, as they become coated with marine growths. They have to be lifted to inspect or recapture the fish to transfer them to smaller working cages for examination and treatment, or to other large cages.

A derrick or davit and a mechanical winch can be used where cages are moored to a shore-walkway. Nets are also easier to haul when offshore cages are anchored in flotillas round a solid, stable, floating-platform. Single offshore nets, anchored in lines, have to be worked from a boat, although they should each have a stable walkway round the floatation collar.

Salmon farmers use ordinary 35-40 ft fishing boats which can come alongside a cage and winch up the net. A special work boat for sea farming should be 30-40 ft in length, have a wide beam, a flat bottom and a flat, clean deck. The bow should be hinged so that it can be raised and lowered.

A working cage is usually used to sort fish and for medication. It can be rectangular, about 4 m x 4 m and not more than 2 m deep. It should have a stable walkway on three sides joined along the fourth side by a bar. The working cage is brought alongside the main cage net, a section of which is unlaced from the above-water net and joined to the working-cage net. The main cage net is lifted and fish are shifted over into the working cage.

Feeding Systems (Sea Fish Feeding and Nutrition)

Feeding salmonids in seawater creates problems. Some farmers are forced to feed only dry, pelleted food but the most successful results have been achieved by feeding either fresh pellets of moist food or wet feeds and dry feeds alternately.

During the summer months, the Norwegian system is to feed wet food mixtures during ordinary working hours of the day. The wet food is dispersed by hand, more or less continuously, by men working in shifts. Out of working hours and at week-ends the fish are fed dry pellets, through automatic feeders, four times an hour, except for the period 2300 – 0500 each night when the fish are not fed. In winter, when the days are shorter, wet food mixtures only are hand-fed to the fish.

Automatic feeding, usually by compressed-air, gun-type

feeders, is only possible in enclosures, or cages anchored to shore-walkways. In some large and very successful salmon farms, no dry food is used and hand-feeding with wet food mixtures is continued for as long as it is possible to persuade the workers to keep at it, usually at least twelve to fourteen hours a day. The fish are not fed at night.

Growth Rates

Large rainbow trout grown in Norwegian sea farms make an average weight at slaughter of 3·5 kg after one and a half years of sea feeding.

Norwegian Atlantic salmon marketed after two years in the sea average 4·5 – 5·0 kg.

In Scottish water, Atlantic salmon smolt put into seawater in April at a weight of 40 gm, reach a weight of 0·5 kg by December of the same year. First sales of grilse are made in June of the following year when the fish are 1–1·5 kg. Salmon sales start in January and continue to April of the third year when the fish average 3–3·5 kg. The cages are then re-stocked with smolt.

Fish Slaughter

Many methods of humane fish-killing have been tried. These have included the use of suffocating gas such as carbon dioxide and electric-shock (which works well in freshwater). Nothing really satisfactory has as yet been devised.

The Norwegians use a method which, although it appears cruel, is said to cause the fish very little distress. A knife is inserted behind the head which severs the main blood vessels. This is done with lightning speed and the fish are then returned to the water, where they rapidly weaken and die through loss of blood. The Norwegian fishermen always bleed the wild salmon they catch as this is thought to improve the quality of the meat.

Scottish and Irish salmon farmers usually use the simple and primitive club that salmon netsmen have used for centuries. In the hands of an expert, one quick blow in the right place is all that is needed and the dead fish are virtually unmarked.

Brood Stock

If special strains of fish are to be retained as brood stock in sea cages, a separate cage should be allocated to each group right from the start when they are introduced as smolt. Even though this may be wasteful of space, it is the only way to guarantee separation throughout their sea life. The growing brood stock do not require any special attention but should be kept at a reduced density, compared to market fish, when they reach large size. A reduction in density can normally be achieved by culling.

Unwanted Guests

A problem which arises for salmonid farmers using enclosures or cages for their fish in the sea is the uninvited entry of unwanted sea fish. Some of the fish species involved, notably saithe (*Pollachius virens*) and pollack (*Pollachius pollachius*) get into the cages as young fish, and grow to large size on the food supplied for the legitimate tenants. They can be a nuisance as well as consuming expensive food, particularly if valuable stocks of brood fish are being held in sea cages which they have invaded.

The only way to remove unwanted species is to shift all the fish into a small working cage and extract the interlopers. Salmon can be badly stressed if hunted round a small cage with dip-nets. The correct procedure is to net-out the unwanted species, not try to net the salmon, although they may be greatly outnumbered.

Chapter 11

Disease Control and Hygiene
in Sea-going Salmonids

Disease is an abnormal and physically damaging condition which can be caused by changes either inside or outside the body of an animal. Diseases in fish may result from any of the following conditions:

Bacterial or viral infection.
Infestation by internal or external parasites.
Environmental conditions such as lack of oxygen, entrained gases in the water or physical damage following skin abrasion or gill clogging.
Toxic algal blooms.
Deficiencies or toxins in the diet.

Much of the disease risk to cultured fish is the direct result of their being held at farm densities, in enclosures from which they cannot escape. Viruses and bacteria known to be present in wild fish stocks only occasionally cause epizootic outbreaks or large casualties. The same applies to diseases resulting from infestation by parasites and naturally adverse conditions in the environment.

Some disease pathogens are present only in freshwater, some in the sea and others in both fresh and saltwater. The sea-going salmonids are doubly at risk. Diseases can be transferred from fresh to saltwater with the young fish, or the pathogenic effects of a disease which infected the fish while in freshwater may become apparent when they are stressed on removal to the sea.

Fish pathogens can be separated into two main groups. Those which are termed obligate are normally absent from water in which there are no diseased fish or carriers of disease.

Many of the common bacterial and viral diseases belong to this group. The second group is termed facultative. These are pathogens which are naturally present in the water and may infect fish and cause symptoms of disease when they are stressed or there are physical changes in their environment, such as abnormal fluctuations in temperature or salinity.

Viral Diseases

Fish diseases caused by viruses seldom if ever respond to treatment, although secondary infections can sometimes be successfully treated. The only method of control is by isolation and destruction of infected stock. Samples of diseased fish must be submitted to a pathological laboratory for definite diagnosis, using live cell-cultures. Reporting the presence or suspected presence of a viral fish disease is a legal obligation in many countries. Some salmonids may resist infection or carry a virus disease, without showing symptoms, which is deadly in other species.

Infectious Haematopoietic Necrosis (IHN)

The disease is endemic in North America and Japan but has not yet been reported in Europe. The species mainly at risk are Pacific salmon and rainbow trout. The virus can be carried in eggs, sperm or faeces and shed into the water, or transmitted by feeding on infected fish tissue. Fish can become healthy carriers. It is a low-temperature disease and does not manifest itself above 15°C.

Symptoms. Frenzied, erratic swimming (flashing); fry float upside-down, breathing rapidly prior to death; early signs are opaque faecal casts trailing from the vent and seen floating on the water or collected on outlet screens; areas of bleeding on the body surface at the base of the fins and vent; fluid in the body cavity; areas of bleeding in the wall of the body cavity and internal organs which are pale in colour; in alevins, signs of bleeding in the yolk-sac which is distended with fluid.

Infective Pancreatic Necrosis (IPN)

The disease is endemic in North America, Europe and Japan. Rainbow trout are at greater risk than salmon. Infected fish can become healthy carriers. The virus can be transmitted through eggs or shed into the water with faeces. It is resistant to adverse conditions and probably remains active in a damp environment for some time outside the body of a host. Mortality is high among very young fish with a death rate of up to 85%. Survivors become carriers probably for life. It is not clear whether the disease can be transmitted in saltwater, but otherwise healthy fish, carrying the disease, may develop symptoms when stressed by transfer from freshwater to the sea.

Symptoms. Erratic swimming; corkscrew movements (flashing); fish sink to the bottom before death; internal bleeding.

Many salmonid farmers have to learn to live with this disease. Stocks appear to build up a degree of immunity and this has been confirmed by the inoculation of adult rainbow trout with live virus. Fish over six months old are naturally resistant to the disease.

It has been suggested that iodophors may reduce losses in salmonid fry when sprayed on dry food pellets or crumb at a rate of 1·5-2·0 gm of undiluted commercial iodophor per kg of food fed for fifteen days. The 'treatment' may do no good but it will not do any harm as the fish would probably die in any case and the iodophor will at least act as a disinfectant.

Viral Haemorrhagic Septicaemia (VHS)

The disease occurs only on the mainland of Europe. It is also called the Egtved Disease after the village in Denmark where it was first reported. The virus was isolated by the late C.J.Rasmussen working at the Research Trout Farm in Brøns. The common mode of transmission is by live fish through the water or by wet, infected equipment. The virus is not transmitted in eggs. It is a cold water disease and outbreaks occur most frequently in winter, particularly when fish are stressed by grading or transportation. Fish of all ages are susceptible and the death rate in bad outbreaks can be up to 90–95%.

Symptoms. Darkening of the skin; eyes bulging, with bleeding in or about the sockets; pale gills; fish become weak and lethargic; body cavity filled with clear or yellowish fluid; swollen and discoloured liver and kidney; flecks of blood and bleeding from the walls of the body cavity.

Bacterial Diseases

Furunculosis

The disease is cause by infection with *Aeromonas salmonicida*. It is mainly a disease of salmonids and is endemic in wild as well as farmed stocks in most countries, with the exception of Australia and New Zealand. It can occur in freshwater and in the sea, and is the most common bacterial disease in farmed fish. Outbreaks are likely when the water temperature is 15°-18°C or above. The disease spreads through the water or by direct contact between the fish. Salmon are more prone to furunculosis than trout. Fish can retain low concentrations of bacteria in their tissues and become carriers. Infection most commonly occurs when the fish are kept in freshwater derived from a river holding wild salmon.

Symptoms. The disease develops after an incubation period of three to four days and salmon parr or young trout may die in large numbers without showing any symptoms other than a slight loss of appetite. Sub-acute infections can cause inflammation of the intestines and reddening of the fins. Large fish or brood stock may develop the typical symptoms of the disease in its acute form. There are swellings or 'furuncles' which can occur anywhere on the fish's body. The swellings, which contain a reddish pus, may burst either before or after death, releasing a mass of bacteria to the water and spreading infection.

Treatment. If the infected fish will continue to eat, the disease can be easily treated and cured with the use of sulpha-drugs mixed in the food. The drug most commonly used is sulphamerazine. A preventative dose can be given when conditions are ripe for an outbreak. The prophylactic dose is 200 mg per kg of live weight of fish for three to four days, with an interval of fourteen days before the next treatment. The same dose can be given therapeutically for three days followed by an interval of one day before the next treatment. Alternatively, a loading dose of 200 mg per kg of live fish weight can be given for one day followed by 100 mg per day for the next ten to fifteen days.

Other treatments:

Furazolidine.	Prophylactic dose 10-20 mg per kg of live body weight. Therapeutic dose 100 mg per kg of live body weight for five to ten days with the food.
Oxytetracycline.	50-75 mg per kg of body weight for ten days with the food.
Inoculation.	Valuable brood stock can be treated by a single intra-peritoneal injection of soluble terramycin dissolved at 10-30 mg/litre.
Immunization.	Oral vaccines have been tried out experimentally with some success.

Bacterial Septicaemias

These diseases are caused by bacteria belonging to the aeromonas and pseudomonas groups. They are universally present in most surface waters holding fish. They are unlikely to cause disease unless the fish are stressed. Their activity is similar to furunculosis in that disease symptoms seldom appear below 10°-12°C, although fish can become infected at lower temperatures. Infections are usually by *Aeromonas liquifaciens* or *Pseudomonas fluorescens* which produce much the same symptoms in infected fish.

Symptoms. Surface lesions on the body, sometimes produced by bursting furuncles but usually first observed as open sores.

The diseases respond to the same treatments used as a preventative and as a cure for furunculosis.

Bacterial Kidney Disease (BKD)

This disease is caused by a *Corynebacterium sp.* so far inadequately described. It affects salmonids in Europe and North America in both fresh and saltwater. It is a serious disease of salmon held in enclosures or cages in the sea. It can be carried over from fresh to saltwater. Previous infection during parr life can cause large losses of smolt with damaged kidneys as they fail to stand up to the osmotic stress of transfer to the sea. In saltwater the disease generally appears during the first winter. Low-grade (relatively few but steady) losses can occur in rainbow trout.

Symptoms. Chronic infections of young fish in freshwater may go unnoticed until casualties occur after the fish are transferred to the sea. Smolt which die will be found on dissection to have whitish lesions in the kidney and bleeding from the kidney and liver. Infected fish in sea cages may cease to feed and swim near the surface. They can appear dark in colour when viewed from above and show swellings on the sides. The eyes may bulge. There can often be no external symptoms and large fish in saltwater may continue feeding actively, until they suddenly die for no apparent reason. When dissected the kidney will be badly diseased and a gram-stained specimen under the microscope shows gram-positive rods.

Treatment. The disease cannot be treated in the sea, although some temporary arrest has been achieved by orally administered sulpha-drugs.

Professor Klontz working at the Circle Salmon Hatchery on Rapid River in Idaho, USA has achieved considerable success in preventing pre-spawning deaths of adult Pacific salmon (spring-chinook *O. tshawytscha*) by sub-cutaneous injection of erythromycin phosphate at 11 mg/kg of fish weight.

Freshly-stripped eggs of that species which were placed to swell (harden) in a solution of 1 mg/litre of erythoromycin phosphate immediately after fertilization, showed a much reduced incidence of bacterial kidney disease during subsequent parr life.

Proliferative Kidney Disease (PKD)

The cause of this disease is unknown. The symptoms are similar to those of BKD with which it can be easily confused. On dissection the kidney is swollen and grey in colour and there is fluid in the body cavity.

Vibriosis ·

This is the most dangerous and damaging disease of salmonids farmed in seawater. It is caused by the bacterium *Vibrio anguillarum* (and possibly other Vibrios) which is present world-wide generally in marine or estuarine environments. The disease can infect all species of sea-going salmonids in fresh and saltwater. The bacterium usually gets in through skin lesions or abrasions caused by the fish rubbing against the concrete walls of tanks or cage nets, or following loss of scales due to grading or handling during transportation. Some strains are observedly more virulent than others. At least two strains have been recognized in Pacific salmon, one of which may infect fish in freshwater but produce no pathogenic effects until they are transferred to the sea. The other infects the fish during their sea life.

Symptoms. The fish cease to feed and become lethargic. Haemorrhagic areas appear in the skin and there is a reddening at the roots of the fins, the vent and sometimes in the mouth. Bleeding occurs in the gills and intestine. Deep red sores may appear on the body. Outbreaks of the disease in acute form, such as can occur among young pink or chum salmon reared in saltwater in shore-based tanks, may produce no external symptoms other than large-scale mortalities.

Treatment. A preventative dose of 40-45 mg of sulphamerazine per kg of live weight of fish per day given in the food. Furazolidine given as 0·02% of the diet over a period of two weeks. There is a risk of producing resistant strains by the continued prophylactic use of either of these drugs. General therapeutic treatment is as follows:

Sulphamerazine. 100 mg per kg of live weight of fish per day for ten days or up to 300 mg per kg of fish while they are still on dry starter diets in freshwater.

Terramycin.   80–90 mg per kg of live weight of fish per day for ten days.

Nitrofurazone.   56 mg per kg of live weight of fish per day.

Furanace.   Short duration baths.

Immunization.   An oral vaccine incorporated in moist pellets has produced some degree of protection in Pacific and Atlantic salmon.

Myxo-bacterial Diseases

Bacterial Gill Disease

The cause of this freshwater disease is infection of the gill filaments by a hitherto unidentified myxo-bacterium. It may occur as a result of irritation following abrasion from debris in the water. It is most likely to occur when the fish are kept in crowded conditions.

Treatment. Avoid over-crowding. Short-term baths. Furanace or hyamine 1 ppm for one hour, or some other quaternary ammonium germicide.

'Cold Water Disease'

This is caused by bacteria of the *Cytophaga spp*.

Treatment. Sulphamerazine or oxytetracycline orally administered. Quaternary ammonium germicide or furanace baths.

Columnaris Disease

Caused by *chondroccoccus columnaris*.

Treatment. As for 'Cold Water Disease'.

Saltwater Myxobacteriosis

The disease is caused by marine myxo-bacteria of the

Sporocytophaga spp. It occurs in Pacific salmon and also possibly in Atlantic salmon in North America. Epizootic outbreaks can occur among salmon in sea cages or enclosures.
Treatment. As for 'Cold Water Disease'.

Other Bacterial Diseases

Tuberculosis

Tubercular lesions can be caused by either *Myco-bacterium piscium* or *Nocardia asteroides*.
Treatment. Avoid infection which usually comes from feeding infected, minced raw trash fish or fish waste, particularly salmonid offals.

Pasteurellosis

This is a rare disease caused by *Pasteurella piscicida*. It has been reported from salmonid sea farms in Europe as well as in North America. It is probably caused by feeding infected wet-fish diets.
Treatment. Avoid infection.

Redmouth Disease

The disease is caused by an enteric bacterium.
Treatment. Sulpha-drugs in the food.

Diseases Caused by Parasites

All disease organisms are in fact parasitic on the host animal but the term is more usually used to include protozoa and metazoa.

Freshwater Protozoan Parasites

Young salmonids intended for on-growing in saltwater are generally too valuable to rear in conditions which might lay them open to infestation with parasites. External parasites that could, in the event of bad hygiene, cause losses to young salmonids are as follows:

Costia. A microscopic pear-shaped protozoan living on the skin of the fish.

Chilodonella and trichodina. Larger more slow moving protozoans on the skin.

Treatment. Baths in formalin or formalin and malachite green solutions.

Ichthyopthiriasis – 'Itch' or 'White Spot'

The disease is caused by an intra–dermal protozoan *Ichthyophthirius* which lives in the skin of the host. Part of its life cycle is spent as a free-swimming organism in the water. Acute infestation can cause severe losses, particularly in hot weather.

Treatment. Killing the free-swimming stage in the water. Otherwise as for external protozoans.

Intestinal Protozoan Parasites

Hexamitiasis. Caused by hexamita (*Octomitus*) which lives in the lumen of the gut of infected fish.

Treatment. Enheptin (2-amino 5-nitrothiazole) 0·2% in the food for three days.

Systemic Protozoan Parasites

Myxosporidae, ceratomyxa, myxosoma (Whirling disease), henneguya (which lives in muscles near the skin of salmon and trout) are all common protozoan parasites in wild salmonids. They can only be controlled in farm stock by good hygiene. There is no treatment for infested fish.

Diseases caused by Parasitic Flukes and Worms

External Flukes

Dactylogyrus and discocotyle are gill-flukes attached by

hooks and suckers to the gill filaments of fish. Gyrodactylus lives on the skin.

Treatment. Prevention of infection by good hygiene. Some treatment is possible using potassium permanganate or organo phosphorus compounds in short-term baths or dips.

Internal Freshwater Flukes

Diplostomum, the 'eye fluke', should never be present in water used to rear young salmonids intended for on-growing in the sea. Water carrying the water-snails (*Lymnaea spp.*), which are the secondary hosts of the parasite, should never be used as a supply for a salmon parr rearing unit.

Acanthocephala

This is a highly specialized type of helminth which can infest the intestine of marine fish. The parasites attach themselves to the gut-lining with thorny hooks that can cause damage which results in poor growth in farm fish. The larval stage of this parasite occurs in marine crustacea. Infestations of farm fish have occurred when they were fed raw shrimp or prawn waste as a source of astaxanthin.

Treatment. Valuable brood stock can be treated with di-n-butyl tin oxide (dibutylin, butyl tin oxide, etc.). Dose: 25 mg per kg of live weight of fish fed for three days. This treatment is also effective in cases of infestation by other helminths.

Crustacean Parasites

The Salmon Sea-Louse (Lepeophtheirus)

This is a large copepod shaped like a miniature crab which lives on the skin of the host fish. The females are about 3–5 mm in diameter and are distinguished by a pair of egg-sacs. The eggs are probably shed in the summer or autumn. Free-swimming nauplius and metanauplius stages are followed by the first chalimus stage when the copepod attaches itself to a host fish.

Parasites in the chalimus stage can be seen on the fins of the fish and are about 1·5 up to 3 mm in length. Several moults occur during the chalimus stages and are followed by numerous others before they attain their maximum size. The parasites feed on particles of skin and possibly blood drawn from the host fish. They can probably migrate from one fish to another.

Heavy infestations can occur in farm fish held in cages or enclosures in the sea and sometimes in wild fish. The parasites can be attached anywhere on the body but the females are often concentrated on the sides and belly particularly between the vent and the tail. The fish are weakened and eventually may die as a result of a bad infestation. The wounds caused by the sea-lice themselves, or by the fish rubbing against the sides of nets or tanks to try to get rid of the parasites, can be centres for bacterial infection.

Treatment. The principle difficulty in treating sea-louse infestations is that chemical baths have to be given in freshwater. Various methods have been tried. These include lifting nets and putting a polythene cover under them, or shifting the fish to smaller, floating containers made of polythene sheet. The saltwater is then pumped out and replaced with freshwater. Aeration is needed while the treatment is being given.

None of these methods can be of much use when the fish are in large, separate off-shore cages but they are possible with fish in cages anchored to a shore-walkway or in enclosures where they can be fairly easily captured without too much stress and brought ashore. There is no problem giving treatment in shore-based tanks provided there is an adequate supply of freshwater. The seawater supply can be replaced with freshwater, aerated if necessary, until the sea-lice are weakened and fall off the fish.

The most successful chemicals so far tried out for treatment are organo phosphorus compounds such as masoten. This commercial preparation is a crystalline powder, soluble in water. The manufacturers' recommended dose for the treatment of external parasitic copepods on salmonids is 1 gm dissolved in 4,000 litres (1 gm per 4 m^3) of water.

Internal medication with a similar compound (dipterex)

has been tried experimentally, fed as a single dose in the food of salmon in sea cages, at 0·08 gm per kg of live fish weight.

The Salmon Gill-Maggot (Salmincola salmonea)

This parasitic copepod grows to maturity attached to the gill filaments of adult Atlantic salmon. Its eggs are shed in freshwater and give rise to free-swimmming larvae which then re-infest adult fish when they return to the river on spawning migration. The parasite survives in the spawned-out fish when they return to the sea and is itself mature if they return to spawn a second time. It has never been reported in Atlantic salmon parr and is very unlikely ever to pose problems for sea farmers, unless they keep their adult brood stock for any length of time in freshwater containing the larval copepods. The parasite might cause difficulties if Atlantic salmon are farmed in freshwater.

Fungal Diseases

Parasitic Fungi

A common cause of loss in freshwater, particularly of eggs and alevin (yolk-sac fry) is infestation with *Saprolegnia spp.,* the spores of which are present in the water.

Treatment. Malachite green (zinc-free) has been generally used to control *Saprolegnia*. It can be made up as a dip 1 : 15,000 (67 ppm) for thirty seconds or as a bath 1 : 500,000 (2 ppm) for fry and parr (fingerlings). The bath concentration can also be used as treatment for incubating eggs after they have reached the eyed stage.

Malachite green is now being replaced for human medical reasons by the use of Furanace as a bath in a concentration of 1-2 ppm for five to ten minutes. It can also be used for more prolonged treatment at a concentration of 0·05-0·1 ppm.

Ichthyophorus

This fungus occurs as a parasite in marine fish but can also invade the organs of farm salmonids in the sea, or in freshwater, fed on infected sea fish.

Fungus Poisonous

Fish food kept for too long in store can become contaminated by the fungus Aspergillus. The afla-toxins produced by this fungus cause hepatoma in salmonids.

Diseases caused by Algae and Dinoflagellates

Fish in enclosures or cages in the sea, unlike wild fish, cannot escape from a sudden wave of poisonous or damaging material entering their confined environment. Dinoflagellates have caused massive losses of salmonids in sea cages. The fish may be killed by a nerve toxin produced by some dinoflagellates such as those forming the so-called 'Red Tides'. Blue-green algae have also been reported as causing losses.

The kill of fish in cages or enclosures is not only caused by direct poisoning but may also be due to suffocation following the complete removal of all the oxygen in the water by the respiration of the algae during the night. The physical clogging of the gills of the fish can also cause suffocation, either by the algae or by mucus produced in the gills of the fish as a result of irritation.

Algal blooms can occur at any time in bright spring or summer weather and little is known of the causes. It seems likely however that sudden changes in water temperature or salinity may act as triggers. Nothing can be done to protect the fish in cages or enclosures sited in an area subject to poisonous algal blooms. The only course of action is to move the cages to a safer place.

Some other diseases

Nephrocalcinosis

The disease is caused by carbon dioxide (CO_2) in alkaline water derived from springs or bore-holes. Calcium carbonate is deposited in the fish producing visceral granulomas. The particles of calcium carbonate can easily be seen on dissection and the kidney has white streaks and lumps and feels gritty.

The normal concentration of CO_2 in average hard surface waters is 4-5 ppm. If the CO_2 level rises 12 ppm there can be some damage to the kidney. Almost total loss of functioning effective kidney tissue results from a CO_2 content of 50-60 ppm.

Salmonid fry reared in water with a high CO_2 content, sufficient to cause granulomas in the kidney, will recover and the calcium carbonate granules will dissolve if the fish are transferred to acid water with a low level of CO_2.

'Gas-bubble' Disease

This condition which appears as minute bubbles of gas under the skin, which sometimes cause the eyes to bulge, is quite common in fry in water from bore-holes or springs. It is due to gas, usually nitrogen (air), entrained in the water at greater than atmospheric pressure.

Ulcerative Dermal Necrosis (UDN)

The lesions which are characteristic of this disease are not the cause of death in the fish. The fish die from secondary infections by pathogenic bacteria and fungi. The lesions will in fact heal up in completely clean, slightly acid water.

An exactly similar lesion to that caused by the unexplained condition known as UDN has been produced experimentally by exposure of live salmonids to UV – A light. It is suggested that photo-sensitization of the skin of the fish may be due to the consumption in the diet of one of a number of photo-toxic compounds now known to exist in their marine environment. This possibility is of considerable importance to sea farmers. Should the condition known as UDN be the result of UV – A light, salmon held in cages would certainly be exposed, as long wave U V light penetrates to a depth of 20-30 m. It is therefore vital that the diets of salmonids in sea cages or enclosures should not contain photo-toxic substances.

Fish Diseases Dangerous to Human Beings

Bacteria

Infection with *Vibro parahaemolyticus* is quite common in human beings in Japan where most fish are eaten raw.

Helminths

There are several worms and flukes common in fish which can be dangerous to man. These include the trematode worm anisakis which is present in the viscera of salmonids in the sea and can be transferred to human beings. The metacercariae of the fluke cryptocotyle, which become encapsulated in the skin of marine fish causing typical black spots, may develop into mature flukes in the human intestine. Both are destroyed by proper cooking. The tapeworm *Diphyllobothrium latum* occurs in freshwater fish in some northern countries and is often met with in people there who eat raw or smoked fish.

Botulism in Fish

The toxin botulin formed by *Clostridium botulinus* can be deadly to human beings, and can also poison salmonids fed on wet fish or fish offal which has had time to become putrid in warm weather. The risk to human beings does not come from the fish which are suffering from the poisonous effects of the toxin, but from eating healthy, smoked or improperly cooked fish which may have become contaminated and contain botulin.

Immunization

The methods of immunization against fish diseases so far tried out experimentally have been intra-peritoneal injections and hyperosmotic infiltration. The diseases involved in the tests were vibriosis and furunculosis. The species tested were coho and chinook salmon. Both methods of immunization gave hopeful results in field tests. Hyperosmotic infiltration gave the best protection in coho salmon with an 83·3% survival compared to 28·7% in a control. The growth rates of the immunized fish were not significantly different from the controls.

Both species of Pacific salmon were immunized as fry. The infiltration of the bacterins was carried out in a vacuum chamber. The fry of both species were kept in freshwater for periods of four to five weeks before being transferred to sea cages. Significant protection against vibriosis and furunculosis was subsequently provided to both species during sea life.

TABLE IX

A Checklist of Useful Chemicals for Controlling Fish Diseases

Chemical	Use or Dose
Betadine (Iodophor)	100 - 200 ppm in water depending on iodine content by weight
Betacide	Dip. 1: 2,000. Time 1 - 2 min Bath. 1: 10,000. Time 20 - 30 min
Calcium cyanamide (Disinfectant)	Drain but leave wet sides and bottoms of tanks or ponds. Rate 200/m^2
Butyl tin oxide (di-n-butyl tin oxide)	250/kg fish wt. orally. 0.3% in food for 5 days
Dipterex (organo phosphorus compound)	See Masoten
Enheptin	0.2% in food for 3 days
Formalin	See special Section
Furanace	See special Section

Chemical	Use or Dose
Furazolidine (Furoxone)	20 - 30 mg/kg fish wt. per day with food. May deteriorate rapidly when mixed with wet diets
Hyamine 3500	1·0 - 2·0 ppm (on basis of product strength). Time 1 hour
Iodophors	See special Section
Malachite Green (zinc-free)	Dip. 1 : 15,000. Time 10 - 30 sec. Bath. 1 - 5 ppm. Time 1 hour
Malachite Green with Formalin	See special Section
Masoten	Bath. 1 gm in 4,000 litres (1 gm in $4m^3$ of water)
Nifurpirinol	See Furanace
Nifurprazine (Nitrofuran)	Bath. 0·01-0·1 ppm. Indefinite period 10 mg per kg of food. 3 - 6 days
Oxytetracyline (Terramycin)	50 - 75 mg/kg fish wt. 10 days with food (treatment must be stopped 3 weeks before slaughter)
Potassium permanganate $KMnO_4$	Dip. 1 : 1,000. Time 10 - 40 sec. Bath. 10 ppm. Time up to 30 min
Roccal (Benzalkonium chloride)	See Hyamine
Sulphamerazine	200 mg/kg fish wt. with food for 14 days (treatment must be stopped 3 weeks before slaughter)
Terramycin (alternative to chloramphenicol)	Single intra–peritoneal injection of soluble form. 10 - 30 mg/kg fish wt.
Wescodyne (Iodophor)	See special Section

Dangers in the Use of Anti-biotics

The same anti-biotics used to treat fish diseases are used in human medical treatment. They generally work by directly poisoning the bacteria without side-effects in the host animal. Resistant strains of bacteria can develop through the constant use of particular drugs and render them less effective in the treatment of diseases in human beings. Chloramphenicol (*Chloromycetin*) should never be used for the oral treatment of fish diseases or released into the water as a prophylactic. It is too valuable a drug in the treatment of human diseases, particularly in children. Its use in fish farming is banned in EEC countries.

It is particularly important to remember that people can suffer harm from eating fish containing residues of the drugs used for oral medication. The fish normally eliminate concentrations that might be harmful to human beings over a period of ten to twelve days, at temperatures of 10°-15°C. The period taken for elimination in colder water between 4° and 10°C is much longer and may exceed thirty days. The average period over which drug treatment should cease before the fish are slaughtered is twenty-one days.

Disinfection of Live Fish

It should not be necessary to treat fish for external parasites, if the water supply is free from any organic pollution and saturated with oxygen, provided the fish are not overcrowded and a good standard of hygiene is maintained on the unit. If fish become infested the first step must be to consider whether treatment is worthwhile in relation to their commercial value.

The condition of the fish and their environment must be taken into consideration, particularly the chemistry of the water. If the oxygen content is low aeration will be essential during treatment. The chemical used in dips or baths can be more or less active according to the pH, and in acid waters may reach toxic levels even when made up at recommended concentrations. The stress of treatment may itself cause an unjustifiable increase in the casualty rate. Kill or cure is a waste of money and it may make better economic sense to deliberately slaughter larger fish and salvage any that are marketable.

Advice should always be sought if a fish farmer is not completely certain of the diagnosis of the disease and the correct treatment. It is essential to make sure that the fish are not suffering from more than one infestation of parasites at the same time. Gill parasites should always be treated first. As a general rule, the fish should be starved for one or two days prior to treatment as this will reduce the ammonia content of the water.

The strength of the solutions used to make up disinfectant dips and baths should be carefully checked. It is usually too late to do anything about it when the fish begin to show signs of distress.

Dips. The fish are held in a net or sieve and lowered into a concentrated solution, usually for not more than about thirty seconds.

Baths. The fish are immersed in the chemical solution for up to one hour (sometimes longer). The oxygen level must be monitored in static water and aeration should be available for use if needed.

When the fish are in tanks or raceways a calculated 'drip' of the chemical at the correct concentration can be added to the water supply. This is expensive but treatment can usually be given in freshwater, without the stress of capturing the fish. Low-level disinfection can be provided over a longer period. Care must be taken with the effluent water containing the chemical solution as this can be a source of pollution.

Formalin

A most useful compound which is commonly used for the chemical treatment of external parasites on fish and is a 40% solution of pure formaldehyde, uncontaminated by paraldehyde which is poisonous to fish.

Formalin should be carefully handled as it is a respiratory

irritant. It must be completely mixed so that the concentration is evenly distributed through the fish tank. In order to make sure that this happens, a little malachite green can be mixed with the formalin as a tracer.

The concentration in the fish tank should not be greater than 1 : 5,000 and the concentration should be reduced to 1 : 6,000 if the water temperature is over 15°C. The time of treatment should be not more than one hour.

Formalin reduces the oxygen in the water and aeration should be provided during treatment.

Formalin and Malachite Green

Stock Solutions for Control of External Protozoan Parasites on Salmonids.

Water above 15°C	Water below 15°C
1 part Malachite Green to 300 parts Formalin	1 part Malachite Green to 200 parts Formalin
Mix together – 1 litre of Formalin (37% Formaldehyde) with 3·3 gm Malachite Green	Mix together – 1 litre of Formalin (37% Formaldehyde) with 5·0 gm Malachite Green
Dilution for Treatment 0·015 ml/litre 15 ml/m^3	Dilution for Treatment 0·020 ml/litre 20 ml/m^3
Final dilution Formalin 15 ppm Malachite Green 0·05 ppm	Final dilution Formalin 20 ppm Malachite Green 0·1 ppm

Treatments with these concentrations of active ingredients should not exceed six hours in tanks with running water, or with aeration. Look out for signs of stress in badly parasitized fish.

Hyamine 3500

This is a quaternary ammonium germicide. Other commercial preparations include Roccal.

The safe use of these compounds at a given concentration depends very much on the hardness of the water. The mixture becomes increasingly toxic in soft water. The final concentration of a bath solution should not exceed 2 ppm in water of a hardness of 100 ppm calcium carbonate, but can be increased to 4 ppm in water containing 200 ppm calcium carbonate.

Furanace

This is the trade name of a nitrofuran manufactured in Japan. It was primarily intended as a disinfectant for the external treatment of fish diseases. It has proved successful in the treatment of fin-rot, bacterial gill disease, external protozoan parasites and saprolegnias. Used as a bath the concentration is 1-2 ppm for five to ten minutes. A more prolonged treatment lasting for some hours, or even days, can be given using concentrations of 0·05-0·1 ppm.

The drug has been used orally, given with the food, to treat bacterial diseases including those caused by aermonas spp. and vibriosis. The recommended dose is 2-4 mg/kg of fish weight per day for three to five days. Furanace has also been used prophylactically, fed with the food at a rate of 0·4-0·8 mg/kg of fish weight per day.

Commercial Iodophors

These are disinfectant solutions containing 1-1·6% iodine (I_2) in an organic solvent. The dose depends on the concentration of iodine in the product which can vary from about 50-200 ppm. An average concentration for use in practice is 100 ppm.

Iodophors can safely be used to disinfect eyed eggs under incubation but are very poisonous to alevins (yolk-sac fry) and fry.

Iodophors in solution are acid and must be neutralized. The usual recommended duration of treatment is ten to twenty minutes in water buffered to a pH of 7·5 to 8·0.

Iodophors given orally in the diet of fry suffering from

IPN are said to reduce losses. The dose is 1·5-2 gm of undiluted iodophor per kg of food over fifteen days.

Hygiene and Disinfection of Installation and Equipment

Like any other domestic animal, fish do best if kept under hygienic conditions. This applies particularly to salmonids which are cold water fish and will not tolerate an adverse environment.

Hatcheries. Suspended solids should be filtered out of the water supply. Debris should not be allowed to accumulate at the bottom of troughs below egg trays. It is particularly important to prevent any accumulation of waste food or faeces in troughs or small tanks when these are used for initial fry feeding. Hatchery equipment should be disinfected and stored dry when not in use.

Fry Tanks. The bottom of tanks and outlet screens should be kept thoroughly clean. After a season's use tanks and screens should be scrubbed out with a disinfectant solution and left dry. The insides of fry tanks should be given a coating of a neutral anti-fouling paint during the off-season to prevent algal growth.

General Equipment. Separate cleaning utensils should be provided for each tank and kept in a weak solution of disinfectant. Buckets, transportation tanks and any other equipment which comes in contact with the fish should be disinfected after use.

Food Hygiene. A common cause of loss is through bad food being given to the fish which has either deteriorated during storage or been prepared under foul conditions with dirty equipment. It is particularly important to store fish food with as good or better attention to hygiene than is paid to human food. This applies to both fresh, wet or deep-frozen foods and to dry foods.

The mincers and mixers used for wet food preparation should be cleaned after use and kept clean. Damp dry food should not be allowed to collect on automatic feeders. This easily happens particularly with oily diets. It is a simple matter on some fish farms to see why the fish are not doing as well as they should. One look at the filthy food preparation room provides the answer.

Saltwater Shore-Tanks. The general degree of hygiene that can be applied in shore-based tanks, using pumped seawater, is the same as for freshwater tanks. The accumulation of marine growths creates special problems as these not only impede the flow of water but also collect waste food and faeces. There is no way round this problem other than to design the unit as simply as possible so that it can be kept clean and to use such non-toxic anti-foulants as may be available.

Sea Cages and Enclosures. There is little that can be done to keep enclosures from becoming fouled with accumulated waste food and faeces. These may eventually have to be dredged or pumped out. Cage nets have to be changed periodically, on average once or twice a year (much more often in warmer waters), depending on the marine growth in the area. Marine plants will grow on the nets in spite of anti-fouling treatment. They are best cleaned off by immersing the nets in freshwater and then if possible getting them thoroughly dried out.

Cage nets on smaller cages can be made with a 'cod end' or tapered bottom ending in a funnel of net. This is closed with two or three turns of cord and a pin. The end of the funnel is connected to the cage-walkway by a rope. Debris collects in the funnel at the bottom of the cage and from time to time it can be hauled up and emptied.

Disinfectants

It must be borne in mind that residues of strong disinfectants used on fish farms may be toxic to fish. Tanks should be washed out with clean water before being re-stocked and fish-handling gear should also be washed after being disinfected.

Disinfectants used on fish farms will cause pollution if they are released undiluted into water courses.

Potassium permanganate. A fairly concentrated solution

1 : 50 is a useful, non-corrosive disinfectant for troughs, tanks and equipment.

Chlorine as sodium hypochlorite. 1 – 2% solution in clean water can be used for troughs, tanks and equipment. It is very corrosive and poisonous to fish. It must be kept away from metals and protective clothing should be worn.

Quaternary ammonium compounds. These can be used at the strengths recommended by the manufacturers.

Iodophors. With an average iodine content of 1 – 1·6% they can be used as general disinfectants at a dilution of 250 ppm. Iodophors are expensive and should only be used for valuable equipment.

Calcium cyanamide and calcium oxide (quicklime). These can be distributed on the bottom and sides of tanks or ponds which have been drained but are still wet at a rate of 200 gm/m^2.

Chapter 12

Salmon Ranching

Ranching sea-going salmonids starts by releasing the young fish at or near their smolt stage, just before they would naturally migrate to sea. The fish then complete the sea-feeding part of their life cycle on free-range and 'home' to the place they were released. This can be a river, or possibly a sheltered bay or fjord. Success in economic terms depends upon enough salmon surviving to return to the point of release, at a place where they can be captured in commercially profitable numbers. The return of the fish not only depends upon natural survival but on their not being caught by other people, either on the high seas or on their way home.

Ranching is based upon the complete freedom of the fish to migrate to and from their marine feeding grounds. The improvement over nature is obtained by artificially incubating and hatching the eggs of the fish, and rearing the young in captivity during the period of greatest natural loss in the wild. It must not be confused with what is called 'enhancement'. This means planting the eggs, fry or parr of anadromous salmonids in sections of the river which the adult fish cannot reach on their spawning migration, or which are unsuitable as spawning ground but could provide useful rearing areas for young fish.

The development of artificial spawning-channels for some species of Pacific salmon is a half-way stage between full ranching and enhancement. A typical spawning channel is an artificial canal made beside the natural river, or across the loop of a wide bend. The bed of the channel is covered by graded gravel of the correct size to be used for redd or nest construction by the selected species of salmon. The inflow and outflow of water is controlled by sluices or valves, and the length of the channel may be divided up by weirs and screens.

A pre-determined number of adult fish returning on spawning migration is allowed into a channel, where they spawn naturally. Alternatively the fish can be stripped and the fertilized eggs planted in artificial redds or nests made in the gravel. The use of spawning channels has substantially increased the marine harvest of some species of Pacific salmon. The method is only of real value for the species which migrate directly to sea as fry (pink and chum), or leave the spawning area in a river to feed in lakes (sockeye). If the fish have to be fed artificially, this is probably better and more easily done in tanks, where the fish are under direct control.

Marine Growth

Feeding on the 'sea-range' depends, as it once did for cattle and sheep on the open range, on the climate of their environment. Salmon production in the sea is dependent on the changes in ocean currents and temperatures that make up the shifting climate of the sea. All ocean-going salmon follow the animals on which they feed, whether their food consists mainly of crustacea in the plankton or species of shoaling fish. Salmon bred in rivers at the southern end of the range go north to feed in the sea and may have a long journey to and from their marine feeding grounds compared to members of the same species from northern rivers. This is an important consideration in ranching because the fish will be in better condition if they have a short return migration. They will burn-off so much fat under conditions of semi-starvation while they are travelling.

TABLE X
The Pacific Salmon

Species	Max. wt. kg	Av. wt. kg	Av. age yrs	Parr life	Marine food	% Commercial value
Pink O. gorbuscha	5·4	2·7	2	Nil	Plankton, small fish	40

Species	Max. wt. kg	Av. wt. kg	Av. age yrs	Parr life	Marine food	% Com- mercial value
Chum O. keta	15·9	5·9	3 - 6	Nil	Plankton, small fish	32
Sockeye O. nerka	6·8	3·6	4 - 6	1–2 yrs (in lakes)	Plankton, small fish	100
Coho O. kisutch	11·3	4·0	3 - 4	1–2 yrs (in rivers)	Mostly fish	88
Chinook (Spring) O. tshawytscha	45·0	8·0	3 - 8	Some months (in rivers)	Mostly fish	72

The older average ages are for fish belonging to colder rivers in the northern part of the range of the species. Sockeye are the most valuable species and their commercial value is taken as 100%.

A good deal is known about the marine environment of the Pacific salmons, because the most valuable species are fished for commercially by drift-netting in their feeding areas. The sea-feeding areas of Atlantic salmon are less well-defined. Drift-netting in the North Atlantic, outside territorial waters, has been banned by international agreement between the main fishing nations. Only inshore feeding grounds, such as those off the coast of Greenland and north Norway, are well-documented from the results of commercial fishing.

The richest feeding grounds in the northern seas are in areas where the cold, less saline water from the melting ice-cap meets the warmer, strongly saline water brought up by the ocean currents circulating from south to north and west to east. Changes in the pattern of the meeting of these waters, such as cooling due to an increase in the influence of the Arctic ice-water and a weakening of the warm currents, could greatly influence the quantity of the food animals available to sea-going salmonids. The marine food supply is, of course, not

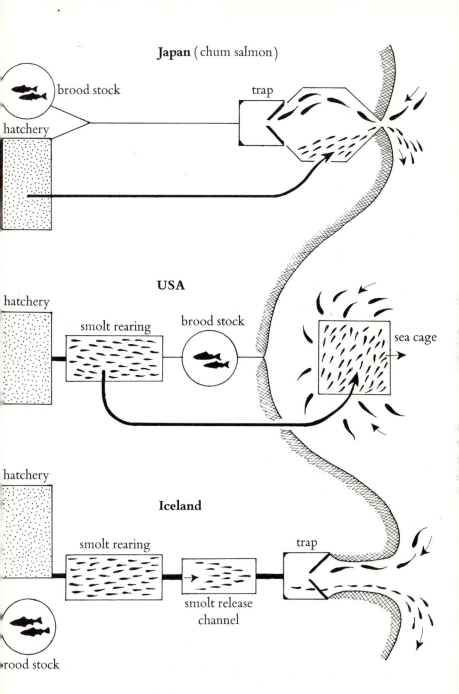

Fig. 26 Salmon ranching methods

only of vital importance to ranched salmon, but to all stocks, including those which are completely wild and not managed in any way by human beings.

Breeding and Rearing Salmon for Ranching

Ranched species need not only be those which have a parr-life period in freshwater. Very large numbers of chum salmon fry, hatched artificially and released in Japanese waters, form the basis of a multi-million fishery for returning adult fish. Pink salmon fry are being released at the mouths of rivers in west and south Norway in order to replace stocks of Atlantic salmon destroyed by acid rain, from the atmospheric pollution arising in other countries, that falls over their upland catchment area. Atlantic salmon, as well as the Pacific species, can be used for ranching.

Culturing the parr intended for ranching, particularly of Atlantic salmon, requires the employment of rather different techniques to those needed for salmon which are grown-on to market size in captivity. The fish to be released on approaching smoltification must be hardier and able to survive to adult life in worthwhile numbers in the wild, without artificial feeding or protection from predators.

The modifications needed to produce viable smolt are basically very simple. Environmental conditions in the hatchery and rearing unit, in terms of water temperature and chemistry, should be as close as possible to those encountered in the wild. The food given to the fish must be similar in protein and fat content to the natural food. The use of sources of protein containing carbohydrates should be avoided. The fish should not be over-crowded and should have room to adopt aggressive, territorial behaviour in order to promote some element of competition similar to that in the wild habitat.

Differences in body chemistry between artificially reared and wild smolt, or pre-smolt parr, have to be rectified after release and the change to a natural diet. It has been shown that the body chemistry of young hatchery-reared coho takes about three months of wild feeding to revert to the natural state. The percentage return from artificially-reared smolt released at smoltification seems likely to be lower than that for fish released as pre-smolt parr several months before smoltifying that have had time to correct their metabolism before having to endure the added stress of moving into saltwater.

It is evident from the results of Atlantic salmon smolt-rearing in Sweden and Iceland that large smolt survive better than small smolt. This applies not only to older smolt but to smolt in the same year class. The optimum smolt weight for subsequent survival in the wild may be as high as 80-90 gm at release. This indicates that there is an advantage to be gained in using S2 Atlantic salmon smolt, or pre-smolt parr in their second year, for ranching.

Natural losses during the freshwater life-period of Atlantic salmon can amount to about 99% from the time the fry emerge from the gravel of the redd to smolt migration. In a well-run hatchery and smolt-rearing unit losses in the same period should not exceed 10-15% and certainly not be greater than 25%. The main causes of loss in the wild are starvation due to competition for food and living space by their own or other species, and predation.

The main disadvantage in artificial rearing is that it takes away the important element of natural selection which weeds out the weaklings and leaves the strongest and most vigorous fish to survive and become smolt.

Releasing Pre-smolt Parr and Smolt

It is futile to release artificially reared pre-smolt parr into water where they will have to face heavy competition with wild fish for the available supplies of natural food, or are under constant attack from predators. They should if possible be released into shallow lakes which do not contain predatory fish species, apart from eels and small trout.

The systems developed in Iceland and in Ireland for releasing smolt have proved very successful. The fish are removed from their rearing tanks to release ponds shortly before smoltification is complete. The release ponds are constructed by excavating an area beside the lower part of the river to which the adult fish are expected to return. The ponds are fed with a freshwater supply at the upstream end. The downstream end is open to the sea or a tidal estuary and is usually controlled by a sluice-gate. Saltwater enters the pond at high tide. Smolt can shift gradually into water of increasing salinity by moving down the pond and are free to go to sea when they feel inclined.

The same pond, with a trap at the upper end and a diversion fence across the river, can be used to retain and capture returning adults.

Survival of Ranched Atlantic Salmon in the Sea

It has not yet proved possible to arrive at a completely accurate estimate of the survival of ranched Atlantic salmon from smolt to returning adult, except possibly in the Icelandic fisheries. The problem has been firstly to develop a satisfactory mark or tag to put on migrating smolt, by which they can be recognized when captured, and secondly to persuade fishermen, who may catch the adult fish away from their parent rivers, to admit to the capture and to return the tags.

A further difficulty is that it is now quite certain that external tags attached to the body of the fish when they are pre-smolt parr can reduce their chances of survival by a factor of as much as ten, in comparison with untagged fish. This of course makes a nonsense of the use of external tags that are sufficiently obvious to be seen on casual examination by a commercial net-fisherman.

The Icelandic salmon ranchers use a very small wire tag which is inserted by a special gun into the nose of the salmon. This type of tag, which is almost microscopic in size, does not inconvenience the fish in any way, but it is quite invisible on the body surface and leaves no scar. All returning fish have to be checked for tags with a sensitive metal detector or by x-ray.

There is no offshore netting for salmon in Icelandic waters, so the catch or count of returning adults made in rivers can give a true indication of the percentge survival of the fish from smolt to adult. Atlantic salmon smolts tagged at an

Icelandic smolt rearing station at an average length of 13 cm produced an adult return of only 1·9% but fish tagged at 15 cm produced a return of 13·2% and those tagged at 17 cm an adult return of 15·6%

Returns of tagged Baltic salmon smolt released from Swedish rivers have averaged 12%, but returns would probably have been much higher had it been posible to use internal tags. In one experiment the return was as high as 40%. The survival of artificially reared smolt in Ireland has been about 6%, but the results are not truly relevant because of the large proportion of adult recaptures made by drift-nets in coastal waters that go unrecorded. The percentage returns of farm smolt from Scottish and Norwegian rivers suffer from the same discrepancies. The true recapture percentage of artificially reared smolt from rivers in these countries is probably not much different from that demonstrated in Iceland.

Ranching has been tried out with varying success using the species of Pacific salmon which spend some time as parr in freshwater before migrating to the sea. The difficulty is that these species can be fairly well advanced towards spawning by the time they return to their parent rivers. Releases have been made from cages or enclosures in the sea in the expectation that sufficient adults could be recaptured in the vicinity of the cage areas. The most successful species for ranching seems likely to be coho which has a life cycle not unlike that of Atlantic salmon. Recaptures of ranched coho have been in the region of 4%.

Ranching with Steelhead Rainbow Trout

The homing behaviour of steelhead trout is not as accurate as that for salmon but is comparable to sea-going brown trout (*Salmo trutta*). Approximately 80% of steelhead smolt in the Oregon rivers in the USA go to sea between mid-April and mid-May at the age of two plus years. The mean weight of smolt at migration was found to be 43·2 gm and the maximum was 107·5 gm. The optimum weight resulting in the highest survival percentage (10%) was 60 gm at smolt migration.

Areas Suitable for Ranching

It is a waste of time and money to try to start ranching on a river in an area where there is already large-scale legal or illegal salmon fishing with nets in the sea, either drift-nets offshore, or fixed gill-nets and trap-nets. The salmon must have a clear run home from their sea-feeding grounds, without being exploited to any extent by outsiders. There are not many places where ranching is possible, particularly if private fishing rights are neither respected or protected, and governments are not prepared to enforce conservation laws, either national or international.

It is not necessary to ranch on a large river and it is quite feasible to induce a return of adult salmon to a small stream (or possibly to a place in the sea), provided the fish will return to a circumscribed area where they can be easily captured. Small streams that are fed by a lake can be made more attractive to returning salmon, and the entry of the fish can be facilitated, by artificial spates given through a sluice-gate in a low dam.

Homing

Ranching is based on the ability of salmon to return to their parent rivers on spawning migration. It has been demonstrated beyond doubt that a sense of smell is the means by which salmon recognize the waters where they were hatched and from which they migrate to sea. The imprint of the home-base must be made by some species in the very short time they spend as fry in freshwater. Evidence from the results of transporting smolt to alien rivers before they are released, indicates that the imprinting process may take longer and that mistakes can subsequently be made by the returning adults.

The olfactory basis for homing may create problems for ranching, if smolt are not released in the river in which they were reared. It would be possible for fish to make mistakes if the volume of water leaving the release stream closely resembled the water coming from another neighbouring catchment area. There is also the possibility of the olfactory stimulus from the home water being masked by some source of pollution.

Homing to a particular part of the coast must be governed by other means than the sense of smell. If smolt, released in the sea, are expected to return to the release area as adults, it seems likely that something more positive than the general marine guidance system may be needed to get them back to the right place.

Returning Adults

The returning adult salmon which were released as smolts must be checked for internal tags when they return, and a proportion retained alive as brood stock. Alternatively, if the river to which they return is also used for angling, some fish may have to be released for the rods, and to spawn naturally.

The proportion needed for brood stock is quite straightforwardly based on the rearing capacity of the unit. The number which may have to be released to satisfy anglers is problematical. In the case of Atlantic salmon, the evidence from rivers where accurate counts can be made is that rod fishing will take 30-40% of the salmon that enter the river, and a smaller proportion of the grilse. This would normally leave a surplus of more fish to spawn than is needed to maintain the stock. The best course of action is to take a straightforward, arbitrary decision as to the proportion of fish to allow upstream for angling, based on what the anglers will pay for their fishing, compared to the commercial value of the fish.

Trapping and Counting

A simple inscale trap is needed to take returning adults. This is a box with slatted sides through which water can pass, with the entrance in the form of an inward-pointing V through which the fish can pass, but through which they cannot find their way out. The returning fish have to be guided to the trap entrance by grids forming a fence across the river. More than one trap may be needed over the width of larger rivers.

Fish can be directly counted in the trap and a proportion released upstream, or an electronic counter can be used in a gap in the upstream wall of the trap. The only satisfactory counters for salmon are those of the so-called resistance type. These are based on the principle that the body of the fish contains a hypertonic salt solution and has less resistance to the passage of electricity than a similar volume of freshwater. The fish are guided to swim through a tube or an open channel which has metal electrodes buried in the sides and base. A very small electric current passes in these electrodes and this increases when a fish goes through the counter. The increased current is amplified and is used to operate a recorder.

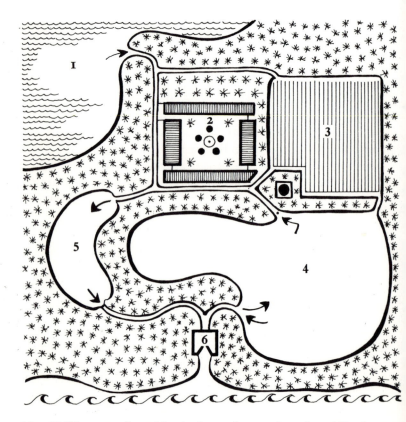

Fig. 27 Diagram of combined salmon farm and ranch: **1** Freshwater supply **2** Hatchery and fry rearing **3** Raceways or tanks for parr **4** Tidal pool **5** Release basin **6** Trap for returning adults

The Future of Salmon Ranching

Ranching salmon, which is a means of taking advantage of the natural growth of the fish in the open sea is an attractive proposition, and one of the most exciting possibilities open to salmon farmers. The future success of any kind of ranching or of the world's stocks of sea-going salmonids depends upon the perhaps unattainable goal of mankind, co-operation between nations in the conservation and utilization of the world's natural resources.

Chapter 13

Markets, Costs and Profits

The capital cost of a fish farm is primarily a reflection of its size. A project should first be investigated from the point of view of marketing the product. The initial questions must be: is the product saleable? where can it be sold? how much will it fetch in the market? The answers should provide the base from which to build an economically viable enterprise of the right size. The most profitable fish farms in simple terms of cash return on investment are probably small family units, although the total turnover of such enterprises may be very small. In direct contrast, very large farms achieve some economies from the scale on which they operate. The minimum size of fish farm which can provide a reasonable living when operated by itself, without some other source of income, is about ten to fifteen tonnes annual production. A sea farm of this size can only be made to show a profit if the capital investment has been kept very small and the proprietor is prepared to put in a great deal of hard work.

The most successful fish farmers manage to operate with a small labour force. Production per man year is a measure of a farm's efficiency but there are jobs which cannot be done by a person working by themselves. The most useful size of small farm is one that can be worked by two people. Many very small fish farms are operated profitably and efficiently as part of some other enterprise, such as land farming or sea fishing.

Farming in the sea is generally more labour intensive than in shore-based tanks, but the additional labour cost can be more than offset by the cost of pumping. Production per man year varies from four to five tonnes or less on a small unit run by part-time work, to fifteen to twenty tonnes per man year on the largest farms, with an annual output of more than one hundred tonnes. Average production per man year on a well-run medium-sized farm would be ten to twelve tonnes per man year, although this level of production can only be expected from larger units operated at maximum efficiency.

A principle item in the production cost of a farm fish is the fish food. Between three and four times the weight of wet feed is needed to produce a given weight of fish than dry feed, but wet feed is proportionately a good deal cheaper than dry feed and the total cost of wet and dry feeds, in terms of tonnes of fish produced, is consequently roughly the same. Dry feed can be transported and stored much more cheaply and easily than wet feed, but it is fair to assume that a farmer intending to use wet feed will site his farm in a place where he can get fresh supplies. Although the situation may be isolated, any additional expenses in marketing will be compensated for by not having to import food for long distances. The only justification for high-cost capital investment in fish-farm construction and equipment is that it results in a corresponding economic gain in efficiency of operation. Some of the most profitable farms are constructed on the simplest lines and have the most primitive equipment for fish feeding, grading and handling.

Sea Farm Profitability

The basic elements of the cost accounting in a sea farm must differ widely according to its location. The interest rates on capital may be at much the same level at any given time in countries with similar economic systems, but there are likely to be much greater differences in the other basic cost elements, such as fish food and labour, although the sale value of the fish may be relatively compatible.

The capital cost per tonne of annual production varies greatly according to the design of the unit. Monetary comparisons have little relevance in times of change, particularly in terms of the currency of any one country. There are no basic criteria for design, and large farms are frequently planned by people lacking in essential, practical knowledge of the subject. Such units are often over-complicated in an attempt to achieve sophistication and are usually grossly over-capitalized. They may have fundamental in-built faults which are the seeds of financial disaster. The most common failing is that actual production never reaches the design capacity of the unit and the farm is always under-producing. The capital cost of a sea farm, producing a given tonnage of salmon or trout in saltwater, can be as much as five times greater than for another farm producing the same tonnage, but the cost is to some extent a reflection of the location and it may not be possible to construct a low-cost unit on a particular site.

The basic elements of running costs can be broken down as follows:

Fixed Costs	*Variable Costs*
Interest on capital	Fish food
Depreciation	Electricity or other power
Rent and rates	Transport
Fixed charges for electricity	Repairs and maintenance
Labour and management	Disposable equipment
Insurance	Dry and cold storage
	Loss of fish

Depreciation on saltwater farms is approximately as follows:

Concrete and steel sea enclosures	7%
Net enclosures in the sea	20%
Sea cages	25%
Shore-based concrete tanks and ponds	6%
Saltwater pumps	20%
Pipes and valves (corrosion-resistant materials)	7%
Cold stores and processing plant	10%
Boats	10%
Vehicles	12%

Fish losses vary with the type of unit. The risk of one kind of loss can be greater on some units than others, or only apply to particular methods.

Charges on Investment

Interest on invested capital can be an important item in production costs. The capital invested in order to produce a given tonnage of fish per year can vary, according to design and circumstances, from less than half the gross value of each year's fish production, at the most profitable end of the scale, to about four times the value of a year's fish production at the least profitable end. The most expensive production system, in terms of return on capital, is a shore-based salmon farm, with a pumped seawater supply. The lowest-cost units are sea cages and small sea enclosures.

Distribution of Operating Costs

The division of running costs is very much a matter of the location of the farm. An apportionment of production costs in fresh and saltwater farming of salmonids in Europe is approximately as follows:

Distribution of Costs	Salt	Fresh
Interest and depreciation	26%	24%
Fish feed	34%	56%
Labour, management and other overheads	40%	20%

It can be seen from the figures that saltwater farming is more labour intensive than freshwater farming.

Accounts of Sea Farms (1980 values)
Shore-based Units

Experience indicates that the most expensive and least profitable type of saltwater salmonid farm is one which involves pumping to shore-based ponds or tanks. Financial success or failure rests on pumping costs. The cost of pumping at a shore site will depend on the price of electricity, and the head at which the pumps have to operate in relation to the average tidal range. Complicated and expensive units become progressively less likely to meet with financial success and there is no apparent economy of scale. Only farms with simple concrete ponds, sited close to the shore, are likely to prove economically viable. (Pumping seawater from beach wells has proved profitable, but only with small fish farms.)

Examples:

1 A medium-sized shore-based unit with simple concrete ponds (rainbow trout)

Approx. capital value	Annual prod. tonnes Planned	Actual	Labour force	Gross value fish sales
£105,000 ($236,250)	50	50	4	£132,000 ($297,000)

2 A large shore-based unit, with raceways (salmon)

Approx. capital value	Annual prod. tonnes Planned	Actual	Labour force	Gross value fish sales
£1,000,000 ($2,250,000)	200	75	16	£363,000 ($816,750)

Enclosures in the Sea

Very small enclosure-type farms can be highly profitable because they cost little to construct and need only a minimum labour force. Very large units can remain profitable, in spite of high capital and running costs, by economies of scale.

Examples:

1 A small enclosure-unit with tidal interchange of water. The farm buys-in fish at a weight of about 80 gm to grow-on in saltwater (rainbow trout)

Approx. capital value	Annual prod. tonnes Planned	Actual	Labour force	Gross value fish sales
£6,000 ($13,500)	10	10	1½	£17,600 ($39,600)

2 A very large salmon farm with tidal flows supplemented by pumping through the enclosures. The farm produces its own smolt and sells the surplus to other fish farms.

Approx. capital value	Annual prod. tonnes Planned	Actual	Labour force	Gross value fish sales
£2,000,000 ($4,500,000)	500	600	30	£2,904,000 ($6,534,000)

Cages in the Sea

The most generally-profitable type of saltwater salmonid farm uses floating net cages in the sea, but the risk of fish losses is higher than in enclosures or shore-based units. Smaller cages are more expensive in terms of capital cost per tonne of fish production than large cages. The most economical type of net cage is supported on a polygonal walkway and has a capacity of between 300 and 400 m^3. The capital cost per tonne of production increases rapidly in cages below 200 m^3 capacity. The capital cost of producing fish in a 70 m^3 cage is double the capital cost of producing them in a 350 m^3 cage.

Examples:

1 A rainbow trout farm using medium-sized net cages (180 m^3). The unit rears young fish in freshwater but has substantial losses on transfer to the sea and poor growth rates.

225

Approx. capital value	Annual prod. tonnes Planned	Actual	Labour force	Gross value fish sales
£84,000 ($189,000)	60	40	3	£79,200 ($178,200)

2. A salmon farm using large, polygonal net cages (300 - 400 m³), catching and freezing its own industrial fish as fish food, processing salmon on the farm and selling most of the product smoked.

Approx. capital value	Annual prod. tonnes Planned	Actual	Labour force	Gross value fresh fish sales
£540,000 ($1,215,000)	135	135	11	£44,000 ($99,000) smoked fish sales £1,031,250 ($2,320,313)

Analysis

The examples are not modelled on any existing salmon or rainbow trout farms, but an analysis of the figures from working farms indicates that there is a relationship between the gross value of an average year's production of fish and the current capital value of the unit. If the gross value of the product is less than the capital value then the farm may be losing money. The more profitable the farm, the greater will be the proportion by which the gross annual value of fish sales exceeds the capital value.

A short-fall in actual production compared to planned production may be due to mistakes in the original design of the farm. It can also stem from a number of other failings, some of which can be corrected, while others are inherent in local conditions. Short-falls most commonly result from losses of fish by disease or escape, and from poor fish-growth. Such losses may be due to bad husbandry, in which case they can be reduced or prevented.

If the water quality is not up to the standard essential for the fish being farmed, it may be possible to change to some other less demanding species. Little or nothing can be done to improve the situation if it has come about as the result of the failure to make an adequate initial survey, and to properly assess the potential of the site.

If fish fail to make the expected growth, or take too long to reach market-size, it may be due to short-comings in the site, but is more frequently the result of incorrect feeding. It may prove very difficult to find a solution to this problem if there is no alternative source of fish food available to the farm.

Losses of Fish during Rearing and On-growing

Fish can be lost due to a wide variety of causes. They can be taken by fish-eating birds and large marine mammals particularly seals. Cages can be damaged and fish escape due to the presence in the area of whales and basking sharks.

The water may be polluted by the discharge of oil, chemicals and waste products from ships at sea or the effluent from shore-drains. The water may become turbid or full of debris during storms. Poisonous algal blooms can occur in the site area.

Failure of a power supply, mechanical breakdown of the pumps or other machinery can result in the death of fish through lack of oxygen. Structural failure due to faulty construction or lack of maintenance can result in the escape or death of fish.

Human error is one of the commonest causes of loss. The following conditions can cause catastrophic losses of fish:
Storm damage
Sudden changes in temperature and salinity
Algal blooms
Turbidity
Failure of the water supply
Disease

Fish Farm Insurance

The premiums charged for fish farms are high because of the risks involved. Various ways are offered by which premiums can be reduced such as the 'Franchise' principle in which the loss of fish has to reach a certain percentage of the total of the stock held on the farm at the time of the incident before the loss can be indemnified. Another method is the so-called 'Deductible' which simply means that the farmer has to bear an agreed initial percentage of any claim.

For practical purposes fish farm insurance is best treated as a form of disaster cover. The fish farmer should decide the most likely causes of a possible catastrophic loss of fish on the farm, at a stage when it is most financially vulnerable. The farmer should then try to negotiate specific cover at an agreed rate for these eventualities only.

*The Economic Advantages of Cold-storage
and Processing on the Farm*

Marketing freshly killed salmonids in perfect condition is difficult and expensive. The fish have to be properly packed in ice, which means having an ice-maker on the premises. Melting ice only staves off deterioration for a relatively short time. Fresh fish are highly perishable and delays in public transport can result in a total loss. Insurance rates are understandably high.

Cold-storage makes sales independent of immediate market considerations. The fish can be slaughtered and processed when labour is available. Prices can be negotiated and agreed in advance with customers and the fish sold direct from cold-store. Bulk transport of frozen fish is cheap and free from the risk of spoilage.

Processing

The greatest advantage of processing is that the value of the fish produced can be greatly enhanced before they leave the farm. A profitable treatment for large trout and salmon is cold-smoking. There is a loss of about 25% in the gutted weight of the fish, but the value per kg is increased by more than 100%. The best quality smoked fish, as far as European and American markets are concerned, is achieved by the method known as wet-brining in which the fish are immersed in a brine bath before being smoked, instead of the usual dry-salt treatment. Other processing includes cutting and packaging in fillets and steaks.

Processed fish does not have to pass through a chain of wholesalers, and markets can be found where there is a direct sale to retail outlets. Besides increasing the profitability of even small fish farms, an additional advantage is that, in competition with other high quality deep-frozen salmon or trout, processed fish on sale to the public can be labelled with the producer's brand name.

A Look into the Future

Fish of the salmon family have come to be regarded as a luxury food. This is a result of scarcity. At one time salmon, like oysters, were a staple part of the poor man's diet. At present they are still relatively expensive to rear because they require a high protein diet. A substitute source of protein is already available in the single-cell 'yeasts' cultivated on oil and natural gas. Other proteins may soon be developed from marine algae.

Human beings cannot maintain themselves on the earth without farming the waters for food. The value in nutritional terms of salmonids farmed in saltwater is almost equivalent to best steak. They are very good to eat and the taste is similar or better than that of wild fish. The relatively high cost of production is reflected in the market price, but scarcity is rapidly bringing this into line with the cost of wild fish. In the future other species, with greater potential for domestication and attraction for fish farmers, may appear on the scene. For the time being salmonids evidently offer the best economic return for farming, where their culture is possible in the cooler parts of the world.

Bibliography

The Salmons, Trouts and Charrs

Salmon

'The Salmon of Ungava Bay.' G. Power, Arctic Inst. N. America, 22/1969.

State of Washington. 13th Annual Report of the State Fish Commissioner, 1902.

'Migratory Behaviour of Adult Fraser River Sockeye.' P. Gilhousen, *Int. Pac. Salmon Fish. Comm.*, Prog. Rep., 1960.

'Mechanisms Controlling Migration of Sockeye Salmon Fry.' E.L. Brannon, *Int. Pac. Salmon Fish. Comm.*, Bull XX1, 1972.

'On the Origin of Kokanee, a Freshwater Type of Sockeye Salmon.' W.E. Ricker, *Trans. Roy. Soc. Can.*, Sec. V, 1940.

'Factors influencing the Upstream Spawning Migration of the Pink Salmon, *Oncorynchus gorbuscha* (Walbaum).' A.L. Pritchard, *J. Biol. Bd. Can.*, 2 (4), 1936.

'Physical Characteristics and Behaviour of Pink Salmon Fry at McClinton Creek, B.C.' A.L. Pritchard, *J.Fish. Res. Bd. Can.*, 6 (3), 1944.

'Synopsis of Biological Data on the Chum Salmon, *Oncorynchus keta* (Walbaum).' R.G. Bakkala, U.S. Dept. of Int., *FAO Fish. Synop. 41*, Circ. 315, 1970.

'An Investigation of the Life History and Propogation of the Sockeye Salmon (*Oncorynchus nerka*) at Cultus Lake, B.C.' R.E. Foerster, *Contr. Can. Biol., N.S.*, V (1), 1929.

'Natural Reproduction of Quinnat Salmon, Brown and Rainbow Trout in Certain New Zealand Waters.' D.F. Hobbs, N.Z. Mar. Dept., *Fish. Bull.* 6, 1937.

Trout

'Rainbow Trout in Mexico and California.' P.R. Needham and R. Gard, *Univ. Col. Pubs. Zool.*, 67 (1), 1959.

'Fecundity of Steelhead Trout, *Salmo gairdneri*, from Alsea River, Oregon.' R.V. Bulkeley, *J. Fish. Res. Bd. Can.*, 24 (5), 1966.
'Age and Size of Steelhead Trout in the Babine River, B.C.' D.W. Narver, *J. Fish. Res. Bd. Can.*, 26 (10), 1969.
'Relationships of the Far Eastern Trout, *Salmo mykiss* (Walbaum).' R.J. Behnke, *Copeia* 2/1966.
'World Distribution of Rainbow Trout (*Salmo gairdneri*).' H.R. MacCrimmon, *J. Fish. Res. Bd. Can.*, 28 (5), 1971.

Charr

'Migrating Behaviour of Sea-Running *Salvelinus fontinalis*.' H.C. White, *J. Fish. Res. Bd. Can.*, 5 (3), 1941.
'Observations on the Speckled Trout (*Salvelinus fontinalis*) in Ungava.' G. Power, *Nat. Can.*, 93 (3) 1966.
'The Arctic Charr, *Salvelinus alpinus L.* of Matamek Lake, Quebec.' L.H. Saunders and G. Power, *Nat. Can.*, 96/1969.
'The Char (*Salvelinus*) of Great Britain.' C. Tate Regan, *Ann. Mag. Nat. Hist.*, Ser. 8. 111, 1909.

All Species

Fishery Resources of the United States: Report to the Senate, Doc. 51, 1945.

Hybridization

'Hybrids.' Francis Day, *British and Irish Salmonidae,* 1887.
'On Races and Hybrids among Salmonidae.' Francis Day, *Proc. Zool. Soc.* 11/1884.
'Results of Species Hybridization within the Family Salmonidae.' K. Buss and J.E. Wright Jr. *Progve. Fish. Cult.*, 18 (4) 1956.
'Hybrids between Salmonidae Species. Hatchability and Growth Rate in the Freshwater Period.' T. Refstie and T. Gjedrem. *Aquaculture*, 6/1975.
'Artificial Hybridization between different Species of the

Salmon Family.' G. Alm, Inst. Freshwater Res., Drottning-holm, 36/1955.

'Inter-Specific Cross-breeding of Pacific Salmon.' *Trans. Roy. Soc. Can.*, (3) (5) 29/1935.

Genetics and Stock Improvement

'Further Studies on the Multiple Components of the Haemo-globins of *Salmo salar* (L.).' H.J.A. Koch, N.P. Wilkins, E. Bergström and J.C. Evans, Swed. Salmon Res. Inst. 2/1976.

'*Artsstrukturen i Atlantisk Laks-Betydning for Kulturarbeidet.*' (Racial Characteristics in Atlantic Salmon – Significance for Fish Culture.) D. Møller, Swed. Salmon. Res. Inst. Rep. LFI. MED., 5/1970.

'Genetic Improvements in Salmonids.' T. Gjedrem, *Proc. Roy. Ed. Soc.* (B) 75 (4) 1976.

'Den Norske Laksestamme.' S. Sømme, *Landbruksdepartemen-tets Småskrift* 93, Oslo 1946.

'Genetics and Fish Farming.' C.E. Purdom, Min. of Ag. Fish and Food, Lab. Lft. 25/1972.

Low-temperature Storage of Fish Sperm

'An Improved Extender for Freezing Atlantic Salmon Sperm-atozoa.' H. Truscott and I.R. Idler, *J. Fish. Res. Bd. Can.*, 26 (12), 1969.

'Cypro-preservation of Fish Spermatozoa and Ova.' H.F. Horton and A.G. Ott, *J. Fish. Res. Bd. Can.*, 33/1976.

Sex Control

'Sex Reversal in Salmonid Culture.' R. Johnstone, T.H. Simpson and A.F. Youngson, *Aquaculture,* 13/1978.

'Sex hormones encourage a salmon run.' *New Scientist,* Feb., 1977.

Smolts and Smoltification

'Growth, Mortality and Migrations of the Anadromous Char, *Salvelinus alpinus, L.,* in the Vardnes River, Troms, Northern Norway.' K.W. Jensen and M. Berg, Inst. Freshwater Res., Drottningholm, 56/1977.

'Factors Influencing Descent of Atlantic Salmon Smolts.' H.C. White, *J. Fish. Res. Bd. Can.,* 4 (5), 1939.

'Tagging of Migrating Salmon Smolts (*Salmo salar L.*) in the Vardnes River, Troms, Northern Norway.' M. Berg, Inst. Freshwater Res., Drottningholm, 56/1977.

'Biochemical Analysis of Young Salmon at the Smolt Stage.' E.M. Malikova, *Trudy Latviiskovo Otdeleniia VNIRO,* 2, Riga, 1957.

'Smoltification and Migration of Young Salmon.' N.V. Evropeitseva, Uchenye Zapiski Leningradskovo Gosudarstvenno Universiteta (LGU), No. 228, *Seria Biologicheskikh Nauk,* 44/1957.

'Influence of Body Size on Silvering of Atlantic Salmon (*Salmo salar*) at Parr – Smolt Transformation.' C.E. Johnston and J.G. Eales, *J. Fish. Res. Bd. Can.,* 27 (5), 1970.

'Influence of Photoperiod on Smolt Development and Growth of Atlantic Salmon (*Salmo salar*).' R.L. Saunders and E.B. Henderson, *J. Fish. Res. Bd. Can.,* 27 (7), 1970.

'Field Measurements of the Basal Oxygen Consumption of Atlantic Salmon Parr and Smolts.' G. Power, *J. Arctic Inst. N. America,* 12, (4), 1957.

'Some Physiological Consequences of Handling Stress in Juvenile Coho Salmon (*O.kisutch*) and Steelhead Trout (*Salmo gairdneri*).' G. Wednemeyer, *J. Fish. Res. Bd. Can.,* 29 (12), 1972.

'Development of Ionic and Osmotic Regulation in Juvenile Steelhead Trout (*S. gairdneri*).' F.P. Conte and H.H. Wagner, *Comp. Biochem. Physiol.,* 14/1965.

'Influence of Salinity, Temperature and Exercise on Plasma Osmolarity and Ionic Concentration in Atlantic Salmon (*S. salar*).' J.M. Byrne, F.W. Beamish and R.L. Saunders. *J. Fish. Res. Bd. Can.,* 29/1972.

'Development of Osmotic and Ionic Regulation in Juvenile Coho Salmon (*O. kisutch*).' F.P. Conte, H.H. Wagner, J. Fessler and C. Grose, *Comp. Biochem. Physiol.*, 18/1966.

'The Importance of Size in the Change from Parr to Smolt in Atlantic Salmon.' P.F. Elsom. *Can. Fish. Cult.*, 21/1957.

'Smolt Transformation, Evolution, Behaviour and Physiology.' W.S. Hoar, *J. Fish. Res. Bd. Can.*, 33/1976.

'Photoperiod and Temperature Regulation of Smolting Steelhead Trout (*S. gairdneri*).' H.H. Wagner, *Can. J. Zool.*, 52/1974.

'Osmotic and Ionic Regulation in Embryos, Alevins and Fry of the five species of Pacific Salmon.' M. Weisbart, *Can. J. Zool.*, 46/1968.

'The Relation of Temperature to the Seaward Migration of Young Sockeye Salmon (*Oncorynchus nerka*).' R.E. Foerster, *J. Fish. Res. Bd. Can.*, 3 (5) 1937.

Nutrition and Growth

Vitamins and Amino-Acids

'The Vitamins in Fish Nutrition.' J.E. Halver, Academic Press 29/1972.

'The Nutrition of Trout 1V. Vitamin Requirements.' A.M. Phillips and D.R. Brockway. *Progve. Fish. Cult.*, 19/1957.

'Vitamin and Amino Acid Requirements of Pacific Salmon (*Oncorynchus*).' J.E. Halver, Eifac 66/Sc 11 – 3.

'Effect of Graded Levels of Supplemented Ascorbic Acid in Practical Diets fed to Rainbow Trout (*S. gairdneri*).' J.W. Ailton, et. al. *J. Fish. Res. Bd. Can.*, 35/1978.

Proteins, Fats and Carbohydrates

'The Protein and Amino Acid Needs in Fish Nutrition.' E.T. Metz, Academic Press, 105/1972.

'The Nutrition of Trout 11. Protein and Carbohydrate.' A.M. Phillips and D.R. Brockway, *Progve. Fish. Cult.*, 18/1956.

Growth Factors

'Essential Fatty Acids in the Diet of Rainbow Trout (*S. gaird-neri*). Growth, feed conversion and some gross deficiency symptoms.' J.D. Castell, et. al., *J. Nutr.*, 102/1972.

'Sockeye Growth Responses to Diet.' J.R. Brett, *J. Fish. Res. Bd. Can.*, 23 (10) 1971.

'Calorie-to-Protein Ratio for Brook Trout (*Salvelinus fontinalis*).' R.C. Ringrose, *J. Fish. Res. Bd. Can.*, 28 (8), 1971.

'Growth Rate and Body Composition of Fingerling Sockeye Salmon, *Oncorynchus nerks,* in relation to Temperature and Ration Size.' J.R. Brett, J.E. Shelbourn and C.T. Shoop, *J. Fish. Res. Bd. Can.*, 26 (9), 1969.

'The Effect of Fat and Cholesterol on the Growth of Young Salmon.' E.R. Norris and L.R. Donaldson. *Am. J. Physiol.*, 129 (1), 1940.

Food Mixtures

'Dry Concentrates as a Complete Trout Food.' A.M. Phillips, et. al. *Progve. Fish. Cult.* 26/1964.

'Formulating Practical Diets for Fish.' J.E. Halver, *J. Fish. Res. Bd. Can.*, 33 (4/2), 1976.

'Mineral Compositions of Oregon Pellet Production Formulations.' D.L. Crawford and D.K. Law, *Progve. Fish. Cult.,* 25 (4), 1963.

'Replacement of Fish Meal by Single-Cell Protein in a Diet for Yearling Atlantic salmon (*Salmo salar*).' D.J. Piggins, *Salmon Res. Trust Ireland*, XX11, 1977.

'Feeding and Feed Composition of Trout and Salmon in the Production of Fish for Food.' F. Utne, Vitaminlaboratoriet, Bergen, Norway.

Moist Pellets and Mixtures

'Bløde foderpiller til ørreder : Ørredernes ernaeringsbehov, og nogle foreløbige resultater.' S.O. Solberg, *Forsøgsdambruget*, Mdde 56, 1976.

'Development of the Oregon Pellet Diet.' W.F. Hublou, et.

al., *Res. Briefs, Fish. Comm. Oregon*, 7 (1), 1959.

'Intermediate-Moisture Foods : Principles and Technology.' N.N. Potter, *Food Prod. Dev.*, 4 (7), 1970.

'Storage and Nutritional Characteristics of Oregon Moist Rations as an Intermediate-Moisture Product.' D.L. Crawford et. al., *Progve. Fish. Cult.*, 35 (1), 1973.

Red and Pink Pigmentation

'Indirect Pigmentation of Salmon and Trout Flesh with Canthaxanthin.' P.J. Schmidt and E.G. Baker, *J. Fish. Res. Bd. Can.*, 26 (2), 1969.

'Pigmentation of Salmon and Trout Flesh – Experimentation with Different Moisture (Water) contents in the Feed of Rainbow Trout (*Salmo gairdneri*) reared in Sea Water.' S. Ugeltveit, Norsildmel, Bergen, Norway.

'Pigmentation of Brook Trout (*Salvelinus fontinalis*) by Feeding Dried Crustacean Waste.' A. Saito and L.W. Regier, *J. Fish. Res. Bd. Can.*, 28 (4), 1971.

'The Yeast Phaffia Rhodozyma as a Dietary Pigment Source for Salmon and Crustaceans.' E.A. Johnston, et. al., *J. Fish. Res. Bd. Can.*, 34/1977.

Dietary Deficiencies

Trout Farming Handbook. S.D. Sedgwick, Seeley Service, London, 1973.

Fish Husbandry, Farm Planning and Costing

'Anaesthetics for Fish.' G.R. Bell, *Fish. Res. Bd. Can.*, Bull. 148, 1964.

'Salmon Stripper, Egg Counter and Incubator.' A. Lindroth, *Progve. Fish. Cult.*, 18 (4), 1956.

'Feeding Response of Atlantic Salmon (*Salmo salar*) Alevins in Flowing and Still Water.' D.M. Rimmer and G. Power, *J. Fish. Res. Bd. Can.*, 35/1978.

Warm-Water Rearing

'Försök med kläckning och uppfödning av laxungar i varm-vatten. (Investigation of hatching and rearing young salmon in warm water).' B. Carlin, *Vandringsfiskutredningen Mdde*, 3/1956.

Re-circulation and Water Heating

'A Compact Recirculation Unit for the Rearing and Maintenance of Fish.' K.R. Scott and D.C. Gillespie, *J. Fish. Res. Bd. Can.*, 29 (7), 1972.
'Salmon Farming and Smolt Rearing in Arctic Norway.' S.D. Sedgwick, *Fish Farmer*, 2 (6), 1979.
'The Use of Solar Water-heating at a Scottish Atlantic Salmon Smolt Rearing Unit.' S.D. Sedgwick and R.H.D. Sedgwick, *Fish Farmer*, 3 (4), 1980.

Saltwater Farming

'Saltwater Rearing of Rainbow Trout and Salmon in Norway.' K.W. Jensen, EIFAC 66/Sc 11 – 4, 1966.
'Single-handed Salmon Farming.' S.D. Sedgwick, *Fish Farmer*, 3 (2), 1980.
'Opdrett av laksefiske i norske kystfarvann miljø og anlegg-styper. (Cultivation of Salmonids in Norwegian Coastal Waters. Sites and types of installation).' B.R. Braaten and R. Saetre, *Fisken og Havet,* Ser. B (2), 1973.
'Large Floating Structure for Holding Adult Pacific Salmon (*Oncorynchus spp.*).' C.J. Hunter and W.E. Farr, *J. Fish. Res. Bd. Can.*, 27 (3), 1970.
'L'élèvage des Salmonides Migrateurs Amphibiotiques en Amerique du Nord.' Y. Harache and J-J. Boulineau. *Rapp. Scient. techn.*, CNEXO, 5/1971.

Fish Feeding

'Hånd-eller maskinfodring i Damme. (Hand or Machine Feeding in Ponds).' S.O. Solberg and J.B. De Neergaard, *Forsøgsdambruget*, Mdde 54, 1975.

Fish Marking

'Rapid Cold-Branding of Salmon and Trout with Liquid Nitrogen.' J.L. Mighell, *J. Fish. Res. Bd. Can.*, 26 (10), 1969.

Costs

'Damfisknaeringen i Norge. (The Pond-Fish Business in Norway).' L. Berge, Inst. Fish. Economics, Bergen, Norway, 1968.
Trout Farming Handbook. S.D. Sedgwick, Seeley Service, London, 1973.

Fish Diseases and their Control

Virus diseases

'Pathology of Infectious Pancreatic Necrosis. 1. The Sequential Histopathology of the Naturally Occuring Condition.' F.I.J. McKnight and R.J. Roberts. *Br. Vet. J.*, 132/1976.
'Nogle foreløbige undersøgelser over regnbueørredens virussygdom (Egtvedsygen).' C.J. Rasmussen, *Forsøgsdambruget*, Mdde 10/1959.

Bacterial Diseases and their Control

'Furunkulose hos damørreder.' C.R. Rasmussen, *Nordisk Veterinaermedicin*, Bd. 16., 1964.
'Fish Furunculosis.' D.H. McCarthy, *J. Inst. Fish. Mgmt.*, 6 (1), 1975.
'Report on the attempted control of an outbreak of Furunculosis amongst impounded adult salmon (*Salmo salar*).' A.C. Leaman (unpublished).
'Freshwater Fish Diseases caused by Bacteria belonging to the Genera Aeromonas and Pseudomonas.' S.F. Snieszko and G.L. Bullock. *U.S. Fish. Div. Lft.* 459/1971.
'Bacterial Kidney Disease of Salmonid Fishes.' K. Wolf. *U.S. Fish. Div. Lft.* 566.
'Control of Bacterial Kidney Disease in Adult and Juvenile

Spring Chinook Salmon at the Circle C Salmon Hatchery on Rapid River. An Interim Progress Report covering 1 July 1974 through 30 September 1978.' G.W. Klontz, Univ. Idaho, 83843, U.S.A.

'Proliferative Kidney Disease in Rainbow Trout, *Salmo gairdneri* (Richardson).' H.W. Ferguson and E.A. Needham. *J. Fish Diseases.* Vol. 1, No. 1, 1978.

'An Established Cell-Line from the Atlantic Salmon (*Salmo salar*).' B.L. Nicholson and C. Byrne. *J. Fish. Res. Bd. Can.*, 30 (7), 1973.

'Vibriosis in Fish.' A.J. Ross, *U.S. Fish. Div. Lft.*, 29/1970.

'Differences in Resistance to Vibrio Disease of Salmon Parr (*Salmo salar*).' T. Gjedrom and D. Aulstad, *Aquaculture, 3/* 1974.

'Occurence and Control of *Chondroccus columnaris* as related to Fraser River Sockeye salmon.' D.J. Colgrove and J.W. Wood, Int. Pac. Salmon Fish. Comm., Prog. Rep., 15/1966.

'Tuberculosis in Pacific Salmon and Steelhead Trout.' J.W. Wood and E.J. Ordal, *Fish. Comm. Oregon Cont.* 25/1958.

Parasites and their Control

'The Life-History and Ecology of the Salmon Gill-Maggot *Salmincola salmonea* (L.) (Copepod crustacean).' G.F. Friend. *Trans. R. Soc. Ed.*, LX – 11 – (15), 1940 – 1941.

'Life-History of *Lepeophtheirus salmonis*. H.C. White, *J. Fish. Res. Bd. Can.*, 1/1942.

'Use of Formalin with Malachite Green (Oxalate) for Control of External Protozoan Parasites of Fishes.' F. Leteux and F.P. Meyer, *Progve. Fish. Cult.*, 34 (1), 1974.

Fish Fungus

'Saprolegnia in Salmonid Fish in Windermere : a Critical Analysis.' L.G. Willoughby, *J. Fish. Diseases*, 1 (1), 1978.

Environmental Diseases

'Nitrogen Gas Bubble Disease Related to a Hatchery Water

Supply from the Forebay of a High-Head Regulating Dam.'
E.J. Wyatt and K.G. Beiningem, *Res. Reps. Fish. Comm. Oregon*, 3/1971.
'Gasblåsesjuka vid Höllelaboratoriet 1955.' G. Carlsson, *Vandringsfiskutredningen Mdde*, 2/1956.

Other Diseases

'Ulcerative Dermal Necrosis (UDN) of Salmon (*Salmo salar*).'
R.J. Roberts, *Symp. Zool. Soc. Lond.*, 30/1972.
'Induction of UDN-like lesions in salmonid fish by exposure to ultraviolet light in the presence of phototoxic agents.'
A.M. Bullock and R.J. Roberts, *J. Fish Diseases*, 2/1972.
'Clostridium Botulinum and its Importance in Fishery Products.' G. Hobbs, *Advances in Food Research*, 22/1976.
'Histological Studies of the Pancreas and Associated Tissues of Wild and Experimentally Fed Young Chinook Salmon.'
L.R. Donaldson, *Am. J. Physiol.*, 138 (3), 1943.

Immunization

'Vaccination af fisk.' P.E. Vestergård – Jørgensen, *Forsøgsdambruget*, Mdde Nr. 59/1977.
'Immunization of Pacific Salmon: Comparison of Intraperitoneal Injection and Hyperosmotic Infiltration of Vibrio anguillarum and Aeromonas salmonicida Bacterias.' R. Antipa and D.F. Amend. *J. Fish. Res. Bd. Can.*, 34/1977.
'Infectious Pancreatic Necrosis: Clinical and Immune Response of Adult Trouts to Inoculation with Live Virus.' K. Wolf and M.C. Quimby. *J. Fish. Res. Bd. Can.*, 26 (9), 1967.

Practical Disease Control

'Diseases of Fish and their Control in the USA.' S.F. Snieszko. Two Lakes Course, 1973.
Trout Farming Handbook. S.D. Sedgwick, Seeley Service, London, 1973.
Handbook of Trout and Salmon Diseases. R.J. Roberts and C.J. Shepherd, Fishing News Books, England, 1974.

'Efforts to Limit Outbreaks of Disease in Fish Rearing Installations.' T. Håstein, *Norsk Veterinaer Tiddskrift.* 85 (2), 1973.

Salmon Ranching

'Some observations on the Olfactory Perception in Migrating Adult Coho and Spring Salmon.' J.R. Brett and D. MacKinnon, *Prog. Reps. Pac. Coast Stns.*, Fish. Res. Bd. Can., 90, 1972.
'An Electrophysiological Basis for Olfactory Discrimination in Homing Salmon : A Review.' T.J. Hard, *J. Fish. Res. Bd. Can.*, 27 (3), 1970.
'Chemical Basis for Homing Atlantic Salmon (*Salmo salar*) to a Hatchery.' A.M. Sutterlin and R. Gray, *J. Fish. Res. Bd. Can.*, 30 (7), 1973.
'Anadromy in North American Salmonidae.' G.A. Rounsefell. U.S. Fish and Wildlife Service, *Fish. Bull.* 209 (62), 1958.
'Anadromous Salmonids.' H.H Wagner, *Oregon Wildlife,* 30 (7), 1975.
'Pink Salmon (*Oncorynchus gorbuscha*) in Northern Norway in the Year 1960.' M. Berg, Acta Borealia A. Scientia 17 Tromsø, 1961.
'Differentiation of Early and Late Running Salmon (*S. salar*).' S.D. Sedgwick, *S. and T. Mag.*, 137, 1953.
'The Seaward Migration and Return of Hatchery-Reared Steelhead Trout, *Salmo gairdneri,* in the Alsea River, Oregon.' H.H. Wagner, R.L. Wallace and H.J. Campbell, *Trans. Am. Fish. Soc.*, 92 (3), 1963.
'Fecundity of Coho Salmon (*O. kisutch*) from the Great Lakes and a Comparison with Ocean Salmon.' T.M. Stauffer, *J. Fish. Res. Bd. Can.*, 33 (5), 1976.
'A Summary of Investigations of the Use of Hatchery-Reared Steelhead in the Management of a Sport Fishery.' H.H. Wagner, *Oregon State Univ. Fish. Rep.*, 5, 1967.
'Tagging Experiments with Salmon.' T. Refstie and D. Aulstad. *Aquaculture*, 4, 1975.
'Survival and Propensity for Homing as Affected by Presence or Absence of Locally Adopted Paternal Genes in Two Trans-

planted Populations of Pink Salmon (*Oncorynchus gorbuscha*).'
R.A. Barns, *J. Fish Res. Bd. Can.*, 33, 1976.

'Estimates of Maturation and Ocean Mortality for Columbia
River Hatchery Fall Chinook Salmon and the Effect of No
Ocean.' K.A. Henry, *Res. Reps. Fish Comm. Oregon.* 3, 1971.

'Marine Growth of Atlantic Salmon (*Salmo salar*) in the North-
west Atlantic.' K.R. Allen, R.L. Saunders and P.F. Elsom.
J. Fish. Res. Bd. Can., 29 (10), 1972.

'Stillehavslaks på Norskekysten. (Pacific Salmon in Norwegian
Waters).' B. Rasmussen, *Fisken og Havet,* 5, 1961.

'Farming Ocean Ranges for Salmon.' T. Joyner, *J. Fish. Res. Bd.
Can.*, 33 (4/2), 1976.

'Migration – Orientation of Atlantic Salmon (*Salmo salar* L.)'
A.B. Stasko, et. al., *Int. Atlantic Salmon Symp., 1973.*

INDEX

Numbers in italics refer to illustrations

Northern Michigan University

3 1854 003 592 766

EZNO
SH167 S17 S43
The salmon handbook : the life and culti